Day Trading for Beginners 2019:

3 BOOKS IN 1 - How to Day Trade for a Living and Become an Expert Day Trader With Penny Stocks, the Forex Market, Swing Trading, & Expert Tools and Strategies.

Bill Sykes

Timothy Gibbs

Under no circumstances will any blame or legal responsibility be held against the publisher, or author, for any damages, reparation, or monetary loss due to the information contained within this book. Either directly or indirectly.

book has been derived from various sources. Please consult a licensed professional before attempting any techniques outlined in this book.

By reading this document, the reader agrees that under no circumstances is the author responsible for any losses, direct or indirect, which are incurred as a result of the use of the information contained within this document, including, but not limited to, — errors, omissions, or inaccuracies.

Books Included:

How to Day Trade Penny Stocks for Beginners: Find Out How You Can Trade For a Living Using Unique Trading Psychology, Expert Tools and Tactics, and Winning Strategies.

Day Trading for Beginners: Want to be a Day Trader? Learn How to Trade for a

Living and Discover These Powerful Day Trading Tips and Strategies in 2019

Forex Trading for Beginners: What Everybody Ought to Know About the Day Trading Business, How to Understand the Forex Market, Scalping Strategies, and the Secret of Making Money Online

How to Day Trade Penny Stocks for Beginners

Find Out How You Can Trade For a Living Using Unique Trading Psychology, Expert Tools and Tactics, and Winning Strategies.

Bill Sykes

Timothy Gibbs

Table of Contents

Are you okay with letting it ride?

Conclusion

References

Introduction

Congratulations on downloading your personal copy of *Penny Stocks for Beginners: A Complete Guide to Investing in Penny Stocks, Day Trading, Passive Income, and Massive Wealth.* Thank you for doing so.

In this guidebook, we're going to spend some time learning about penny stocks and why they are among the best options to consider when deciding to get involved in investing. While there are many choices within the world of investing, penny stocks can be an interesting one to decide upon and one that has the possibility of bringing in a lot of profit. This guidebook contains everything you need to know about penny stocks so that you can learn how to start using this investment tool for your own benefit.

First, we will start with some of the basics concerning penny stocks and how they are different from other stocks that are available. We will also discuss the two main options for penny stocks - namely the pink sheets and the Over-the-Counter Bulletins. Once you've had a chance to learn about these basics, we will delve deep into the topic of penny stock investing. We'll touch on how to get into the game and find a good broker before moving on to some of the top strategies you can implement to put your money to work and find out which penny stocks will work best for you. The guidebook will conclude with some basic tips that can help you really see results, even as a beginner.

Investing in penny stocks is a great way to open up your portfolio so that your money can grow more than ever before. However, it does take some time and effort in order to learn this method and make it work well for you. This guidebook is going to give you the tips that you need to get started creating a good income with penny stocks.

There are plenty of books on this subject available on the market, so thank you again for choosing this one. Please enjoy!

Chapter 1: Get Familiar with Stocks

Have you thought about using any passive income sources? Do you have a desire to be part of a profitable investment? If so, you should definitely consider investing in the stock market. Though investing in stocks is a profitable venture, it is a difficult one. You will be required to learn several things in regard to stock investments before you can begin buying the quoted shares in the stock exchange market. Do not make the mistake of buying stocks before understanding the basics; you will regret it in the long run.

To put it simply, one share of stocks is the representation of a partial claim that the owner has towards the earnings and assets of the issuing company. If the number of shares available in the market is higher, then it means a single share will have less worth. If one has a higher number of shares for a particular company, then that individual has greater control over the company. Any owner of stock in a particular company is regarded as a shareholder, implying that they own a portion of the profits of the company (Hayes, 2013). Such portions are normally called dividends. The payment of dividends is made on predetermined points of any particular year. If you have shares of a specific company, you may have voting rights regarding the decisions of the company, in which case you can influence its future progress.

You should note that owning shares of a particular company does not give you an active say in the daily operations of the company. Owning shares provides you with entitlement to a profit share and voting shares. During the annual shareholder meeting, you have the possibility to vote for the members who constitute the board of directors. This is the moment where you have the chance to express your satisfaction or dissatisfaction towards the current setup of the company or how it's run.

When you decide to invest in the stock market, it is paramount that you understand the risk. Be considerate of the companies you resolve to invest in, and identify whether they pay out dividends; not all companies do so, and it's not a guarantee that one that paid out dividends previously will continue doing it. This is because, when talking about the stock market, profits are never 100 percent guaranteed. It is impossible to count on continuous stock appreciation in generating more value. There will be reasons that may contribute to the slipping of a given stock. It's also possible that the company could declare bankruptcy.

Don't consider the risk with negative thoughts, though; consider it as a tool that can help you evaluate the potential of a given stock. If a particular stock presents a greater risk, then the possibility of reward is high if it moves in the direction you want it to. If you carefully take the time to understand the risk, you will generate a return that's higher than the standard 7 percent promised by many investments; you may even reach a profit of 12 percent.

Why Do Companies Sell Stock?

A company sells stock when it needs to raise money. It can also do this by borrowing funds from a bank or another source (Metcalf, 2019). However, if its owners choose to sell stock, there are no repayment plans you'll face in the future.

There are a few different ways to sell stock. If a company's owners want to control who is offered a piece of the pie, they sell stock through "private placement," which allows the management to choose to whom the stock is offered.

Chances are that if you've purchased stock or plan to do so in the future, you've done so through a public offering. Companies initiate public offerings, as was noted, in order to raise money. They may need money for a variety of reasons, including expansion or any other kind of further growth, or to pay back owners or investors who had a hand in starting the company.

Companies set up an initial public offering (IPO), which is the first offering of stock, but they can also continue later with a secondary public offering if they need to raise more capital.

A company that has stock that's performing well is usually considered a stable company and tends to have an easier time raising money through lenders, as well, aside from the sale of stock.

The stock market

The stock market is the place where stocks and bonds are "traded" (bought and sold). Simply put, a stock market links buyers and sellers, facilitating the exchange of securities between these two groups of investors.

A stock market may be termed as a physical place where face-to-face trading happens, such as the New York Stock Exchange in New York City, or more likely a virtual location, or a network where trades are made electronically.

There are two aspects of the stock market: the primary market and the secondary market.

The primary market is where new issues of stock are sold through the aforementioned initial public offerings or IPOs. Institutional investors – those who have extremely large dollar amounts to spend – use the primary markets to purchase shares at initial public offerings and are given preferential treatment due to the dollar amount they plan to purchase.

The secondary market is where the "little guy" makes his or her purchases. After the IPO, all subsequent trading happens on the secondary market, with offerings available to individual purchasers.

Chapter 2: Investing Versus Trading

Most individuals use the terms "investing" and "trading" interchangeably, inferring that the two are synonymous with one another. However, those well-versed in penny stocks know that they're two markedly different things that entail various risks, different time commitments, and most certainly some mixed results.

Being an Investor

Investing in penny stocks without doing lots of constant trading requires an individual with plenty of patience. Investors tend to "let it ride" rather than cashing out for small gains. The investor is the researcher and the wearer of rose-colored glasses. He's in it for the duration and, as such, stands to make more considerable gains than the trader.

Investing is wise in the penny stock market, especially for those new to the realm. Though it tends to be easier than being a trader, that doesn't mean there isn't work involved. The work tends to be more up-front at the beginning of the investment process. For example, an investor needs to jump into the often tedious task of investigating penny stock companies in which he would like to invest. This involves making calls, poring over figures, and putting it all together to make wise purchasing decisions. This takes time to do correctly but generally results in a better feeling about the stock purchased. Potentially, there may be less risk involved, as well.

Investors stand to recognize more gains than traders, because they tend to keep shares for a longer amount of time and, hence, they see prices rise over and over again rather than jumping to cash in at the first or second gain, fearing that it might be their only chance.

Most experts note that investing really is the best approach in the penny stock market.

Being a Trader

While the investor is the painter content to hone his masterpiece a few strokes at a time over several months, the trader is the child who spends his money as soon as he gets it without waiting to amass a considerable sum with which he could buy something much bigger - if only he had the patience. However, for him, those small rewards are much more exciting.

Traders are in it for the short-term gains and are discontent with waiting to see what happens. They are impatient players who rarely take the time to thoroughly research each penny stock company as investors do. Therefore, they depend mostly on the information available on trading charts to make their decisions about which shares to buy and which to pass up.

You might think that this takes less work. Well, it certainly does at the beginning of the process. Trading demands a much more active role in the health of one's stock portfolio. Because traders are only looking to make these short-term gains, they spend much more time buying and selling. They may even buy and sell several times in a day or dozens of times per week. For them, it's a nail-biting process they enjoy being part of that allows for perhaps a 10 or 20 percent gain each time (small tidbits that are less likely to result in significant profits, even over the long stretch). Nonetheless, it's a game that keeps the adrenaline pumping.

Again, investing is the better strategy for the novice, especially one who has entered the market with some trepidation; but trading - with all of its excitement - seems to be best suited for those who have a considerable amount of stock market know-how, even if that know-how hasn't been developed in the world of penny stocks.

Chapter 3: The Basics of Penny Stocks

Penny stocks are the gateway to a hidden sector of the stock market. Penny stocks differ from other types of stocks in that they're open to public investment, but they do not become available before they are a well-known brand. The reason that companies open themselves to investment before they are popular is to secure funding and continue developing a product. As a penny stock investor, you are investing in a company at its early levels of developing its product. It is for this very reason that penny stocks can be so profitable - you are a starting investor and have the opportunity to earn returns far greater than on any well known publicly traded stock.

Penny stocks get their name from their price. Although the Securities and Exchange Commission officially defines a penny stock as having a value of less than $5 per share, many penny stocks trade at or below $1 ('What are Penny Stocks and How Do Penny Stocks

Work?', 2019). You will typically be buying penny stocks in large quantities of shares, but this does not mean that you will get majority ownership in nearly any penny stock company, nor would you want to do this. Nearly all of these small businesses have diluted the value of their shares; this is why they are worth so little individually. Also, their shares are not listed on most of the traditional stock exchanges. Most penny stocks are traded through the Over-The-Counter Bulletin Board and the Pink Sheets. If they were to become a corporation with influence all around the world, a long process would take place. To make money consistently and quickly, you won't be worried about companies that progress this far. The goal is to be interested only in the very beginning stages and then to get out of the market before the company becomes more popular.

The products that penny stock companies produce are vast and diverse. Businesses exist in everything from social media websites, to a chain of national party promoters, to a company that works to create more accurate global positioning systems. What is common amongst all of these companies is that large venture capital firms have passed on their ideas. Penny stock companies rely on a large swath of investors spread out across the country and the globe. Their market capitalization is a numbers game based on their total number of investors. Do not think all of these companies are destined to fail, although you should know that most of them will. For your purposes, you will be pulling out of a specific company long before they become a large success or before they fail and fade away.

The Securities and Exchange Commission has come to heavily regulate penny stocks in the last three decades. Many of these regulations regard starting investor count, the quality of market exchanges, and market capitalization prior to listing, which is a huge benefit to traders like you and me. There is one significant drawback to the added involvement of the SEC, however, and this is that they can stop trading on highly volatile stocks. There are specific cases of stock manipulation in the last twenty years that has put the SEC on high alert for penny stocks that are trading upwards in an irregular manner quickly. The SEC will halt trading on these stocks and will only reopen after they have looked at the underlying company being traded to see whether or not manipulation was used to raise the price. Yet again, the SEC has our best interests at heart, but this detail can be a real nuisance to traders.

When the SEC halts a stock, not only do traders lose the option to buy, but investors also cannot sell the stock that they've already purchased. The frequency of these events is limited, and this book will discuss specific strategies you can use should this ever happen. While it may seem like penny stocks have developed a bad name for themselves, you should understand that this view is extremely outdated and that present-day penny stock trading is generally well regulated, and investors are better protected. Actually, there is no better time to get involved in penny stocks than right now.

Traditional Markets

Traditional markets house large public companies that are known on an international scale. These are the companies that you've heard of, the companies that you shop at, and ones that might even include your employer. The traditional stock exchanges are very difficult to break through for many reasons, ranging from a lack of investor technology to limited capital, reducing potential profitability. Now, most trading is done online, and most trades are not executed by human beings. Mathematicians have created complicated algorithms that are programmed into a computer, executing trades based on complex theories about stock trends. These trades are conducted by the thousands per second, and they make it very difficult to compete. However, as a new trader, by far the biggest hurdle will not be technology, but rather a lack of capital.

Trades on standard stock exchanges are mostly made on very small margins per each share. To earn a good profit, you will need to purchase a lot of shares and invest thousands of dollars. Furthermore, to limit losses, you would ideally be purchasing options for sell prices in case the value drops, buy prices in case the stock continues to go up, and the entire time you will be dealing with numerous brokers - both online and over the phone. These are the reasons that most people eventually decide to invest in penny stocks. Most people have enough capital to create decent profits on good trades, but too many competitors are being replaced by machines. As a starting investor, stay away from these exchanges and look to penny stocks instead.

Why Penny Stocks Are So Profitable

Penny stocks are profitable because of their high volatility, their limited entry price, the size of the market, and the limits in human competitors. These are just some of the myriad of reasons these stocks are valuable for traders like you and me. Penny stocks are today what the traditional stock market was in the 1960s, 70s, and 80s - fast moving and taking on new investors every day. This increase in market capitalization spread out across various penny stocks is precisely why you'll be able to earn a decent profit through trading.

Today's large stock markets operate using a variety of complicated financial products, such as derivatives. These products were created to compensate for a slowing market or one that does not display as much volatility. As trading became more advanced and computers started making most trades, distance to the central exchanges become a prime concern, where investment firms are now purchasing property locked in New York City simply because they can make trades a hair of a second faster than their competitors.

This information does little to add why penny stocks are so profitable, but it does paint a picture of what has happened to traditional markets. As they have slowed down and grown more competitive, new tricks have been created by established investors that make profits much more difficult to come by for the average person. Penny stocks are an alternative that takes us back to the early days of the stock market where trades were done more slowly, and investors had more of an equal opportunity; this truly is why penny stocks are so profitable, especially compared to traditional markets.

Shortcomings of Penny Stocks

While the potential profit from penny stocks is good, you should also consider the disadvantages of investing in this kind of stock.

Below we have outlined some of these downsides.

Most penny stock exchanges do not require companies to submit regular reports - Companies listed in the major stock exchanges are required to pass regular financial reports. The transparency of the companies' financial dealings allows investors to make informed decisions regarding when to buy and sell stocks.

Because penny stocks are not listed with major exchanges, these companies aren't required to submit reports. Financial news companies also do not give a lot of attention to these small companies. When investing in them, you should be the one doing the research regarding the nature of the business of the companies you invest in.

Aside from the financial reports, it may also be difficult to find information about the leadership and history of the companies you are investing in. You need to call these companies or go straight to their offices to gather this information. Learning about the leadership and history of a company is also important because they provide you with clues on the progress the company has made.

With bigger companies listed with the major exchanges, you can check the history of the company for bankruptcy and changes in leadership online. Their business transactions are well documented by the media. You can also check the track record of the company's current leaders. With a penny stock company, this information may not be available. A company that's trying to hide its past will successfully do so in this market.

The market may lack liquidity - The lack of market liquidity is a common problem in the penny stock market. Investing in major stock exchanges is easy because there are always buyers for the stocks you are selling. Even if local investors are feeling cautious about investing, there are always international investors who are interested in buying US shares.

International funds are not interested in buying penny stocks due to their extremely speculative nature. The lack of information for companies listed in this market makes investing in them too risky for most institutional investors.

Due to insufficient players in the market, you may discover there are no buyers for the stocks you want to sell, especially when the market is down. The lack of buyers will push the prices down, which will lead to major losses on your part.

The Pump and Dump Scheme

Because of the low liquidity in the penny stock market, it's also easier for organized crime groups to execute a pump and dump scheme with certain penny stock companies.

This is an illegal practice in the stock market where a group of stockbrokers or marketing companies buy a big chunk of the stocks of a company when the prices are still low. The sudden buying up of large amounts of shares of the said company increases its market value. Using their sales teams, these groups increase the hype further for the company by offering its stocks for sale through the phone, fake news, newsletters, and other means of marketing.

They target people who can afford to buy the funds but who are not financially savvy enough to invest in the penny stock market. When these people check the stocks that the sales team is offering, they may see an upward trend in its prices. Because of this, many beginning investors may be fooled into buying the shares of the company.

The continued promotion of the shares of the company keeps fueling its price increase. This is the pump part of the process. When the price of the shares gets to a given point, the masterminds of the scheme begin to dump their shares of the company while the prices are still high. They also use their marketing teams to dispose of their shares. Due to owning a large chunk of the company, selling their shares affects the price of the shares.

When the masterminds of these schemes sell all of their shares, they stop marketing the stocks. The hype for the shares also decreases, and people start to sell the ones they own. However, the share prices will now be lower than their buying price. Usually, late buyers are the ones that suffer from most of the losses in these schemes.

While the SEC keeps an eye out for pump and dump schemes in the stock exchange, it is difficult for them to differentiate true investors from pump and dump masterminds. The task is even more challenging in the penny stock market. The lack of liquidity in the market makes it easier for criminal groups to fake price increases in the market.

A Short message from the Author:

Hey, are you enjoying the book? I'd love to hear your thoughts!

Many readers do not know how hard reviews are to come by, and how much they help an author.

Customer Reviews

⭐⭐⭐⭐⭐ 2

5.0 out of 5 stars ▾

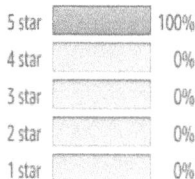

5 star		100%
4 star		0%
3 star		0%
2 star		0%
1 star		0%

Share your thoughts with other customers

Write a customer review ⬅

See all verified purchase reviews ›

I would be incredibly thankful if you could take just 60 seconds to write a brief review on Amazon, even if it's just a few sentences!

>> Click here to leave a quick review

Chapter 4: Personality Traits of a Successful Penny Stock Investor

Penny stocks are clearly not for everyone. Many investors prefer safer investments that are likely to grow steadily over long periods of time and have almost no chance of going belly-up. The penny stock investor is cut from a slightly different cloth. If you're wondering whether or not you're a penny stock investor in your heart of hearts, then consider the following factors (Leeds, 2019).

Do you enjoy actively managing and monitoring your portfolio?

The typical medium-to-large cap investor (someone who buys stocks in larger companies) doesn't really need to spend too much time researching their investments and monitoring their day-to-day performance. Perhaps once a quarter, they'll make some trades and evaluate how their stocks have performed, but it won't be a particularly heady endeavor. The successful penny stock investor, by contrast, actively monitors and manages their portfolio. They know that even if a penny stock looks good one week, a few factors can shuffle around quite quickly, and the stock will look like a disaster the next week. This investor will want to get out before it's too late. This type of active monitoring and frequent buying and selling requires time and also money, as you'll presumably be paying more commission for more frequent trading.

Will you be satisfied with a modest return?

It's important to set up reasonable expectations for your penny stock investment. Since there's so much hype behind penny stocks, many new investors expect big returns right out of the gate. The odds that you're going to stumble upon a big winner are incredibly low. If you're smart and diligent, then you have a decent chance of seeing some modest growth in the value of your portfolio over time. It is an incorrect assumption that you'll get rich quickly by investing in penny stocks.

Can you tell when someone's lying to you?

A good penny stock investor needs to have an adequate internal lie detector because a lot of lies get flung around in this space. Get ready to confront and size up a lot of over-hyped reviews about how a certain company is poised to change the world and the like. Stories are important, but you should never make an investment based on that alone. You're going to need to see important financial metrics, such as price-to-book, price-to-sales, and other important measurements that allow you to size up the company's true potential. This book discusses these and other metrics in the subsequent chapters. However, for now, just know that you can't be gullible if you want to succeed as a penny stock investor.

Do you cope well with risk?

If you're delving into penny stocks, then you need to accept that there's a certain amount of risk involved. You may wind up watching your investments go up in smoke left and right, but you may also watch them multiply aggressively. If you flinch at risks and prefer securities that are more, well, secure, then penny stocks may not be for you. As a good rule of thumb, you should only invest in penny stocks if you have enough disposable income to support your investments. If you're taking money out of crucial household budgets, such as rent, food, or your car payment, in order to buy more penny stocks, then you're acting irresponsibly.

Are you okay with letting it ride?

Unlike larger securities, penny stocks are not so easily liquidated. For common stocks, you can usually buy or sell on any day that the market is open. Penny stock investors don't enjoy the same level of liquidity. You may find yourself in the incredibly frustrating position of watching your stock rise aggressively but being unable to sell it before it dips back down again. This just comes with the territory.

Chapter 5: Pink Sheets

Pink sheets are termed as an OTC market that enables the electronic connectivity of broker and dealers; everything, including price quotes, is done virtually (Murphy, 2019). There is no trading floor required. However, because of the virtual environment pink sheet trading has to offer, it differs from the New York Stock Exchange (NYSE). The required criteria for pink sheet-listed companies aren't the same as the required criteria for companies listed on the NYSE (LIOUDIS, 2019). Because of these innate differences, you'll want to spend some time familiarizing yourself with the nature of pink sheets. That is what we'll to discuss in the following chapter - the securities, benefits, risks, and profitability ratios pink sheet trading has to offer to investors.

Who Can Be Pink Sheet-Listed?

Generally speaking, you'll find that most pink sheet-listed companies are small companies either starting out or struggling to obtain positive profit margins. They're typically thinly traded, tightly held companies. Especially for the struggling company, pink sheet trading is a bonus, as companies that are pink sheet-listed don't need to meet or maintain any particular requirements in order to obtain or remain pink sheet-listed. In order to be listed, all an interested company needs to do is submit a Form 211 with the OTC Compliance Unit with the current financial information included - that's it.

You should know that when you delve into the world of pink sheet trading, you'll find that some companies eagerly and willingly show you their financial books—their financial records, so to speak—while others don't. Unfortunately, pink sheet-listed companies are not obligated or required to show you their books upon request. You'll also inevitably encounter problems with finding annual reports on pink sheet-listed companies that interest you since these companies don't file the yearly or periodic reports as required. Unfortunately for the investor (you), this makes it nearly impossible to gain all the necessary financial information regarding the company of interest; unless they're willing to give it to you, of course.

The Difference between Pink Sheets and OTCBB

Whereas OTCBBs, a topic we learned about in the previous chapter, are owned and operated by NASDAQ, pink sheets are owned by private companies; and because OTCBB is organized by NASDAQ, the second largest exchange platform in the world, it makes sense that strict rules, regulations, and standards follow. It's compulsory for issuers, for example, to register with the Securities and Exchange Commission. No registration is required for pink sheet-listed companies, nor do such rules or regulations exist.

The Benefits of Pink Sheets

Pink sheets can be extremely cheap per share, with some even costing less than a dollar. This makes pink sheet trading highly beneficial and incredibly advantageous to the potential investor looking to invest in small increments while wishing to reap potentially high financial rewards. Volatility levels are very high with pink sheets, so increases in even penny amounts may result in great financial returns for an investor.

If you're looking to reap dramatic benefits and are willing to take oftentimes bold financial risks in order to do so, you might want to look for companies that have recently suffered from negative financial events but that have the potential to make a comeback. Companies that were once listed on the NYSE, for example, might be good starting points. You can purchase shares from those companies and hope that they make a comeback.

One of the best things about pink sheet-listed companies is that you can invest your money in a small or unpopular company, but still achieve a positive return rate. If a company is small and less known, you have a higher chance of success, because the competition is low. Investing in these small companies can turn out to be quite profitable if the growing process continues over time. In the future, and with gradual growth, that same company might be listed on a key exchange.

Risks Associated with Pink Sheets

As an investor, you should be well aware that there can be many disadvantages to pink sheet trading, as well - especially when investment opportunities and endeavors are approached in inappropriate or unknowledgeable ways. One of the biggest disadvantages of pink sheet trading is the limited amount of information that listed companies are required to share with investors and dealer-brokers. A company's decision to not report their financial status or publish annual reports makes it far more difficult for investors to access the information they require to consider the company, make vital financial decisions, and take risk-free actions. In other words, without these annual reports, you will not have all the crucial information about what you are purchasing and how the company is doing.

These pink sheet-listed companies are also thinly traded. You can purchase 500 shares from a company that promises to become the next Microsoft, but what happens if you gain a good profit and then decide to sell? When you sell, the price of the stock goes down. When a large number of investors continually do this, stocks and companies gain the title of being thinly traded. Regardless of what the market is when you do decide to sell, if you don't find a potential buyer for your stocks, you won't be able to get out of the position you put yourself in.

This situation becomes even more complicated when it comes to pink sheet-listed companies. It's a hard task to initiate a stock position when the bid-ask spreads are high. If you want to invest in those companies, you should be aware of the fact that they usually may not be covered by analysts. For example, if you watch or read the daily financial news, you'll already know that they almost never cover companies that aren't listed on a major exchange. This means that you will need to do some extra research in order to find the important information you need to make knowledgeable decisions and take successful actions.

The Workings of the Pink Sheet Tier System

The tier system was mentioned synonymously with the pink sheet trading system earlier, but let's stop for a second and take a closer look before moving on. In recent years, the pink sheet system has adopted something called "market tiers," an organizational method that lists and separates the companies that have higher risk levels from those with lower degrees of financial risk.

With these tiers, you can gain a sense of increased clarity regarding the type of company you are investing in (Beers, 2018). As its name suggests, there are certain levels, or tiers, that a company can fall under (Basenese, 2017). There are five in total, which are detailed below.

Tier #1: Trusted Tiers - Just like their name suggests, these tiers are confirmed by the pink sheet OTC market to be trustworthy and highly appealing to investors. The companies that fall under this tier have both international companies and ones in the US. With this in mind, the trusted tier can then be divided into two sub-categories, as follows:

- **International Premier QX**: These consist of overseas companies that are listed on an international exchange, though they still cover the required financials of the listed worldwide standards noted and regulated by the NYSE. These companies conduct an independent audit and are able to present an immediate CEO certification to anyone who refuses to comply with corporate governance.
- **Premiere QX:** This includes companies that are based only in the US and continually meet the standards of NASDAQ's capital market. It is not necessary for those companies to report directly to SEC, although they have to adhere to the requirements that NASDAQ lists.

Tier #2: Transparent Tiers - Transparent tiers are below the trusted tier. It consists of:

- **OTCBB pink quotes**: This represents companies that are listed on both the OTCBB and pink sheet systems. OTCBB makes it necessary for these companies to give frequent reports to the SEC.

- **OTCBB:** As you've learned throughout this book already, these companies are simply found on the OTCBB market only.
- **Information right now:** Such companies have daily and current information, meaning that they provide the given information with the OTC Disclosure or the Securities and Exchange Commission. The information that's provided is less than six months old. If a company wants to keep itself up on this exact tier and not move down, it needs to file an annual report within the period of 75 days after the ending of the final quarter. The information will be verified as posted by the pink sheets OTC market.

Tier #3: Distressed Tiers - These are next on the tier and are tough to manage. The companies listed within this tier include:

- **Companies with limited information:**
  - The information that's listed may be available for everyone to view, but it

is generally older than six months and often doesn't meet the pink sheets OTC market requirements.

- A company might file a report to SEC, but they still haven't kept that report updated frequently.
- Broken and bankrupted companies oftentimes pop up on this list. These companies must promptly file information with both the News Service and OTC Disclosure.

Tier #4: Defunct Tiers - Only two kinds of companies are included in the defunct tiers:

- **Companies without information**: This category can be easily recognized by its stop signal sign. Companies that fall under this tier are either defunct or haven't filed any kind of update on current information to the OTC Disclosure, the Securities and Exchange Commission, or the News Service in the last six months. If you are considering any investment in these types of companies, proceed with caution.
- **Gray markets:** This second market, much like the previous tier category, has

its own symbol, too, and that is the exclamation point. The companies listed in the gray market are missing a market maker and are not listed on either OTCBB or pink sheets. As a bonus, there is no transparency within the markets.

Tier #5: Toxic Tiers - Just like the name indicates, toxic tiers are tiers that have an extremely high level of risk. Its symbol, the skull and crossbones, suggests the risk investors take when pursuing companies listed within this tier. Only one category falls under this tier:

- **Caveat emptor:** The translation of this tier's title to English is quite clear: "buyer beware." On pink sheets, these tiers are described as stocks that can be a scam, have an unclear promotion, undergo regular suspensions, and many other things that reveal their risk level. Many of the companies listed within this bottom-most tier are all too often scams.

Now that you know a little more about the 5 types of tiers within the investing and penny stocks world, you need to learn about the brokers. That is, if you decide to invest in pink sheet stocks, you should consider hiring a broker. If you have already made a broker account, your broker is supposed to grant you an allowance to trade pink sheet stocks. However, be aware that this might not be possible, as some brokerage companies can only grant their most loyal customers to trade in the pink sheet market. If you do find an opportunity to delve into the pink sheet trading market with the help of your broker, you will be asked to sign another form that states that you understand and agree that pink sheet stocks can be risky investment endeavors.

There are many companies out there who simply don't want to give out any information concerning their business and financial matters. Be careful about investing in companies like this. Pink sheet companies are highly appealing due to their low price, and many investors find them interesting investment opportunities because they want to step up into a current and potentially rising company. The possibility that you may lose portions or all of your investment if you don't make the right buying choice means that you need to think carefully before proceeding with any decision.

You'll always want to avoid speculative stocks. Pink sheet trading has made major progress in the last few decades, and there have been more standards set, and there is more information circulating about pink sheet-listed companies, thanks to the help of the OTC market. If a pink sheet-listed company is introduced to one of the tier systems we discussed earlier, the more likely an investor will find it to be attractive. Be sure to pay attention to the tier system you select and ask for professional help before making any financial decisions. Be wary of some of the "expert" advertisements, as many are unreliable or scams. Sit down and do the research yourself. You can also take a look at the OTC Markets Group website; they have a detailed list of many OTC stocks. For now, though, you'll want to focus mostly on the two main stock categories: OTCQX and OTCQB. The other categories will not provide much information, and there may not be many strategies for them.

Chapter 6: Getting Started

Now, you have come to the part of this book where you will learn all there is to know about starting your penny stock trading venture. You might think that penny stock trading is complicated, with all the rules, things to look out for, complicated stock exchange terms, and everything else involved, but it is actually quite simple (Murphy, 2018). Read on to find out the four basic steps in starting your undertaking in penny stocks.

Research

Like when you start doing anything that you are unfamiliar with, you first need to do some research. In this book, the word "research" refers to two kinds of research. Before going to battle, you must first get your weapon ready, and in the world of penny stocks, there's no better weapon than knowledge.

The first kind of research is general research. This involves gathering general information about penny stocks, such as what it entails, how to go about investing in them, and most especially, the risks involved. Through this book, you ought to already have the proper knowledge for your general penny stock research.

The second type of research is the specific stock research. This kind of research should be done when you're actually looking for prospective penny stocks to invest in. Researching about the stock you are going to invest in should essentially be done when dealing with all kinds of stocks, but this is especially important for penny stocks. That's because, as you might recall from the previous sections, information about penny stocks is quite lacking and more difficult to find when compared to other kinds of stocks.

While researching about penny stocks, there are two things you need to look for. For one, you should look for any accessible public data about the stock. The second thing you need to look for is information regarding the stock's historical performance. While looking for this, you should observe and take note of the kinds of events that occurred and the reactions of the share price. An example of these events was instances when the price of the share remained as it was when there should have been an increase. An event such as this may suggest that investors have looked over the stock's information and decided to steer clear from investing in the stock.

Choose a Broker to set up an Online Brokerage Account

As soon as you have done enough research, the next thing to do in order to start your penny stock investments is to set up your own brokerage account just as you would at a bank. A brokerage account is a platform from where you will be able to buy stocks and other investments. It's also here that your money will be held, along with your investments. When you buy shares, your money will be taken out of your account and exchanged for company shares. Then, when you successfully sell your shares, they will be converted into money.

There are different kinds of brokerage accounts out there. One kind is brokerage accounts that you can manage yourself, though this is not recommended for beginners. For novice penny stock investors, it's best to select a broker for yourself. These paid professionals will be the people who directly buy or sell your stocks as they are told. Of course, you also have to provide them with their payment, called "commissions" or "commission fees." These payments can range from $5 to prices in the hundreds.

Two types of brokers exist that you can choose from full-service stock brokers (known as traditional brokers) and discount stock brokers.

Full-service brokers offer a much more extensive array of services, including the offering of advice and suggestions on what shares to buy and which investment can be more profitable for you. Due to these services, traditional brokers tend to have a higher commission fee compared to discount brokers. Enlisting these kinds of brokers is only good for investors who plan to do only a few trades and can afford to spend a lot of money. If money is a concern for you, hiring a full-service stockbroker is not advisable. Commission fees for brokers like these can cost you around $100 for purchasing stocks and an additional $100 for selling, and that doesn't even include other service fees.

A good choice for beginning investors would be to employ discount stock brokers. Although they offer a very limited number of services, you'll have more freedom when it comes to making decisions. If you prefer to be more independent in your decision-making process, you should opt to hire discount stock brokers, as their services only include giving limited investment advice. Consequently, their commission fees are cheaper, and you as an investor can save more money.

A much better option for you would be online discount brokers, partnered with an online brokerage account. Using the power of the internet in these times will be to your advantage, as you will be the one mainly managing your account, and using the internet is the most effective way to do so. Online brokerage systems can help you keep an eye on your account and execute orders to your broker. Here, you can see market indexes, monitor buy orders that are open, stay updated on quoted stock prices, and obtain access to analyses and research done by your broker anytime you want help making your decisions. With this arrangement, you can save a lot of money on commission fees while also making your transactions simpler.

When you have finally chosen a broker, setting up your brokerage account will become much easier. You only have to contact your broker, and they will provide you with the forms or files that need to be filled out. Most of the time, they'll be the one who creates the account. Of course, you cannot start an account without an initial cash deposit or a minimum investment. This can range from a few hundred dollars to around $1,000. After this, your account will be up and running in approximately three to four days, and you can then start investing.

Buy

After setting up the brokerage account, the next step is to start buying stocks. This is the most crucial part in the course of all your penny stock transactions. The moment you make the mistake of buying and investing in the wrong stocks, you are already bound to lose money.

Buying stocks is quite simple. When you want to purchase shares of stocks, you should first contact your broker and execute a buy order. However, before doing this, you must first ensure that your brokerage account is stocked up with an adequate amount of money - enough to be able to pay for the share costs and commissions that you will eventually incur.

When contacting your broker, you should have already done your research. You should also have the following set of information: the ticker symbol of the organization that executed the stock, the market that the stock is being traded in, the number of shares or the volume that you want to get, the price of the shares that you're prepared to pay, and the order's duration or how long you want it to last (it can be for only that specific day or until the date that you selected).

The ticker symbol is the trading symbol by which organizations are identified within the stock exchanges and bulletin boards. For example, you can tell your broker that you want to purchase 1,000 shares of a specific company with a ticker symbol HYPO at $1 or less. You can go on to say that the stock must be traded on the OTC Bulletin Boards, and you want this order to remain active until Thursday. By this time, what you need to do is wait; it's up to your broker to deal with the transaction.

So, if ever the price of HYPO shares becomes equal to or less than $1, your broker will purchase the shares. If you check on your online brokerage account, you'll discover that you already have 1,000 shares. Consequently, the money in your account, which will serve as payment for the shares and for the broker's commission fee, will also be transferred to the respective recipients - in this case, $1,000 to HYPO and approximately $5 to your broker.

You may now be wondering how you'll know if a certain penny stock is a good investment or not. Four of the primary things that you need to look out for in a penny stock are as follows:

1. The price range must be $0.50 to $2; stocks with prices higher than $2 in the Over-The-Counter Bulletin Board are a bit harder to find.

2. The daily average volume should not be less than 100,000 numbers of shares. (This will be discussed further in the next chapter.)

3. The stocks should be moving higher in the market.

4. Avoid stocks from companies with negative growth rates in earnings; you can obtain this information via data released to the public through the SEC or in listings.

Sell

Similarly to buying penny stocks, selling penny stocks is also very simple, though there is still a lot of information to take into account. As discussed in the third chapter, where we touched on the benefits and risks of penny stock trading, finding a buyer for penny stocks is quite difficult. However, having a broker to do the actual trading for you will make it much easier.

As in buying, all you need to do in order to sell your penny stocks is do a bit of research, contact your broker, and execute a sell order. Also, the information that you gave your broker for your buy order is the same as what you will have to give to them for your sell order. These include the ticker symbol, market, volume of shares you wish to sell, price of the shares, and the order's duration.

As an example, you can notify your broker that you want to sell 1,000 of your shares from your account in a specific company with the ticker symbol HYPO. You can then tell them that the stocks are in the OTCBB and that you wish to sell your stocks at $2 or more, with the order being active until the following Wednesday.

So, if the stock price of HYPO does become $2 or more, it will be sold. The money that's exchanged with the stock will be transferred to your account, and it can then be used for another transaction; however, this money will already be deducted with the broker's commission fee. Consequently, you now have $1,995 in your account.

If you want to know whether or not you made profits from your transactions, you can visit stocks and investment websites to help you gauge your profits, or you can do the computation yourself. To do this, just simply compare or subtract the money you shelled out for your buy order and the money you made from your sell order. For example, if the buy order cost you $1,005 ($1,000 for the stocks and $5 for the commission fee), and you got $1,995 for the sell order ($2,000 for the stocks, subtracted with $5 for the commission fee), after subtracting, you then have a profit of $990.

How to Open up an Account

The first step you'll need to follow when starting your investment in penny stocks is choosing which trading account you would like and then opening up the account. As an investor, it's in your best interest to take into consideration how easy the account is to work with. You should think about how easy it is to transfer to and from the account, the customer service that is offered with the account, and any fees that are associated with opening and running the account. There are times when a broker will choose a fixed rate for a smaller amount of shares, but one that can increase when trading on more shares. Depending on the type of trading that you do, this could make a big difference in the profit you make.

The nice thing about working on a commission per share idea is that it works well for investors who want to get into penny stocks but don't have a lot of extra money for this. As the investor, you will need to shop around in order to find the best broker and the best trading account to help expand your options and maximize your profits, so take the time to look at and talk to a few different companies to determine which one is the best for you to open.

Starting with Paper Trading

To start paper trading, you can go to online broker companies that provide practice software for prospective investors. You should choose companies that do not require initial deposits to download their software. By starting with these companies, you'll also start learning how to use their trading software.

If for some reason this method is not accessible, you could start paper trading manually. All you need is a notebook, a pen, and a stable internet connection. You can start paper trading by following these steps:

1. **Set a trading budget**

You should start by setting a budget that is close to your real-world budget. By setting one like this, you will be able to learn the advantages and limitations set by your budget. Ideally, you should choose an even number like $1,000 or $5,000. These numbers are easier to remember, and they will make it easier to calculate your profits or losses.

2. Set your trading rules

It's also possible to make the trading experience more realistic by setting real-world rules for your practice trading. For instance, you could start by setting the fees of your chosen broker. To learn about these fees, you can shop around for legitimate penny stock brokers. Try asking investors that you know of for recommendations. If you don't know people who invest in penny stocks, you can also try reading some blogs written by penny stock traders.

Aside from the fees, you should also consider jotting down the sources of information that you will use when buying and selling penny stocks. The best information source varies depending on the industry that you're participating in. You should also consider looking into the analytic tools that you'll use in making your decision when picking stocks and timing your selling process. These will be discussed in future chapters.

It's best to focus on one specific sector. By focusing on the healthcare sector, for example, you will be able to limit the amount of time you spend on research and information gathering. You will be able to specialize in your research because you will then have more time to delve into the companies. If you don't focus on one sector or industry, you'll spend all of your time on this task alone. The sheer number of companies out there will end up overwhelming you.

3. Use the best methods for practice trading

When investing in penny stocks, you need to follow certain rules that will increase your chances of making a profit. We have outlined some of these rules below:

- Set a target amount - You should have a goal when investing. A good investor sets his eyes on his goal and never gives up until he achieves it. Your goal will also result in an easier decision-making process. Let's say you want to increase your $100,000 practice money to $150,000. You will need a 50 percent increase in your investment. If you increase your portfolio value by 5 percent every month, you'll reach your goal within your eighth month. If you would like to attain your goal faster, you will need to take more risks by buying stocks with higher interest rate potential.

You will learn about the potential of these penny stocks based on their performance when you practice buying and selling them. By practicing your stock picking skills, you will be able to figure out which stocks perform well before you start risking real money. You will also have an idea of the spectrum of potential in investing in your chosen sector. This will prevent you from setting unrealistic goals when you're already using real money.

- Practice buying stocks only in your chosen sectors - When practicing investing in penny stocks, focus your resources only in your chosen sectors. If you plan to invest in the finance and healthcare sectors, for instance, only focus your practice time in them. This will develop your discipline in investing. When investing with real money, you'll be tempted to buy stocks that are hyped.

Don't feel bad if you missed out on these stocks because they are merely distractions. Instead, focus on the stocks of companies that you're familiar with. This way, you will always be making informed decisions rather than gambling away your money.

- Don't put your money in one company - When practicing, you should make a point to diversify your investments. Beginning investors are always tempted to throw their money into "sure" profits. However, you should learn from this point that there are no sure profits, especially in penny stocks. Because of the lack of information, penny stock companies post higher risks. The risk that comes with this type of investment makes diversifying even more important.

Start developing the discipline to diversify your resources, even when practicing, so that you won't be tempted by big profits when using real money.

- Follow more than one penny stock company at once - In the beginning, you should start following just a handful of companies. For instance, you should begin by following five companies from your chosen penny stock list. These companies should belong to your chosen sectors. As you spend more time following the market, you can expand the number of companies that you're following in these sectors. Eventually, you will know how each company stock performs in specific economic conditions.

Observe how the stock of these companies performs when the market is down. Take note of the best-performing stocks when the market is bullish and also when the market is bearish.

4.   Start buying and selling penny stocks

Now that you have set the trading criteria, you can now start going through the list of your chosen exchange and start researching about the companies that you find interesting. Your goal is to find a company that may be undervalued in the market. You can learn more about the company through research. With the internet, information flows faster. However, many individuals are looking for information about penny stock companies. You want to learn about key information before the rest of the market catches on.

When practicing, you should use your short-term, mid-term, and long-term strategies. Set a budget, and pick stocks that you will buy and sell in the short-term. You will buy and sell these stocks within the next month. You should also select stocks for your mid-term strategy. You will hold these penny stocks for at least one month and up to six months.

You should consider penny stocks for long term investments, as well. These investments are held for at least six months. You will need to hold especially stable companies for long term investments. These companies should have a great product and strong corporate leaders, and they should also show an intention for expansion. This can be in the arrangement of new products to reach new markets. They could also be expanding to more places. In some cases, they may realign their marketing strategy to target new market segments.

If you see that a company is successful in these types of business activities, you may want to consider investing in them for longer periods. In some cases, companies may even transition out of their penny stock status and register in a bigger exchange. This will increase the company's exposure and the value of its stock.

5.   Record your thoughts and experiences

When practicing, your goal is to create a list of guidelines to follow when you are already investing with real money. To do this, you need to record the strategies that you use and the changes that you create along the way. Start by using an investment journal. Choose a dotted journal where you record your thoughts before buying or selling stocks. After each week, record the results of the strategies you used. You should also include additional notes regarding your thoughts on specific strategies, companies, and economic events.

Let's say you practiced buying 100 shares of Company A and 100 shares of Company B. The market was on a downtrend all week long. Company A behaved accordingly, and your 100 shares decreased in value by 1.5 percent. However, Company B performed opposite to the performance of the market, and it increased in value by 0.5 percent.

You should take note of these factors in your journal. You could note the respective performances of these companies in your journal in that week and compare their performance to the overall performance of the sector and the market.

By doing so, you will get an idea of how stocks from certain companies behave during bullish and bearish markets. If the entire sector increased in value by 50 percent and your investment strategies only appreciated by 20 percent, you might be missing out on some key stocks. If you're participating in only one sector, use the sector performance as a gauge of your success. If you play in multiple sectors, on the other hand, use the performance of the market as your gauge.

Take note of the things that you should have done to improve your performance. Consider all risk and reward exchanges when you are noting your experiences. Your insights when practice trading may make you a lot of money when you're already investing real money.

6. Assess the best and worst trades weekly

When trading, you'll want to have a reason for each of your actions. You'll also want to know why the market behaved the way it did. You will learn these insights through experiences in the market.

You can start understanding these insights even while only still practicing. Every week, you should assess your trading performance and try to explain each of your actions, writing them down in your journal. Write down your thought process for why you bought or sold a certain stock of a company.

Aside from this, you should also assess the performance of the companies you bought and sold. Try to explain why a certain company increased in value. If a company performed less than expected, try to explain why it did that.

In this part of the process, you should also assess the value of your information sources. You should keep track of the information that you use when taking trading actions. If the information from a source keeps turning out to be false, drop the source. When using real money, only listen to sources of information that consistently churn out reliable data.

7.   Adjust your strategy based on your personal preferences

When you transition to real money, the fear of losing tends to set in and affect your performance. Take note of the mental factor when investing. More importantly, adjust your strategy based on the changes in your mindset. If you are afraid of losing money, you may perform better if you avoid high-risk stocks or if you transition into a sector with fewer price fluctuations.

If you're invested in tech stocks, for instance, you may be shocked by the sharp price fluctuations of the companies in the sector. These fluctuations will be even greater if you enter the market in an active season. If the fluctuations in the prices of stocks in this sector make you anxious, try practicing in less active sectors, such as the food industry.

Transitioning to Investing with Real Money

After practicing for months or even years, the next step is to process your application to start investing with real money. You need to consider a couple of things:

- Budget - Your budget should cover the initial investment required by your broker. It's possible to invest more, but as this is your first time, it's recommended that you start small. Some brokers have penalties for accounts that have low balances, so make sure that you have this amount covered to avoid unnecessary fees.
- Look for a broker that fits your needs - When selecting a broker, you should pick one according to the type of service that you need. In most cases, you will deal with regular brokers. They don't specify that they cater to only penny stock investors. However, take note of the ones who have special services for penny stock traders.

You will usually find special treatment to penny stock traders based on the fees and requirements that the broker imposes. Here are some of the fees and special requirements:

1.   Minimum balance

If you are just starting out and testing your strategies, you may want to begin with discount brokers. These include brokers with no minimum balance requirements. You can start investing in penny stocks for as low as $100.

2. Commission rate per trade

As you become more active, you may want to choose a broker with a low per-trade commission rate. You should shop around for the perfect balance between the minimum balance requirement and the per-trade commission rate.

3. Fees for low-priced shares

Since we're focusing on penny stocks, you should also avoid brokers that impose fees for low-priced shares. Some brokers have these types of fees to make more money from penny stocks and to discourage penny stock trading.

Choosing a Broker

So you've made it this far. You've read through the pros and cons of penny stock trading and somehow managed to avoid being scared away by the fact that it's so risky. Perhaps you're even enthralled by the possibilities that come along with penny stock trading or the inherent challenge. Well, that's perfect! Before we delve into how to pick the perfect stock in order to multiply your money and hopefully make you millions, there's one essential pit stop that we need to make: choosing the broker that we're going to decide on (Murphy, 2019).

The broker that you decide to use will actually have a lot of sway on the whole process of your trading. Your choice of broker can make a definite difference in how much money you make. You're going to want different brokers depending upon the exact situation that you're working with. For example, if you only have $500 to invest, you obviously don't want a broker with a $1,000 account minimum.

There are a few specific things that you want to be mindful of when you're choosing between various different online penny stock brokers.

The first thing is surcharges. Different brokers will often add surcharges to stocks if they cost less than a certain amount of money. The charges that aren't necessarily huge - usually something like a one-cent surcharge for every share bought - can still add up, especially if you're trading in higher volumes.

Another thing to be aware of is that a lot of brokers put restrictions in place. These may pop up as either restrictions to the volume that you trade or the manner in which you trade. When brokers restrict the volume of your trades, they'll often charge quite a bit extra for particularly large stock purchases. When they restrict the manner in which you trade, there are a myriad of ways in which they can do this. For example, some may require you to call them in order to place an order of a certain size, while others may demand that you only trade so many times per day. Neither is convenient, but sadly, it's the reality of working with online brokers. However, many online brokers won't have such stringent regulations in place, and you can rest assured that the regulations that are there are there for a certain reason.

So what broker will you go with? It depends on exactly what you need.

Overall

Many consider the two best penny stock brokers overall to be Charles Schwab and E-Trade. As an added perk to their other benefits, they both have a very strong customer support team and offer a ton of resources to educate you on how to choose stocks and play the market on your terms.

Charles Schwab is fantastic for a number of reasons. First off, they have a relatively low trade commission of only $4.95 for every trade you issue. The platform that they've established for trading penny stocks is top-notch and will definitely not leave you wanting. The only downside of Charles Schwab is that they have an account minimum of $1,000, which may be a bit out of your grasp, depending on whether you're wanting to get into this trade as a hobby or not. However, bear in mind that compared to some others (which we'll look at momentarily), this still isn't a bad account minimum. If you have the initial speculative investment capital to spend, then Charles Schwab is certainly a great option. As an added bonus, as of the time of writing, Charles Schwab will give you $500 cash with which to do as you wish if you deposit a certain amount of money into your account.

The other overall best option is often considered to be E-Trade. Their trade commission is a little bit higher than Charles Schwab's, clocking in at $6.95 per trade, but it falls down to be equal to Charles Schwab's at $4.95 if you issue more than thirty trades every financial quarter. If you intend on trading more heavily and more often, this may be the ideal route for you. The fact that they benefit people who intend to trade frequently even extends into their current promotion: they will give you sixty days of trades without any commission at all if you deposit a certain amount of money. What does this mean for you? Well, it means that if you're a frequent trader, then you could save hundreds of dollars on trade commissions. There are a lot of reasons that you can benefit from using E-Trade, but the low trade commissions combined with an easy-to-use and powerful platform, alongside an amazing breadth of penny stocks to choose from and a Library of Alexandria's worth of important information for enterprising young traders, all make it a great option.

Low Commissions

If you're specifically looking for brokers who will have a very light footprint on the amount you spend on commissions, then there are two other options you might want to consider. The ones with the lowest commission footprints are typically said to be Merrill Edge and Interactive Brokers.

Merrill Edge has a relatively high base commission at $6.95 per trade, but they don't have any sort of surcharges on top of that. That is to say that, on top of the cost that you're paying for your shares, you pay $6.95, and that's it. So where does Merrill Edge fall short? There aren't many, but one thing that you may find a tad out of reach is their $25,000 account minimum. Merrill Edge also certainly does not take any pains to cater to people who want to play the penny stock market. They allow people with lesser account values to trade on the normal exchanges and also have a mandate that money placed in penny stocks shouldn't be more than 20 percent of their account minimum. Despite all of this, if low commissions are your game, then Merrill Edge just may be the option that you want to look into.

Interactive Brokers is the other choice that has a very light commission footprint. They have no extra charges for penny stocks beyond a $1 minimum payment on every order that you place and a $0.50 cent per share commission. This is not much at all. You could trade 800 shares before it even really touches the base commission of other services, and that's not even including other services' surcharges and costs of a similar nature. They also have a much lower account minimum than Merrill Edge, coming in at only $10,000. However, they do quite a bit to vet the people that trade on their platform, wanting to keep it mainly used by professionals who have the money to spare. They have a monthly commission minimum of right around $10. They also require that you have a certain net worth and amount of income depending upon your age.

Platforms

If you're looking for the absolute best platform - maybe you're a hopeful professional or someone who just really wants to spend a lot of time analyzing the decisions that they make - then there are two services that you'd really be hard pressed to do much better than Ameritrade and TradeStation.

Ameritrade may just be one of the best platforms out there for a lot of reasons. They certainly don't cater to penny stock traders, with a pretty high trade commission of $6.95, but aside from that, they're actually a great choice for multiple reasons, the first of which being that they have no account minimum. Granted, you may pay for this later in surcharges and commission, but if you don't have much to get started and just want to be a weekend trader with some of the extra money you've got lying around, then you and Ameritrade just might become best friends. On top of that, they'll give you a $600 bonus when you deposit a certain amount of money.

We're not here to talk about any of that, though, are we? Ameritrade isn't being listed for its low account minimum nor its hefty promotional bonus. Rather, it's being mentioned for its absolutely incredible trading platform. Ameritrade's thinkorswim is easily one of the best trading platforms out there, regardless of what is being traded. It's equally great for options trading, safer securities trading, and penny stock trading, for the sole reason that thinkorswim is loaded with professional-grade tools that will help you do everything that you need to do and learn everything that you need to know. You'd be wise to try to work with Ameritrade in order to utilize it if a high-tech and limitless platform are among the things that you'd like to see in whatever broker that you choose. If you need something simpler for starting out, they also have an easily usable web interface called Trade Architect, which is far friendlier to newer investors.

TradeStation is the other broker worth mentioning for their platform. They have a trading platform that's immensely and endlessly complex. However, for its complexity, it is one of the most extensive and endlessly useful trading platforms on the market. Even more, it offers a plethora of tools and data that will help you figure out if you're making the right buy every single time.

Ending Notes

We have covered the most worthwhile penny stock brokers to look into. They all have their own sets of features that make them the best in their own right, and all of them have their own sets of pros and cons. I can't pin down the right one for you, simply because I'm not you. You could be a college student with an extra $1,000 from scholarships that you'd like to invest, or you could be a middle-aged man trying to make investments with some early pension money. It all depends on you and what you want out of investing.

How to Select Penny Stocks

In order for you as an investor to have a sense of clarity when it comes to what lies in store for your investment into penny stocks, it's helpful to know a stock's history. As the tried and true cliché goes, history repeats itself. Moving ahead without taking the time to look back will essentially doom you to make the same mistakes that other investors may have already made many times over. Generally speaking, some investors say that trading in penny stocks can simply be different scenarios that repeatedly play out time and again, generation after generation. Some investors are under the impression that the old economy rules will not work with new economy stocks, but no matter what your personal take on this issue may be, there is an irrefutable fact that researching the past proves for a more profitable future. How do you pick a winning penny stock? As stated previously in this book, it all begins with your research.

Share Price

Get to know that prices aren't always what they seem. The general line of logic is that penny stocks are far more cost-effective. However, this isn't necessarily true and fails to take other factors into account.

This is one of the biggest things that people misunderstand about penny stocks. Just because they're cheaper doesn't mean that they're automatically worth more, or that you're getting more for less. Allow me to explain.

People who reduce the entire situation to this simple notion of "share price" don't realize the actual value of their shares. This is where the concept of "shares outstanding" comes into play.

For example, let's consider two companies, one of which has a share price of $0.05 and a market capitalization of $50,000,000. The other has a share price of $50 and a market cap of

$50,000,000. They have identical market capitalizations, so they are actually not faring too badly compared to one another in terms of investiture. Because the first company has a share price of $0.05 and a market cap of $50,000,000, we can surmise that they have 1,000,000,000 outstanding shares, with outstanding shares being defined as the number of shares that have currently been issued. This is different from "authorized shares," which is the number of shares that the company is allowed to issue by the marketplace regulations. Meanwhile, Company B only has 1,000,000 shares issued. Thus, even though the two companies have a similar market cap and are faring similarly in that respect, the shares of Company A have a lower price than the shares of Company B, by virtue of the fact that there are more of them. Thus, the price of a company's shares isn't necessarily indicative of how well it's faring, especially not compared to another with a higher share price.

Side note: market capitalization has two meanings in the world of finance. The first is the sum total of the value of a corporation's stock, alongside its long-term debt and the earnings that it has retained. However, it can also refer to the number of outstanding shares multiplied by the share price to indicate how many have invested in the company and at what price. Here, of course, we're using the second definition, as we normally will throughout these discussions.

Dilution

This is the other thing that a new trader needs to be wary of when working with penny stocks; perhaps even more experienced traders won't have that much of an idea about how this concept works. Dilution refers to when the number of shares outstanding increases drastically and uncontrollably. There are a lot of reasons that this might happen. Among the most common are when companies decide to issue shares to others. This happens most often when they offer their employees stock options or when they start issuing shares as a means to raise the amount of capital that they have.

The second is actually extremely common among small companies as a means to raise the amount of money that they have, which is needed to operate and glide by until they have a meaningful occurrence (product launch, company milestone, new facility, and so forth).

However, when this happens, it can dilute the percentage of the company that's owned by the investors who contributed before the company began to issue shares. This would cause the share price to decline massively in order to maintain a steady market cap.

When you're working with penny stocks, it's incredibly important to be sure that the company you're wanting to use has a strong grip on the structure of its shares and the way that shares are supposed to be handled in different situations. If a company dilutes its shares constantly, the values of the shares will drop for the people who already own some. In other words, you won't be making money, and that's not a good thing. Be super careful about this. A company that dilutes often could make or break your penny stock portfolio.

How to Seek out the Winners

This is what you're reading this book for, I'm sure - to learn how to seek out penny stocks that will make you a lot of money in a short amount of time. Well, I can tell you that there's certainly no formula for doing so in any way, but there are a lot of things that you can do to increase the chances of picking a stock (or a set of stocks) that will give you a noticeable return.

First off, you need to look at how a company works. Look at the bare essentials of the company and its actions in order to determine whether it's a bright move or just a bold move for you to invest in them. For example, if they dilute their share prices often by issuing shares, do you really want to invest? Look at their structure, too. Is the company either drawing a profit, or will it eventually be able to gain a profit just by looking solely at the structure of the business and their current plans? Is it a realistic investiture? Could you see yourself using their product, if it came down to it? Is the company able to make a meaningful statement within its sector? Meaning, will the company be able to compete at a decent level with its competitors and hopefully, come out on top? Research its competitors, too, and see if it genuinely stands an honest chance against them.

If you do this for every single stock that interests you, you almost certainly will be able to find a very promising company with a bright future ahead of it right then and there. It's actually incredible just how much context can do for you as an enterprising investor, so seek it out as much as you possibly can. Knowing the context of a company will help prevent you from making terrible and wasteful investments.

Yet another thing that you can do is consider whether or not the company is in a sector where it's common or reasonable for a stock to be trading for less than a dollar. For example, the mining industry tends to have a lot of companies that trade for extremely low amounts - sometimes even just pennies. Because certain sectors rely quite a bit on the issuing of new shares in order to raise capital alongside hurting from increased competition within the sector, a potential investor must stay very alert as to the specific conditions in which the business they'd like to invest is residing. If the business suffers from poor conditions in a poor sector, then they likely are not a wise investment. If the business is in a sector with an extremely high level of competition, then it's not terribly realistic to expect that some run-of-the-mill company will just start taking over the sector and succeed at the rate at which you'd like it to. Some, however, are particularly good within their sectors and have very strong plans. Such was the case of

HudBay Minerals, which went from a small company with an even smaller micro-cop to a company worth two and a half billion dollars.

This may seem like obvious enough advice, but you'd be extremely surprised by how many investors and traders completely neglect looking into the basics of a company, like how much their shares are actually worth after taking into account shares outstanding or things such as the company's basic structure.

How to Find a Penny Stock Before It Spikes

It is fairly important for a penny stock trader to be able to notice when a stock is spiking. Of course, there is no 100 percent guarantee that will let you know what every single stock will be doing in every single situation (this is the stock market after all), but there are several signals that you can use in order to try and predict when spikes will occur.

The following list includes some ways to find penny stocks before they spike (number 1 is going to sound very familiar):

1.   Do your research

One big reason why most people fail when trading penny stocks is simply because they don't realize how much research needs to be done or because they are just too lazy to put the time in to do it. A lot of penny stock traders just want someone to simply tell them what they should do. The biggest problem with that scenario is this: the same person who is telling that trader what to do is also probably telling thousands of other traders the exact same information. Thus, all of these other traders will have already moved in on the proposed opportunity, which means that all that will be left is mere scraps. This won't be enough to make a profit and will actually most likely end up causing the investor to take a loss.

So the real question, then, is how to find out the next big news before the masses, right? The answer for doing so is, of course, research. Look up a stock's disclosure and filings. Find out whether or not that stock has had any recent news in those filings. You may be able to find out that a stock is about to spike using whatever news you find.

2.   Bet on a stock's price action

Many potential investors make the mistake of attempting to predict when a spike is occurring by paying a visit to their chat room of choice to check in with other members to see what stocks they think may be moving or to see how high they think a specific stock is going to go. Other potential investors may buy alerts from a guru of sorts who might tell them when they should buy, according to their predicted spikes.

This is not to say that all chat rooms are bad. Investors have made a lot of money off of tips from people they trust in certain chat rooms. Ultimately, though, chat rooms are just simply a forum for conversation. Instead, you should really bet on a stock's price action. A stock's price action is its chart movement, and that will give you the actual information about any stock. All of the latest news on every site in the world will not be able to tell you when a stock may break out to a new high or if it has crossed its VWAP, but the chart movement of a stock certainly will.

3.   Seek out stocks with the potential for breakouts that are reaching new highs

As a penny stock investor, it may behoove you greatly to always keep an eye out for those stocks that may be following this trend. This especially applies to the stocks that are holding the morning high and still up on the day. You do have to exercise some caution here, though. If you happen to see this play out on a Friday afternoon, there is a big potential for a short squeeze being worked into the close at that point.

4.   You can piggyback on a stock that has spiked a bit already

Out of these four strategies, this one will certainly take up a lot less of your time than the others. Piggybacking is where an investor finds a stock that's already on its way up. This is really one of the fastest methods of identifying a stock that is about to spike. There are plenty of research tools available online that can help investors find this information. All you need to do is utilize them.

Hopefully, you will put these strategies to use, and they will help you learn how important it is to properly prepare and research before you buy into any stock, penny or otherwise. The majority of penny stock traders decide not to bother with the work it takes to really dig into the SEC filings of a company they may be interested in, much less take the time to attempt to interpret what all of that information will mean as far as the price of the stock moving higher or lower. This is the reason why the majority of penny stock investors will ultimately end up bankrupting their own portfolios - a lack of preparation and research.

There is no need for you to end up with the same fate. While most people may not find research and preparation to be particularly enjoyable undertakings, keep in mind that this book is not claiming to tell you how to get rich quick or how to have the most fun you've ever had; the purpose of this book is to show you how to be successful in trading penny stocks by providing proven rules and methods of seasoned investors and how to be successful in obtaining the financial freedom that you desire. So, what does it take to really be a success in trading penny stocks?

It takes hard work and a lot of determination. Success in trading in penny stocks requires that you, the investor, put in the time and energy that is necessary in order to reap the kind of benefits that you're seeking. Traders who choose not to put in the necessary time and energy will not accomplish the things that you as a dedicated trader will accomplish, and they will never be able to enjoy the financial freedom that you will be able to enjoy - all because they avoided doing what was necessary to succeed. Even though proper planning may not exactly be fun, it is absolutely crucial in order to achieve success when trading penny stocks.

The Payoff Potential in Penny Stocks

Since there is all this risk and hard work involved, you may be wondering why any potential investor in their right mind would be willing to buy into penny stocks. The answer here is simply the volatility. Penny stocks are very much prone to volatility and violent fluctuation. Knowing this, a lot of investors believe in the possibility of lucking out on a certain stock that they think has the ability to jump from a mere $0.09 up to $9 in just a few weeks. While this is certainly not typical, it has actually happened. If you look through enough message boards that are dedicated to investing, then you will definitely be sure to read some success stories where investors talk about how they made a significant amount of money while "playing the pennies."

It is extremely rare to come across a company that can successfully navigate, making the leap from being a penny stock to becoming a power stock, but on the rare occasion that you do find them, those stocks really pay out in a mind-blowing way. Since the numbers in the penny stock world are so volatile and vary so greatly, some very prepared investors have actually seen gains that reached over 1,000 percent in only a few weeks. Of course, the real trick lies in first being able to find a winning stock, which this chapter has hopefully better prepared you to do.

Enjoying this book so far? I'd love it for you to share your thoughts and post a quick review on Amazon!

Chapter 7: Strategies

It's difficult to encapsulate penny stocks into a few "strategies." This isn't some 1990s video game where there's a set way to win a given level, and it's also not some 2019 video game where there are seven different ways to win a level. The hard truth is that there's no such thing as "winning a level" when it comes to penny stocks because penny stock investing is simply just investing in a market. The market will go up and go down, and a win for one is a loss for another, somewhere. There is no market absolution. If you were to invest in the right thing, then sure, maybe you could consider it a win, but what if you sold and the stock continued to rise? Are you now a loser, since you didn't win as well as you could have? If a stock goes down one day, you might consider yourself a loser - but what if it balloons in price the very next day? Are you a winner now?

The truth is that, in many ways, playing the stock market isn't a game, no matter how fun it can be, and because it's not a game, there are no strict win conditions, nor is there even really a way to win, because there's no such thing as winning.

One can, however, do things that appear like winning. You can develop tendencies that will allow you to generally make the right decision, even if you don't ride a stock all the way to the top or even if things go awry and you have to watch it crash to the bottom. You can also develop a deep enough knowledge of not only investing but also of the various industries in which you'd like to invest, such that you can make wiser investment choices. However, to say there's a single investment strategy to win every time is silly, because it dilutes the multi-faceted and beautifully enthralling world of finance and trading into a simple dichotomy of winning and losing, which is false.

With all of that in mind, we will go over some tips. These are strategies to help yourself and to change the way you think so that you can look at the market in a better and more clever way.

So, let's go through these ones by one.

1. *Examine the waves*

The first tip is to watch how the market moves. A ton of studies on penny stocks and penny stock trading have shown that looking at the market with a short-term eye and trading in the short-term is far less risky than trying to trade in the long-term. This is understandable, too. Companies that tend to be based on the penny stock exchanges generally have one of two business models: they are either a new small business with a strong management team and a great product that just need some capital investment in order to get themselves off of the ground or a low-profit small-scale operating company that isn't yielding too much of a result one way or the other.

By recognizing this and trying to trade in the short-term rather than the long-term, you can mitigate the risk that you accidentally invested in the latter rather than the former. Of course, this also should go hand in hand with doing a lot of research on a company and being certain that they're reputable and strong enough to be worth making an investment. However, working in the short-term in combination with a fair amount of research can make a huge difference and make the risky game of penny stocks just a little bit less risky.

So, how do you play in the short term? You play the day trading game of buying low and selling high. It's normal for stocks to be a bit like an ocean wave and fluctuate, going from low to high and back. This is just the life cycle of a stock and is not out of the ordinary whatsoever. When it's in a low, you buy. When it's high, you sell. If you do this with a company that you know well, you can make quite a bit of money.

2. *Block out others*

I don't mean you should quit listening to your family or feeding your dog. Rather, new investors tend to be highly affected by malicious companies who opt to artificially make their stock more valuable than it actually is. This can be tragic for other investors, but great for the businesses in question. After they've gotten a bunch of new and inexperienced investors to invest in a stock for little to no reason other than word-of-mouth and the fact that they said the stock was a good investment, the owners of the company that spread the word about the stock will then sell their shares in order to make an easy profit.

This problem is becoming even more prevalent now that penny stocks have started to be placed in the spotlight more than they were before. Now, there is technology everywhere and constant communication between people. Penny stocks are no longer relegated to over-the-counter exchanges. Much like options, the fact that we've entered into an information age where people can spread their success stories has led to a lot of interest in penny stocks that weren't there before. Of course, this is exacerbated greatly by the fact that penny stocks are very cheap. This makes them rather appealing to people who aren't wealthy and those who would just like to weekend trade. These people normally play the penny stock exchanges like a lottery, putting their money where they think it should vaguely go and not thinking much more about it. They'll come back to it the following weekend and see just how well their investment went. These kinds of gullible hopeful investors have created a perfect audience for greedy and malicious people out in the real world who think it would be perfectly hilarious to find unsuspecting people and con them into investing in a worthless company so that they can earn a quick buck.

This sort of scam is called a "pump and dump," and it's highly illegal. There are a number of different times in history where pump and dump scams have been all over the news and have been major silver bullets to the ever-fragile world economy. Perhaps the most well-known example of this scam is the Enron debacle.

Back in 2001, a company called Enron was one of America's largest electric and gas companies of all time. The executives at Enron decided that they would craft up a lofty scheme that would make them a ton of money, part of which involved a pump and dump. The scheme was so brilliantly devised that even the most clever and experienced Wall Street financial analysts were tricked. The company was going under for various reasons and was quite in debt. The debt was highly covered up by mark-to-market accounting, which is a form of accounting that aims to present balance sheets and company yields not as they actually are, but as the investors and the stock market would like them to be. The Enron executives were reporting profits high enough in order to inflate the price of Enron's stock, and shortly before the company went bankrupt, nearly thirty Enron executives would sell the stock they had for over a billion dollars altogether. They made a hefty profit, obviously. However, the resulting trial would end up landing most of them behind bars.

Another more fun example of this is Jonathan Lebed's pump and dump scheme. Then only fifteen, he was determined to prove how simple it was to use the internet in order to pull off a successful pump and dump scam. He bought many shares of penny stocks and then went on to promote them on message boards and chat rooms. He pointed at the price increase and told people to buy the stocks that he bought, saying that they were good investments; however, they were not, which was unknown to the people who were falling victim to Lebed's scam! He would then sell his shares for a profit, leaving the stock rather worthless and with the other investors losing a lot of money. It was at this point that the young Lebed landed in the eyes of the SEC. The SEC filed a suit against him. He would not end up going to jail, and instead simply paid back some of his gains and made a promise not to manipulate the markets anymore. At the end of the day, he still walked away with hundreds of thousands of dollars - not half bad for a fifteen-year-old, if you ask me. The young

Lebed was very clever, but what he did was highly illegal.

These are just two examples, and the first one shows that you don't necessarily have to be gullible to think that a stock is valuable when it isn't - pretty much the whole of the US investing core thought that Enron was far more valuable than it really was. However, if you keep your wits about you and pay close attention to everything that you're investing in, carefully going over the history of everything that you want to work with, it's highly likely that you can avoid being a money-losing victim in the scheme of someone like Jonathan Lebed.

3. *Don't expect too much*

One of the reasons you probably even picked up this book was because, at some point, you heard somebody say how much of an untapped gold mine penny stocks are. I'm sure that now, you're a little disenchanted with that concept, especially after reading about all of the risks and scams that happen with penny stock trading. However, maybe there's a part of you that's thinking that you can make a ton of money with penny stocks if you do it correctly. That part of you isn't wrong. In fact, it's technically right.

You can make a bunch of money pushing penny stocks, just like your son can make $50 per day by opening a lemonade stand, or your dog could just relax on the couch when you get home from work instead of jumping on you excitedly. It could happen, but that doesn't mean that it's likely to.

This brings us back to the whole part about respecting the market, and there not being winners and losers. The best investors aren't the ones who make $500,000 off of a single trade. No, those are the luckiest investors. The lucky ones are always winners, but the winners aren't always lucky. You don't have to be lucky to be a good investor.

If you try to coast by on luck alone and you do end up making $500,000 on a single trade, you might decide that it played out really well, and so you must be a master investor. Then, you decide to invest $100,000 of the $500,000 you made in profit back into the penny stock market. You choose to invest in a stock which is rising, and it keeps rising, and you don't sell, and then it takes a nosedive. Maybe the owner of the company got caught in a terrible scandal, or they had a major disaster at one of their main facilities. The stock that you bought is now worth less than what you bought it for, and you've effectively lost a few thousand dollars. So, what happened? Well, you didn't play it risky. Instead of setting a minimum and maximum amount that you'd be happy with, you got greedy and waited for a guarantee of gain that wasn't there. Instead of making back 125 to 150 percent of what you invested, you've now lost about 10 percent.

It's a bit of an extreme example, but it happens on a micro-scale every single day. This is even more important in a market such as penny stock exchanges where everything is so volatile and moving from here to there and back again on a daily basis. If you go in expecting the world, you're going to be intensely disappointed and probably will end up being one of the majority of penny stock investors who end up losing money in the process of investing.

Be happy with little bits here and there. Don't get greedy. If you get lucky, then that's fantastic, but don't rely on luck alone. Build up good trading habits now so that you have them when things do get a little rough.

4. *Have a plan*

This tip is understated. It's always smart to have a plan no matter what you're doing. However, it's especially important to have a plan in something so volatile as penny stocks.

Now, it may be a little difficult to imagine having a plan when you're working with these stocks. After all, everything is so erratic all the time, so how can one possibly have a plan?

Well, the fact that it's so volatile means that it's especially important to have one. You always need to have a maximum that you'll be happy to gain, a maximum that you'll be happy to lose, and most importantly, an exit plan.

You need a maximum that you'll be happy to gain so that you don't sit down greedily on a stock when something is going your way. You could easily end up losing money this way - possibly more than you're really willing to lose.

You need a maximum that you'll be happy to lose because you don't want to sit around waiting for the stock coming through the tunnel when it may never do so. If a penny stock loses $0.13, of course, it's hypothetically possible in a volatile market that it could make an utter swing and come out the other side and gain back its value really quickly, in the end making you a profit. Of course, it's possible, but that doesn't mean that it's smart to wait around for this to happen, because it may not. Then, if it doesn't, suddenly the negative $0.13 shares you're sitting on are negative $0.25, and you've lost a ton of money. Is that really something that you want to happen?

You always need an exit plan. Have an idea of what you're going to do when the stock is within the boundaries that you've set, whether it's going in your favor or not. Are you going to sell it and sit on the money, or are you going to reinvest it? If so, do you need to be researching other penny stocks you may be interested in? This isn't as vital for securities as it is for futures, but it's still worthwhile to have an exit plan for your timing and your events afterward. Even one personally stagnant moment in the world of finance can make all the difference.

5. *Don't let your emotions get in the way*

This tip is arguably the most important. You absolutely cannot let your emotions get in the way. What do I mean by emotions? I mean greed, anger, sadness, vindication, happiness, etc. When you're in front of your stock portfolio or your trading platform, all that you should allow yourself to think in are rational absolutes. Anything that isn't a rational absolute isn't worth your time and will only throw you off course.

You may be wondering what is exactly implied by letting your emotions get in the way. Let's say that you suffer a loss on a stock, and so to make up for that loss, you end up pouring even more money into the next investment that you make with the rationale that a profit on that will make up for both the losses and the disappointments of the prior failed trade. You decide to invest in another stock in a rush, only barely looking at the stock's history and the company itself.

Is that rational at all? No, of course not. However, you'd be surprised by how often this happens to people who'd like to be financial traders.

Money isn't an art, but rather a science. Spare your emotions for art. Money is a game of math. The answers to your high school algebra assignments weren't allowed to change depending upon whether you felt happy, sad, or angry on any given day, so why would you allow the way you handle your money to change with your emotions? The basic operations don't change, as they shouldn't, so why would anything else change? That's absurd. Money is money is money, and it is absolute, so treat it absolutely, as you would math or chemistry.

So, what exactly can you do to avoid letting your emotions get in the way? Well, having your investing money detached from the money you need to live can help, hence why earlier in the book, it was recommended that you only use speculative investing money that you can spare in order to invest in penny stocks. Using anything else is not only risky but a wholly bad idea. You need money to get by in life. Therefore, don't make the stupid mistake of mixing your gambling money with your energy bill. That's how you lose your lights, and believe me, you don't want to lose your lights.

Don't forget to take time to decompress each day and get away from your investments. Designate part of your day to meditate and possibly practice the tenets of Zen if you're so inclined. Give yourself a massage to release your tension, or set up a very comfortable couch in front of a bright window and take time each day to sit in front of it and bask in the light, revitalizing yourself and calming your nerves, which are surely on edge from a long day of trading and market unpredictability.

Do whatever you can in order to be certain that you yourself are healthy because your wellness always comes first. When your body and mind are healthy and relaxed, clear decision-making will follow.

6. *Keep a journal*

This is a big one. Keep a record of your trading patterns, both good and bad. Record your thoughts on each trade and how those trades go for you. If something stuck out to you about a company, record that. Do whatever you can in order to document your thought process when you're trading.

Why should you do this? Well, there's hardly anybody better to learn from than yourself. I can guarantee that some of the greatest lessons you'll ever learn are from your own mistakes (and also the mistakes of others, of course). Learn what things go wrong for you, and try to keep up with your own head in terms of what you're thinking (or what you aren't thinking) when you make the good (or bad) decisions that you do.

You'll eventually develop your own style of trading, and this will help you to find out what works best for you. Maybe you find that you're actually rather good at seeking out companies that will be good in the long-term, and your strength is to invest more in the companies that you think will do well. On the other hand, maybe you'll figure out that when you invest a lot, you don't do as well. This might tell you that you need to make smaller investitures and diversify more. Everyone has a different temperament and a different way of thinking about things. By studying your own thoughts and your own tendencies - how much you invest, when you invest, the way in which you invest, whether you take profits or losses - will teach you a lot about the game of trading and about your own way of playing it.

You won't always make the right decisions. In fact, a lot of the time, you won't. That's where this journal will come in handy.

Dollar Cost Averaging (DCA)

Numerous investors, especially the ones who are just starting to invest, are under the wrong impression that in order to gain a high profit in trading, they have to buy and sell shares at the same time. Of course, this strategy can prove useful if you don't want to hire a broker and want to save money by limiting or eliminating broker commission fees. However, you'll find that the advantages are fewer ('Trading Strategy,' 2019).

A better strategy that is proven to work is DCA. As you should know by now, penny stocks tend to be very unpredictable and volatile. You should always avoid the short-term upsides and downsides that a lot of penny stocks have. As an investor, you can benefit by using Dollar-Cost Averaging. The simple process of the DCA strategy is as follows: purchase additional shares of the stock at precise and pre-established set intervals (no matter the activity of the share price) rather than purchasing all the shares at the same time.

Usually, with the DCA, many people buy shares when the stock price is low, and they don't when the stock price is high. Using the DCA strategy, however, you will lower the risk of investing a large amount of money into a single investment that can turn out to be bad and reap negative returns. The average price will be lower than what it would be if you purchased all the shares at a price peak. Overall, keep in mind that you should absolutely avoid the high risk that comes with purchasing a large number of shares when the stock price is at its highest. Invest in small intervals over an extended period of time instead.

There is, however, a downside to the DCA. This relates to the commission you must pay to the broker; every transaction requires a new commission to be paid. Nonetheless, the positives of DCA win over the negatives, because minimizing risk is probably the most important thing, and it cannot (and should not) be compared to a commission cost.

Reverse Mergers

Do an advanced search for penny stocks that match your investment and trading criteria, looking for public stocks that have gained their status through a "reverse merger."

Here is what happens in a reverse merger: a public company that possesses a small or nonexistent amount of assets merges with a private company that not only has assets but also has operations and personnel. When the successful, private company merges with the struggling public company, it becomes publicly traded. If you own stock in a private company and want to make it public, this is a very easy way to do so.

Let's use an example to better clarify this point. We are going to use the private company ABC that has $5 million of earnings and wishes to go public. ABC contacts a small company that agrees to give them a major part of their stock, and in return, the small company will own a small stake in ABC. The public company obtains ABC for around $0.10 a share. After the merger is finished, the reverse-merged company makes a press release stating that the private company went public, that their management team is still the same, and that the company underwent a beneficial and successful merger.

If ABC keeps growing, stocks will move even higher in price since there are many investors interested in buying shares of merged companies. This may not always be the case, however. Sometimes companies that undergo a reverse-merger don't see a profitable rise in their stock prices. In essence, it all depends on the newly created public company; if that company fails, the stock prices will encounter a decline, which will lead to a loss of money for the investors.

Stop-Loss Orders

Stop-losses are something every investor or trader needs to know how and when to manage. They are sell orders that are triggered if the stock or stocks purchased fall any percentage below the original purchase price. Stop-loss orders will save you from financial hardships that occur when shares experience frequent declines. There are two different subcategories of stop-loss orders: automatic and mental. What category you find yourself and your investments under will depend upon your broker; some brokers will let you set up an automatic stop-loss order, while other brokers need to do it manually.

Below we have detailed how both an automatic and mental stop-loss order work:

- **Automatic:** If you are allowed to set up an automatic stop-loss order on a couple of penny stocks, your stock will be put on sale once it reaches your pre-established "stop" price. If this option is available, use it. These are more reliable than the mental.
- **Mental:** With this one, you already have a trigger price in mind. You sell when shares fall below your pre-established price, but this selling is done manually by your broker. There's no system in place to sell your share automatically, hence the difference between automatic and mental stop-loss. However, when you purchase a stock using mental stop-loss, don't forget to set up a price alert at the level you decide to stop at so you aren't caught off guard if and when the time comes.

One of the hardest elements about investing is selling your shares when they hit the mental stop-loss level. Many investors try to either find a way out of the position or keep their investments. If you want to use stop-loss orders successfully as an investment strategy, then stick with it and don't ask questions or make excuses. Like any other strategy, stop-losses are not free of risk. One of the biggest risks that hide among penny stock trading and investing is the possibility of being stopped out. This is referred to as a "fall price swing." This is when you hit your pre-established stop-loss price, and soon afterward, you sell the stock, only to observe the price of shares in that same penny stock go up once again.

If you find yourself entering a situation like this, there are a few things you can do to prevent yourself from getting completely stopped out:

- **Set stop-losses on high trading volume shares** - These penny stocks will have less price volatility in general. Once the stock starts falling, a lot of the observing investors may buy at the lower prices and thus push the shares high once again.
- **Use stop-loss on penny stocks that have a low volatility history** - If a penny stock currently has high volatility, you can count on it to only increase in the future. The lower the volatility, the

better the chances of not being stopped out on price swings.

- **Set up stop-loss on stocks for which you expect a great price decline** - Instead of setting your stop level at 5 or 10 percent below your buying price, think about dropping it down to 25 percent of your original purchase price. This lower stop may put you at financial risk, but it will also lower the risk of getting stopped out if there is a brief fall in shares. You'll need to determine what your personal preferences are and what you think works best in your unique financial situation when following this suggestion.

- **Purchase shares on price dips** - Wait and purchase stock shares after a price dip. This will lead to short-term upsides and won't fall too much in the future. When you purchase penny stocks after they experience price dips, you lower your chance of getting stopped out in the near future.

Position Sizing

Position sizing is probably the best strategy for keeping your portfolio safe, yet it's somehow misunderstood by all too many investors, experienced and inexperienced. With position sizing, you are limiting every purchase to an already determined percentage of your own portfolio. So, for example, let's say you have a $10,000 portfolio and you choose to limit your biggest purchase to $500. This will be roughly 5 percent of your portfolio. Yes, with this strategy, you are certainly limiting your profit opportunities, but you are also protecting your investments from a downfall. This strategy is appropriate for bigger portfolios. If you are a trader with a $240,000 portfolio, for example, you may benefit by purchasing stocks worth $4,000, which means that you'll be able to purchase around 60 different stocks. Doing so will risk just a small part of your portfolio on every single stock. If your portfolio is small, it may not work out in the best way possible with this strategy. If you have only $3,000 to invest, it would be pointless to divide this relatively small amount among 10 penny stocks.

When to Take and When to Sell a Profit

There are highly effective strategies that will help you determine the perfect time to withdraw your profit and when you should sell your stock if the price experiences a gradual and/or steady decline.

- **Stopping at a profit** - If you invested in a stock and its price has risen significantly from the price you bought it at, it would be a safe and profitable investment move to sell and take the profit while you can. Doing so locks in your gains. When shares are trading at a significantly higher price than your purchase price, you should lock in your gains instead of taking financial risks. If the stock looks unfavorable, and financial analysis shows that the company may soon experience a decline, you should absolutely consider taking your profit before any major financial changes occur. Even if you are wrong and the price of the stock goes up, you can rest assured that you've still made a considerable profit and have the funds to pursue further investment opportunities. If there is no loss, you experience no stress.

- **Take your losses** - You'll need to learn to accept your losses when they happen, which means accepting your financial mistakes, learning from them, and moving forward. As already mentioned, selling shares at a loss is probably the hardest thing you are going to stumble upon as an investor. Penny stocks are risky by nature, which means that you should always know what happens concerning the company you are investing in, and if their stock price declines.

Moving Averages (MA)

Moving averages can be very helpful when it comes to penny stocks because they can identify clear buying and selling signals. Moving averages can be described as the average price of your shares over a selected time frame. For example, a seven-day MA will display the average price of stock each day, with the seventh day included. In general, if you have a couple of MAs, they will be applied at the same time, which makes your trades very clear.

The moving averages are looking back, which means that they display the changes in the prices until this point rather than making predictions regarding what the shares will do when they keep moving forward. You'll be able to spot the beginning of a trade if you notice some momentum price changes of a stock, which will be portrayed by moving average lines of crossing lengths that have different timing. The strategy in this technical analysis indicator is when shares start to go up or down significantly, the new prices should outpace the MA that is lagging.

You can see this outpace by the moving average breaking away from the shares price. When a major trend starts, the price of the share will begin to move higher. Afterward, throughout the following days, there will be a movement up in the shorter moving average. In the end, the longer MA will start going up, and the shorter MA will lag. As an investor, you should know a few things about the moving averages:

- **Time length** - If you want to use moving averages successfully, you should select their duration. Rather than looking for the best and most effective duration, you should find the one that will be the most reliable. If you pick a short MA time frame, the prices should be more responsive at the beginning, because in order to calculate the average, a few days will be needed.

- **The number of moving average** - Many TAs involve two moving averages. Of course, there are investors who prefer to use only one, but others think it's more beneficial to use three or more MA lines. If you're investing in penny stocks, in particular, the most effective way to do so is to use exactly two MA lines.

- **Buy and sell signals** - Every time a short MA crosses a long one, it indicates a buy signal. When the MA indicators display the trending up of the short-term prices, this means a stock uptrend. On the other hand, when the short MA goes below the long one, it implies a sell. When the MA indicator displays that the short-term prices are going beneath the long-term average price, this indicates a stock downtrend.

The key to being a successful trader and investor relies upon the strategies you understand and embrace during your time in the stock market.

Chapter 8: Risk Management

Since they are typically issued by small and growing companies with limited resources as well as limited cash, and because their shares are considered to be extremely speculative, penny stocks are known for being very volatile and more suited for those investors who have a high-risk tolerance. All in all, the majority of penny stocks tend to have low trading volumes and also tend to be high-risk investments. As an investor, there are some things that you need to be aware of, including some of the risks that are involved with trading penny stocks. Keep in mind that penny stocks have earned every bit of their bad reputation, but educating yourself will remove a lot of the extra risk involved.

The Risks Associated with Penny Stocks

Aside from the usual risks that come with trading volatile stocks, here are some things that you may not be aware of, even if you're not a total beginner:

- Spam - everyone has seen it, and everyone despises it. As an investor, spam can be found not only in the inbox of your email but also through many places online. Penny stocks are not immune, either. Scammers make a lot of money by promoting sketchy penny stocks to investors that may not know that this practice exists.
- Be aware of dilution. Sometimes a company will need to issue additional stock in order to gain capital. When this happens, it usually leads to the dilution of the stock that's already held by its investors, meaning that the stock decreases in value. This is commonplace and is not considered to be shady dealings at all, but it's certainly something that investors need to be aware of.
- Pink sheets and the OTCBB do not have to meet minimum standard requirements to stay on the exchange. Minimum standards are in place to protect investors and as a guideline for

companies issuing stock. When first starting out, you may want to stick with trading on a major exchange, because they have regulations in place which protect you and your investment.

- The short squeeze is a tricky, calculated situation where a very heavily shorted commodity or stock moves higher very sharply and forces the short sellers to close out their short positions, which only adds to the stock's sudden upward pressure. The term "short squeeze" refers to the fact that the short sellers are effectively being "squeezed" out of their position in the stock, and they typically find themselves at a loss.

- One issue penny stocks are known for is the difficulty in finding necessary information and history about them, which makes it even more difficult to form an educated decision when trading (Staff, 2016). If you paid enough attention to what worked for you and what didn't when you were paper trading and heeded the warnings and advice of trusted sources such as this book, you should be able to make more informed decisions.

- Penny stocks are known for not having much liquidity. This means that it can be really difficult to sell a stock once you have bought it, and you may have to lower your price below your buying price in order for that stock to sell. Low liquidity in a stock also makes it more vulnerable to manipulation and pump and dump type scams.
- The pump and dump scam is probably the most common scam associated with penny stocks, so you need to keep your eyes open and know what to look for. The pump and dump consist of a worthless stock being bought up by an individual or company. Then, the worthless stock is hyped up, and investors who are inexperienced end up buying these worthless stocks at a heightened price - this is the pump. When the inexperienced investors have bought enough of the stock to drive the price up enough, the person or company who initially bought the previously worthless stock then sells all of their shares, which effectively makes the stock worthless again. This is known as the dump. Beware!

10 Ways to Protect Yourself and Prepare for Financial Freedom

Some investors may not be aware of the methods that are available for protecting themselves when investing in penny stocks and can end up getting burned or losing all of their hard earned savings. There is some repeated information made in the following list of pointers that can be found in other parts of this book, but just know that this repetition serves a purpose. Some things just bear repeating. Be mindful of the following points in order to avoid the scams, misleading information, and low-quality investments associated with penny stock investment:

1. **Prepare yourself by doing your research**. Anyone who has ever invested in penny stocks will tell you that you need to prepare and research as much as possible before you buy in. You don't anticipate winding up as one of those super sad statistics where you lose everything

because you got bamboozled. Have you ever wondered why Wall Street is always profiting, no matter what? Wall Street always profits, because there is always someone buying into stocks which have not done their research and, therefore, loses their money. So make sure to do your research.

2. **If you come across a penny stock tip in your email or on social media, just say no.** Do not spend any time at all on these types of tips. Many inexperienced investors buy up these stocks like they're lotto tickets when the jackpot is up to hundreds of millions of dollars. That definitely isn't the right way to handle these tips; just ignore them altogether.

3. **Read the disclaimers on all penny stock newsletters.** In general, penny stocks are sold more than they are bought. A huge contributor to this fact is the misinformation contained in those newsletters that convince potential investors to buy and buy quickly. Keep in mind that penny

stock newsletters do not dole out free advice just to be nice. The disclaimers at the bottom of these newsletters will inform you whether or not someone is just trying to create hype by making a false promise about their worthless companies.

4. **Never listen to what a company's management says about their stock.** This closely correlates with the previous point on the grounds that, yet again, someone is trying to manipulate you as the investor into purchasing what will be a scam. Most penny stocks are actually thought to be scams themselves. They are stocks that are built up by a company so that they can stay in business and created with the sole purpose of enriching only the business' insiders by taking advantage of investors. Be aware that there is a large group of people who run penny stock promotions using all kinds of different press releases (think newsletters, social media, etc.) and

different companies. In fact, one of these people has actually recently returned to the stock market after being convicted of a pump and dump scam while barely in high school.

5. **Be quick to sell.** After all of the unnerving information above, the good news is that it is possible to make 20 or 30 percent of your penny stocks in just a few days. This is the main reason why people are drawn to them. When you happen to see this kind of return, you need to put your curiosity or greed aside and sell immediately; this is because penny stocks can be so volatile that you never know when the 20 or 30 percent may suddenly drop to nothing at all. In penny stocks, it is not very prudent to hold out for a 1,000 percent return. Take your profits and move on.

6. **Do not trade big.** Trading big is also known as trading large positions, and you need to be really careful about your position sizing when it comes

to penny stocks. As a rule of thumb, it is smart not to trade more than about 10 percent of a stock's daily volume. You'll actually want to limit your share size so that it will be easier for you to sell the stock more quickly, which ultimately results in making more money.

7. **Only focus on those penny stocks that have a high volume.** Try to deal with penny stocks that trade a minimum of 100,000 shares per day. Penny stocks with lower volumes are more difficult to sell, and so they're also more difficult to make money on.

8. **Give yourself limits and guidelines.** Learn what risk-reward ratios work for you and stick to them when buying and selling your penny stock shares. While there may be a time or two that you could have made more money if you would have waited for just a little longer, sticking to the limits you create for yourself will end up generating more profit for you in the long run.

9. **Do not get attached to any penny stock because someone tells you to be.** This can be especially difficult to do when a family member or a friend specifically recommends a particular stock and are very enthusiastic about its potential. Also, each and every penny stock company out there would love for you to think that it has the most potentially profitable stock with the most exciting story and that it will revolutionize the known world. As you are entering the arena of penny stock trading, it is extremely wise to be very cynical, to diversify, and to rely on your own research (there's that word, again) before you buy into any penny stock.

10. **Look for the penny stocks that are having an earnings breakout.** A stock that has good earnings will be breaking out to 52-week highs and will be trading at a volume of at least 250,000 shares per day. If you know where and how to look, these types of penny stocks can be relatively easy

to find. However, the challenge comes again in avoiding a pump and dump scam that is behind the 52-week highs of a penny stock.

Chapter 9: Identifying Good Companies

At the heart of all of the metrics and ratios is the search for a good company. As a penny stock investor, all you're really looking for at the end of the day is a business that knows what it's doing and one that just so happens to have cheap stock at the moment. You're looking for a company that's having success serving a market, that's able to grow, and is run by competent people (Lewis, 2019).

Look for Companies Matching a Strong Angle with Financial Competence

The previous chapter listed a multitude of metrics that can help shed light on a business's ability to attain the financial goals it needs to, but if you're looking to invest in a company that's going to succeed big, then you have to make sure that the business itself is clearly viable and that it has a great angle. This type of information about a business can be found in press releases, internet chat rooms, on the company's website, and in the media. Below is a fictional account of what your research process may look like.

Let's say you get a tip in a chat room or on a penny stock investor website that a certain stock trading at $5 per share has great potential. Let's say that the stock is Wellness Express (WEX). According to your source, Wellness Express was set up in the United States to open a string of healthy, quick-service restaurants in small-to-medium-sized towns. They offer a selection of pre-prepared healthy dishes as well as a made-to-order menu to deliver healthy and fast meal options to their patrons. Their angle is that people will choose to pursue healthy eating options on-the-go when those options are presented to them in a convenient way, and they are more comfortable getting food in a small store environment than they are in a large supermarket where they face a busy parking lot, potentially heavy foot traffic, a long checkout line, and limited sit-down space.

The concept resonates with you as a reasonable business angle, so you jump on your broker's website or the website for the exchange where WEX is being traded and check out its numbers. WEX has a quick ratio of 1.3 and an operating cash flow ratio of 0.8, which is not bad from a liquidity standpoint. The company is making sales at $11.50 for every share; that's a price-to-sales ratio of 11.50 to 5, which is indicative of a company that's reaching its market. The price-to-book ratio is just above 1, so you know that the current stock price of $5 is low. Maybe you've found your diamond for the day, so you buy.

Since there are tens of thousands of penny stocks from which to choose, you can't crunch the numbers for all of them.

Note: Some software programs allow you to filter penny stocks by various markets, ratios, and prices. So, if you want to look at a list of all stocks selling at less than $4 per share with a price-to-book ratio of at least 1 and a *quick ratio of 1 or higher, then you can set those parameters in your software and generate a list.*

You have to be able to supplement your quantitative analysis with a qualitative one. You can do this by inspecting the company's image. Has it put any work toward branding? With the fictitious health foods company, WEX, it would be worth a look at the company website and menu. You could also use Google Maps to take a street-view look at where the restaurants are being placed. Does the area look well-trafficked? Does the sign and façade of the restaurant look attractive? Is the restaurant logo and color scheme attractive?

Branding is especially important with penny stock companies because they are usually in the process of introducing themselves to the market and making a case as to why they deserve market share. In the case of WEX, the company is trying to persuade the market that it's possible to eat healthy on-the-go. Therefore, customers must see Wellness Express as a credible source of good food. Below are some ways for an investor to tell when a company is leveraging good branding toward the promotion of a good business.

The company provides relentless value at every interaction point.

A company that's well branded and destined to survive and thrive aggressively delivers value to the consumer at every opportunity. The company should have a website that's easy to use, be ready to add new visitors to their mailing list and give direction to their stores. These may all seem like common sense concerns, but if a company has invested in creating and hosting a website, then it should be maximizing its utility with every customer visit.

The company stands out from the crowd.

A company destined to succeed must have a sense of inspiration about it. It must be distinct from other retailers in its space. In the case of WEX, the company defines itself as a fast food alternative: get the speed and convenience of fast food without the nutritional drawbacks.

The company cultivates focus in its branding.

A company that's going to thrive in its market must be clearly focused on its mission and dedicated to serving a specific market sector. One thing that often leads smaller companies to fail or stagnate is over-diversifying or switching course too frequently. If WEX purports itself to deliver healthy food fast, then it doesn't also offer authentic Chinese food, the best coffee in town, or even the best tasting veggie burger on the market. In reality, there's no reason that WEX can't offer all of these things. In fact, it would be great if it did. But when it comes to the branding of the company, it must remain steady and focused on one particular market entry point.

The company communicates well.

When a company is eager to communicate with its customers via emails, surveys, focus groups, or the like, and also communicates with its investors via reports or press releases, then the company is clearly committed to its own success. That's an important commitment, seeing as not all companies you'll encounter, especially in the penny stock trade, are going to maintain their passion. Look for companies that aggressively seek feedback and new insight into the market they're trying to reach.

The company cultivates its own distinct and consistent style.

A company that's poised to grow is a company with a very clear and consistent vision for itself. This is perhaps the most important qualitative attribute that you can look for in a winning investment, but perhaps also the most difficult attribute to put into words. A company often comes into its own long before it financially matures. This is that rare, elusive point at which the savviest investors have a real opportunity to reap dramatically high returns on a penny stock investment. The key is consistency in branding.

Look for evidence that the company has secured some kind of essential image for itself that creates sparks of eminence and inevitability. These abstract elements can be manifested in a variety of ways. In our WEX example, perhaps the investor notices a rich consistency of branding across the company's in-store experience, its online branding, and its email marketing styles, such as the same colors, the same voice, the same feel, or a sense of a new entity being born and to great purpose. This is where investing, penny stock or otherwise, becomes much more of an art than a science.

The Penny Stock Branding Advantage

One advantage that a smaller, lesser-known, or unknown company has over a larger, established company is the ability to flexibly position its brand. Keeping with the example, let's say that Whole Foods saw the need for a healthy meal-on-the-go option in medium-sized cities. Because it already has a reputation for being a higher-end grocery store, it would face an uphill branding battle if it tried to compete with the smaller and newer Wellness Express. Why? Because Wellness Express has cultivated focus around its branding. Wellness Express is about one thing and one thing only: providing diners with great healthy food. Not to say that Whole Foods couldn't eventually position itself to be a viable option for this market need, but it would require a lot more effort on the part of Whole Foods. The company would have to readjust its floor plan a bit to allow for an expansion of its dining area, and it would need to open a separate checkout station so that diners would be able to check out quickly and eat while their food was still hot. Speaking of hot food, extra care would need to be taken with the preparation and sale of hot food items, since more of these items would be consumed on site, rather than taken home where they could be reheated and microwaved.

Perform Technical and Fundamental Analyses before Buying

"Fundamental analysis" and "technical analysis" are two terms that get thrown around a lot in the investment world. Fundamental analysis refers to drilling down on the essentials that make a company tick. Who sits on the board of directors, who's managing the company, what is communicated by the company's press releases, and how does this company fare within its industry? Technical analysis refers to looking at all the charts and graphs and other goodies showing how the stock's price has changed over time, its trading volume, and other facts that provide give an indication of what the company's future share value will look like. The methods you use largely depend on the type of investor you are - some call this your "investor personality" - and whether you feel more comfortable betting on trends and data or solid people and a good story.

The Typical Penny Stock

One potential problem with the WEX (Wellness Express) example is that we're envisioning a penny stock that, presumably, already has an active retail location and is generating a substantial cash flow. As a penny stock investor, you're more likely to be confronted with companies that are still in the early research and development phases, approaching some untested market with a new concept, and no one knows whether or not it's going to work. You'll also find everything in between. You'll have a lot of options to choose from, so you will need to whittle down your choices some. Below are some ways you can do this.

Trade in market sectors that you know - Being a successful penny stock investor requires a lot of dedicated research time. It's not always fun. Focusing on market sectors in which you're genuinely interested makes it easier for you to stay up-to-date and intrigued. By being an expert in a given area and investing in companies and sectors you understand, you'll be different from most investors who follow the media buzz and move with the swarm from sector to sector, chasing whatever the pundits happen to say is "hot" at the time.

Note: The prices of these media-hyped stocks tend to overinflate and then plummet, and many investors suffer losses. Many stock "experts" print off weekly tip sheets, purportedly telling them where to find the hottest penny stocks. More often than not, the hype results in the stock trading for more money than it's really worth. Its poor fundamentals eventually betray it, and it again plummets in value. So, how do you weather the waves of hype? It's simple - learn how to conduct sound fundamental and technical analyses of the stocks you're interested in purchasing.

Look for critical pre-market success indicators - Depending on the industry, various fundamental factors determine how strong a stock is before its product or service even goes to market. For example, if the company is based on producing and marketing a new invention, then you should check to see that the company has acquired a 10-year patent on the invention. If they haven't received their patent yet, check to see if they're working on improving their product to a point at which patenting is possible. If the company is a bank, a consultancy, or a research group, then inspect the existing and pending relationships. Does the company have financing from a solid source? Does it have sufficient financing to stay afloat for at least 12 more months? Does it have the right partners in place to meet its marketing needs, such as advertisers and agents? Is there any government involvement in the company? Has the company applied for a grant or entered into a dialog with a government entity regarding the future purchase of the company's products? Did it get little more than token attention from these entities, or did it really captivate them?

Make sure the company's debt is serviceable - It's not uncommon for penny stocks to have debts that exceed their assets. Nonetheless, if the company has incurred debt that's over three times the value of its assets, then it's in a very vulnerable financial position.

How and When to Cash In

Investment in penny stocks is quite different from traditional stock investment, largely because of all the strange but potent hype that surrounds them. Because the stock price is so volatile, a little bit of good press can send the price soaring. These media pumps don't always work, and the high price rarely sustains itself before going back down. Winning penny stock investors do not buy in the heat of a price-spiking media parade, but are already holding significant shares of the stock at the time the media parade commences.

When you find yourself holding a penny stock that's spiking high, usually, the prudent thing to do is to sell within one hour (and no longer than 3 months) after the initial spike. The reason for this is because, in most cases, the stock eventually plummets back down. Use the cash you free up to reinvest in other stocks. (Remember, the more you invest, the more experience you gain, and the better your insight and intuition become.) If your exploding penny stock continues to climb higher and higher after you sell, don't fret about it, as this happens. You did the right thing by insulating yourself from undue risk.

Chapter 10: Metrics

This chapter deals with some critical metrics to help you make better decisions when choosing penny stocks (Leeds, 2018). Every good investment is essentially built on a story - a reason why the current price for a particular security is lower than it should be. Even though you can't predict the future, the ability to tell a compelling story that forecasts a probable future outcome can be a powerful tool. However, since you're dealing with dollars and cents and profits and loss, you need to incorporate rock hard data into your stories wherever possible.

Penny stocks usually draw a lot of attention from investors, because they're cheap to acquire. Investors who only have a few hundred dollars to throw into the market are drawn to penny stocks, because they can buy a substantial quantity, and, at times, they can realize astronomical gains. You're reading this book because you want to maximize your chances at realizing a great return. You want a strategy to succeed.

Liquidity Ratios

Understanding how to use liquidity ratios insulates you from one of the major hazards of penny stock investing - investing in a company that cannot pay its short-term obligations. Many stocks are priced low, specifically because they are unable to service their debts. You want to steer clear of these stocks, and you can easily do so by learning how to access and interpret these relatively simple ratios, which are detailed below.

Current Ratio - This liquidity ratio is found by dividing a company's current assets by its current liabilities. You're looking for a value of 1 or higher, indicating that the company has enough value in its assets to cover its currently outstanding liabilities. If the ratio is 1/3, then it's in your best interest to stay away from this penny stock. Its debt is three times as large as the value of its current assets. If the ratio, on the other hand, has a value of 3, then you understand that the firm's assets are sufficient to cover its liabilities three times over.

Quick Ratio - The quick ratio is essentially the current ratio with more restrictions placed upon what qualifies as an "asset." The quick ratio defines assets as only cash, accounts receivable, and marketable securities.

The objective of the quick ratio is to give the investor a sense for the value of a company's assets that can be quickly and expediently liquidated. The quick ratio is thought to be more accurate than the current ratio, seeing as some of the assets included in the current ratio may not be truly liquid and may not have the same value when resold. Like the current ratio, the investor should seek a value of 1 or higher to feel at ease with the company's ability to service its short-term debts.

Cash Ratio - Cash is king, and a good cash ratio makes a penny stock investment even safer than just a good quick ratio. The cash ratio is essentially the quick ratio with accounts receivable removed from the calculation. You're left with cash plus marketable securities divided by liabilities. By removing accounts receivable, you no longer need to worry about whether the company's customers are ever going to pay them. Everything they have immediately on hand is accounted for and nothing else. With penny stocks, it's not necessarily a deal breaker if a company has a weaker cash ratio. A value of at least 1 is a good benchmark to ensure that the company will be able to remain in business and service all of its debts due within a year.

Operating Cash Flow Ratio - Operating cash flow is an even stricter measurement of a company's short-term financial solvency. This liquidity ratio is calculated using only the incoming cash from company operations in the numerator and dividing it by the company's current liabilities. In the case of this ratio, it's alright if your value is less than 1, as other liquid assets can be brought in if needed to service the company's debts; however, if the operating cash flow ratio drops too low, then the company may be facing some serious financial trouble. If the operating cash flow is 1 or more, then the company is bringing in enough cash through normal business operations to service its debts for the next 12 months, which is a really good sign for a penny stock.

Note: As a general rule, investors prefer companies that have solid cash flow and the ability to readily cover all of their debts. If you can find a company in this position that's priced cheaply (see Price-to-Book, Price-to-Earnings, and Price-to-Sales below), then you've found a good penny stock prospect.

There are several reasons why a stock's operating cash flow is important. These reasons have been outlined below:

1. If the company has a strong operating cash flow, then it must be bringing in a substantial income, meaning that whatever products or services are being sold are reaching a significant market, and that market is likely to continue creating a real demand.
2. When operational cash flow is heavy, the firm is able to take advantage of growth opportunities. The company may hire new employees, invest in new assets, or purchase back its own stock shares.
3. A company with a strong operational cash flow is less likely to take on more debt. Without the necessity to raise more money, slowing it down, the company is free to focus on further expansions of its business.

Price-to-Book - The price-to-book ratio, or P/B ratio, is an interesting indicator that can help you determine whether a stock, regardless of its share price, is truly inexpensive. Let's take a look at a fictional penny stock, Brayton Co., or "BYT," that trades for $3. Let's say that BYT is listed on the OTCQX, so you are able to access some decent financial data. To find the stock's P/B ratio, you first need to get its market capitalization (market cap) value, which is listed next to every stock on the OTCQX. Market cap simply refers to the number of outstanding shares multiplied by the share value. Let's say BYT has 3 million outstanding shares and thus has a market cap of $9 million.

Next, you'll need to find the company's "book price." The book price is what the company would be left with after all of its assets were liquidated, and all of its liabilities paid. A company's book price can usually be determined by looking at its most recent balance sheet, which is a listing of all assets and liabilities. Now, let's say that you are able to find BYT's book price and that the company "goes to book" at 12 million dollars. This means that the company is selling at 3/4 of its book value (below book value), which is another way of saying it's inexpensive, or perhaps a good deal.

Note: Sometimes, P/B ratio is calculated using all per share values. Each share's book value has to be established. In our example, BYT would have a per *share book value of 12 million divided by 3 million or a book value per share of $4. The P/B ratio would thus be 3/4. You will always get the same P/B value, no matter which calculation method you use. Some investors like to look at per-share book value and compare it to the stock value.*

In theory, the P/B ratio is exceptionally important for penny stocks because the companies that issue penny stocks are more likely to be on the brink of bankruptcy. If a company's share value is lower than its per-share book value, and the company goes bankrupt immediately, then theoretically, the loss would be smaller than it would have been had the share value been higher than the book value. Therefore, investing in companies with a lower P/B ratio can serve as a stop-loss against risky investments.

As with any financial ratio investors use, a company's price-to-book can bode both well and poorly for the company's future stock value. In our example, BYT's stock is selling for less than its per-share book value. Some investors would say that this is an indication that the stock has been underpriced, and, assuming that the company is still fundamentally in good shape and there aren't any unpleasant surprises, the stock should go up in value. So get in now while it's hot. Another investor may look at the stock and think: it's a penny stock; it's likely to go bankrupt, so in the best case the investors will get some of their money back and take a modest loss. This is not so good.

It's important to realize here that a strategy is not following a fail-safe, inflexible plan of operation, but building a knowledge base in order to make informed decisions. This is the classic difference between "strategy" and "tactics." Tactics refer to a clear-cut action plan that, if executed correctly, produces a very specific result; strategy refers to the more artistic pursuit of gently honing the larger picture toward your vision for success. When it comes to investments, calculating a penny stock's P/B ratio is a tactic, and deciding whether or not to buy the stock is a strategy.

Growth Rates

Anyone can easily understand this metric. What does the penny stock's growth history look like? Has the stock been taking a steady plummet over the last several quarters, or is it ascending to great heights with no end in sight?

When assessing a stock's growth pattern, make sure that you're looking at quarterly markers, if not monthly ones. Looking at a stock's growth on a year-by-year basis can be a bit deceptive, as smaller yet meaningful growth changes can occur within the confines of a year. If you only look at growth benchmarks on a year-by-year basis, then you may miss crucial patterns.

Take, for example, a stock that has a market cap value of $25 million in the spring quarter of 2014. It grows to $40 million in the summer quarter, then begins declining to $35 million in the fall quarter and is at $33 million in the winter quarter. In the spring quarter of 2015, it's at $30 million. The market cap value has declined over the last three quarters. As long as you're evaluating the stock in quarterly increments, you will see this. If an investor fails to review the quarterly increments and only evaluates the stock in annual increments, seeing the spring 2014 quarter at $25 million and then the spring 2015 quarter at $30 million, he may mistakenly assume that the stock is on a steady upward trajectory.

The same mistaken evaluation can occur in the inverse. Let's say the stock has a market cap value of $30 million in the spring of 2014 and then slumps to $15 million by the summer of 2014, and then it's at $20 and $23 million, in the fall and winter quarters, respectively. By the spring quarter of 2015, the stock continues its steady ascent to $26 million, but if the investor were looking at the stock on a year-by-year basis, then they would see that it was at $30 million in the spring of 2014 and $26 million in the spring of 2015. Thus, they may assume that the growing stock is actually stagnant.

So, what really makes a stock go up in value? The simple answer to that question is market demand. If more people are willing to pay more money for a stock, then the stock price ascends. It's commonly thought that higher sales and higher revenue are directly proportional to stock price, but this is not necessarily true. Companies don't need to have growing sales for the stocks to go up, but such growth is one of the signs that may demarcate a big winner.

The Price-to-Earnings Ratio

The P/E ratio allows you to evaluate how hot your penny stock is - at least in terms of its current ability to generate earnings. You have to be a bit wary here with penny stocks, as they can be seriously overvalued. To define the price-to-earnings ratio, divide the company's market cap by its earnings for the most recent year. You may also define the ratio by dividing the share price of the stock by the stock's revenue per share.

Let's go back to our example stock, Brayton Co. (BYT), which trades for $3 and has a market cap of $9 million. Now let's say that BYT's earnings for the past year were $6 million. BYT's price-to-earnings ratio would be 9/6 or 3/2. If you want to calculate its price-to-earnings ratio using earnings per share as the denominator, you simply divide the total revenue ($6 million) by the total number of outstanding shares ($3 million), and you have your earnings per share ($2). The BYT share price ($3) over earnings per share ($2) is 3/2.

Usually, as an investor, what you're looking for is a company that has a low price-to-earnings ratio. You want the company's per-share revenue to outstrip its per share cost. The only assumption you have to make is that more revenue leads to opportunities for more growth, and, of course, more growth means a higher stock valuation. A low price-to-earnings ratio can be another indicator that the stock is a good deal. In the case of BYT, it looks like its stock price is higher than its per share revenue, perhaps because its price-to-book ratio is favorable. Perhaps investors don't see an amazing growth opportunity but are willing to pay slightly more for the stock because its P/B ratio tells them its assets are intrinsically valuable.

Hopefully, you are beginning to see how various metrics connect with one another and can, in tandem, influence a stock's price along with its estimated growth potential. With penny stocks, the investor is faced simultaneously with both an advantage and a disadvantage.

The advantage is that, with good research and attention paid to key metrics, it's easier to spot promising penny stock investment opportunities, as penny stocks are more volatile in general. You're more likely to stumble upon a stock that's both cheap and has good growth potential.

The disadvantage, unfortunately, is related to the advantage. Because the stocks are so volatile and the financial reporting relatively more haphazard, many times, even the most well thought out plays don't have the desired result. You make money with penny stocks by continuing to make smart plays over a period of time and taking your losses with your wins.

When the Penny Stock Doesn't Have Earnings

Sometimes, what makes a penny stock a penny stock is the fact that its earnings are minimal or non-existent. The stock could be taken to market well before the company posts a profit. When this happens, the P/E ratio is, of course, meaningless, because you have a zero in your denominator. Other ratios, such as the price-to-sales ratio and the price-to-cash-flow ratio, are incredibly important for these penny stocks. These ratios can be calculated in the same way as the price-to-revenue ratio; simply replace sales or cash flow data for revenue data. A good benchmark for a strong penny stock is when its share price is half the value of its per-share sales value. The cash flow metric is important to study if the company's earnings are questionable.

Compare the price-to-cash flow and price-to-sales ratios for the company over several reporting periods to determine if they look coherent and are indicative of a healthy company. Then, if the price is right, make sure to buy.

Where Do I Find All These Ratios?

The ratios you use to evaluate penny stocks usually come directly from the exchange and are provided by your broker-dealer. Depending on the exchange, certain reporting practices are mandatory for companies that wish to have their stock traded on the exchange.

Chapter 11: Technical Analysis

When you make a plan to invest in penny stocks, you will most certainly need to know how and when to apply technical analysis, oftentimes referred to as TA ('Technical Analysis and Penny Stocks', 2019). The majority of skilled investors let their initial research on a stock revolve around the basics of technical analysis, so your goal should be to do the same. To do this successfully, however, you'll need to learn what technical analysis is and what practices, observations, and calculations it entails.

As an investor, your aim is to put your money into healthy and growing companies that employ knowledgeable workers, have positive profit margins, and of course, have a market share price that is gradually increasing. You can find all of this information by browsing through a company's annual reports - reports that all American companies and corporations are legally obligated to publish to the general public at the conclusion of each fiscal year. There are, of course, investors who prefer to predict the direction in which a company's share price will go by doing a simple review of the company's trading charts - and then they will apply TA. The shortcoming of this method, however, is that these investors tend to overlook the financial fundamentals of the company they are investing in.

When technical analysis is done correctly, investors who complete TA have an advantage over the research forms other investors sometimes prefer to do. Unfortunately, this doesn't mean TA is a flawless economic approach. Like all things relating to finance and economics, you should always proceed with caution when you take on trading endeavors and opportunities. Oftentimes, a great cautionary approach to financial matters is to combine strategies. In other words, a cautious investor doesn't rely solely on TA, nor does he or she rely solely on the interpretation of a company's trading charts. Instead, a knowledgeable and cautious investor embraces TA and combines it with other approaches as well. It's recommended that you do initial research on a company of interest, applying TA to the current research you've completed, and then combining all of that information with full abstract and fundamental analysis review. This should give you all the vital financial information that you need to know about a company of interest.

The Positives of Technical Analysis

In this section, you'll discover the information and knowledge you need in order to become a more knowledgeable investor who is better prepared to succeed in the marketplace. The following list outlines highly effective and appropriate TA situations that you'll want to strive to meet:

- **Eliminate the required work for fundamental analysis.** Concerns regarding a company's growth, profit margins, and market shares can be eliminated when using TA. This is because you are not going to invest in a company - you are only trying to gain a profit from the share price.
- **Be a day trader, not a long-term one.** Many investment opportunities involve purchasing stocks from a healthy company in hopes of gaining a profit over an extended period of time and, as

a result, an increase in the share price. If you can't wait around for the desired results, then TA is the quick fix for you.

- **Be informed about good buying and selling opportunities.** Pay attention to a company's chart patterns, changes in price directions, and trading volume. Technical analysis often shows very precise buy and sell points. To know when the best time to trade a penny stock is, you have to know how upward trends and drop-off in volumes work. We'll get to this a bit later.

- **Minimize investment exposure.** If you have any sort of investment, whether big or small, you're exposed. The best way to avoid exposure is to make trades in a short amount of time using TA techniques. Keep in mind, though, that while this shortens the time in which your money is exposed, it doesn't help eliminate the risk altogether.

- **Buy shares that trend in desirable price directions.** In other words, you're not buying shares in a specific company, per se. This makes the need to analyze a company's growth, interaction with competitors, and profit margins an unnecessary and altogether avoidable task.

- **Do the work.** If you decide to rely on TA, plan to make the interpretation of trading charts your new favorite hobby. Remember that many of the charts you'll encounter often don't highlight appropriate opportunities. With enough time, though, you'll come across charts (using TA) that show predictable patterns that you can further pursue - and by enough time, I mean about 20-40 hours a week spent in the open stock market.
- **Do what works best for you.** As a new or inexperienced investor, you'll need to spend time figuring out what tools work best for you, including TA. Feel free to use your personal preferences during financial endeavors.
- **It is possible to miss the really big gains.** Using TA means making smaller gains more often. Using this method might result in missing out on major percent moves and highly profitable opportunities. Don't be discouraged when this happens, as it will indeed

happen. Success in penny stocks trading is achieved through patience and mental resilience.

If you find the points mentioned above appealing, then you'll probably find technical analysis equally appealing. However, there is no need to use TA and TA only in all of your investment decisions, but you can absolutely utilize it as a tool. Many investors who use TA to trade stocks avoid owning share overnight or during the weekend, because a lot can change when the market is closed, and those changes can impact the share prices once the market is open again. Take caution to that, because you cannot always react appropriately when events like that occur.

As detailed earlier, the best research approach involves using both a technical and fundamental review. With fundamental analysis, you can identify high-quality penny stocks that are moving in profitable directions. If you apply technical analysis to the trading charts of these stocks, you'll increase your ability to see and engage in highly rewarding buying and profit-making opportunities.

The Negatives of Technical Analysis

The more activity and trades involved in building a technical analysis pattern, the better. No matter the price dip or the resistance level, technical analysis will be more reliable. We can use political polls to demonstrate this. That is, not many people will invest if the results are based on the opinions of 50 people, but if the opinions are based on the polling of 1 million people, most will invest without hesitation. TA is no different; it's more reliable if the amount of the trading volume that generates the pattern is high. In other words, if the trading volume is low, the TA pattern won't appear to be so trustworthy.

Generally speaking, penny stocks have less trade activity than other stocks, which means some TA techniques simply can't be applied. This can be a major restriction at times. In addition to this drawback, some TA indicators can hint at a right price direction in the future, but sometimes this only applies when the underlying shares have been trading for a while. The effectiveness of TA depends on the situation and the stock, along with the factors listed below:

- **The percentage of shares trading hands.** If a single percent of total outstanding shares trade a day, the patterns that may form will most likely be unreliable. If a penny stock reveals a good indicator on 5 percent of shares every day, then this indicator can be considered highly reliable.
- **The daily trading volume.** Don't forget to watch the amount of shares trading hands every day. If you want to put your trust in technical analysis and the patterns it depicts, then you have to observe and understand the thousands of shares being bought and sold every day. The higher the number of shares, the more reliable the TA pattern will be.

Technical analysis with penny stocks is a very involving concept. Some TA patterns may work with some shares while other TA patterns may not. Every stock and every situation is very different from one another. The effectiveness of some financial indicators will vary from one penny stock to another. Like any other investment opportunity and endeavor, you will get better at it with time and practice.

Chapter 12: Working as a Professional

For every corporation that is traded publicly with the capitalization of the market in huge amounts of money, there are countless other small companies with market caps that are a lot more modest.

Since these companies don't have as big of operations or risks as others, they can be traded at much lower prices. I am talking, of course, about penny stocks. In this chapter, we will go over some of the dangers to stay aware of if you wish to become a penny stock pro.

Factors to Stay Aware of When Mastering Penny Stocks

Beware of the myth of the evolving stock, which is something that keeps people coming back time and time again to dabble with penny stocks is the assumption that the companies will grow and evolve into something huge and great. Although this is possible and happens at times, it isn't as common as proponents of penny stocks want you to think.

A lot of public firms choose to avoid going public until they have reached a big enough stance to make it worthwhile. Until this happens, they might opt for raising funds using corporate loans or private investors in addition to their typical operation methods. In general, these companies won't need IPOs initial public offerings) to fund their growth.

When companies offer their stock out at penny stock prices, it's typically due to one of these reasons: the company is on the verge of a huge expenditure and thinks that funds raised from an IPO could be the amount needed to finance this expenditure, or they have reached an apex in their size and want to disperse their earnings or shift the structure of their taxes.

In addition to those two reasons, there are some additional, less noble reasons that a company could opt for IPO when they aren't big yet. It could be because a company has been convinced that they should be involved with an

IPO that's overhyped and overpriced by brokerage firms, hoping to make a quick buck by taking advantage of investors. It could also be the company owner's attempt to shift the ownership of the company over to others, as they don't see a bright future for the business.

It's a good idea to keep in mind that there is a huge range of companies within penny stocks and that the variance is immense. You could, for example, see a corporate structured company that specializes in prospecting oil right next to a farm that is family run and that specializes in crops.

Some businesses like these let investors chime in regarding who runs the show, while others are operations run by one person that falls apart when that person decides to retire. On average, bigger companies aim to please the people who invest in them, and companies using penny stocks don't always care about this aspect of the field.

How to Increase Your Effectiveness and Skill in Penny Stocks

A lot of great companies start off by trading with penny stocks, meaning that choosing to invest in these companies can pay off big time as they grow into larger stocks. But penny stocks don't typically have a positive name in the investment field, and, at times, this is for very good reasons. However, once you figure out a few methods for avoiding the negative possibilities of getting involved in penny stocks, you can find great companies that will pay off as fantastic rewards in the future.

Protection from the Downfalls of Investing in Penny Stocks

People who decide to invest but who don't learn about the most effective methods of protecting themselves from the risks that come along with penny stocks might end up getting burned. However, if you follow the points below, you will be able to avoid most scams, bad investments, and faulty information:

- Stick to higher caliber markets when possible - For the safest bets, try to stick with AMEX, NASDAQ, and

OTCBB for your penny stock trading. While low caliber markets like OTC and the pink sheets can hold promise, it isn't worth the risk when you're first starting out.

- Do research and reach your own conclusions - Although well-meaning friends or family members might have a tip for you, you should never operate based on that alone. Remember to always do research on your own and reach an informed conclusion before investing to avoid losses and maximize your success with penny stocks.

- Stay away from free stock picks - Don't ever pursue these, no matter how alluring they may seem. When you hear about a stock through an email, a mailing list, or a free newsletter, they typically have some type of hidden motive. They'll try to trick people into buying stocks using tactics and false information, planning to get rid of the shares after convincing enough investors to trust them.

- Stick to solid stocks - You should only get involved with penny stocks that have solid fundamentals. If you aren't sure how to find this information, you can quickly look up the company online. Do a check for the position of their financial situation, and make a choice based on that.

- Be wary of story stocks - Watch out for stocks that come along with an incredible story. Very bad investments can have great business concepts, like the curing of a horrid disease or an engine design that will solve the pollution issues of our planet. However, stocks with fantastic stories such as these are most often bad companies in terms of finances, and the tempting nature of their concepts of business will have pushed their value way higher than it is in reality.

- Don't be afraid to call and ask - The more you know, the better. This means that calling the phone number for investor relations for the company you're looking into is a great idea. They should be more than happy to answer your questions, and knowing which ones to ask can allow you to discover quite easily how legitimate the business really is.

A Method for Getting Great at Investing in Penny Stocks

It's possible to practice your trading tactics in legitimate stocks in legitimate time, without risking any money. This is referred to as "paper trading" and involves using fake money for real stocks and learning by staying on top of how your picks do.

When you use this method, you can improve at investing in penny stocks quite quickly. Improving doesn't mean you have to risk actual money. As soon as you have reached a comfortable position in your investment knowledge and enjoy consistent profit with your fake trades, you can confidently switch to using real money. Here is how to do it:

1. Begin with a false amount of money - Keep an eye on the current, real penny stocks out there, and pick which one you would purchase with real capital.

2. Take notes - Start writing down the trades you would have made, including when you would buy and

sell. Make sure to record the name of the stock, the date, the purchase's dollar amount, and the prices per share.

3. Invest in multiple - Do this with a lot of different penny stocks instead of only a couple, so you can get the most experience possible using this method. There is no reason to limit yourself to only one or two different practice stocks. The more you have, the better and faster you will learn.

4. Record which false investments were profitable - Keep track of your success using fake money so you can figure out what methods of yours are successful and which you might be doing incorrectly. Write down your successful methods, so you know what to do more of and what to ease up on in the future.

If you make it a point to learn as much as possible about penny stocks through daily research in combination with trading with fake money using real stocks, you'll be well on your way to becoming a pro. It won't be long before you're ready to make the jump to real money and start earning profit.

Chapter 13: Don't Get Scammed

It's difficult not to consider a penny stock that's being advertised as the next big thing. Although it can easily be considered a scam, a lot of new investors still fall into this trap. There are thousands of publicly listed companies in a major stock exchange. However, so many individuals are still drawn to lesser-known penny stock companies ('How to Avoid Penny Stock Scams,' 2017).

A penny stock company listed on the Over-The-Counter Bulletin Board, an electronic system which shows real-time quotations, volume information, and last-sale prices of securities, is often advertised as being listed. On the other hand, a penny stock listed on the pink sheets isn't regulated by any financial organization or government entity. As such, it is a riskier investment than any other major stock company listed on a stock exchange. The company can post losses, and deficits can be huge. Furthermore, it can easily fold up. An investor can check with the Securities and Exchange

Commission for information regarding a penny stock company.

Tools and Strategies Used In Penny Stock Scams

Spam and junk mail can be distributed by scam artists to generate interest in a particular penny stock. In general, these emails contain fictitious information about the stock. It's highly advised to avoid buying the advertised stock just on the basis of any emails received. In addition, online bulletin boards are used to spread "hot tips" about a certain stock. Scammers use aliases to spread false information. Again, any interested investor must practice due diligence when they intend to invest in a penny stock. Some of these companies also pay stock promoters to offer "unbiased and independent" recommendations through the mass media. Before believing these paid promoters, it's best to investigate if they have financial certifications.

Cold calls and boiler room tactics are also used by fraudsters who have an organized group of high-pressure sales agents. These agents make cold calls to encourage potential investors to buy the penny stock. It's advised to be careful about receiving calls from unknown people. Furthermore, the penny stock company may issue dubious press releases. The potential investor must make it a point to investigate facts on his own so that he won't be scammed.

In case the individual is scammed, he can report the incident to his broker. If the latter doesn't resolve the issue, the former can report it to the Securities and Exchange Commission or the securities regulator of the state.

Why People Become Interested in Penny Stocks

A penny stock offers the possibility to become rich quickly, which is exciting. It's the same concept as a lottery ticket, which offers a better future to the winner (if it's a winning ticket). An individual who invests in a penny stock is usually someone who doesn't perform mathematical computations to find out the penny stock company's intrinsic worth. He often is not one to analyze financial statements, industry studies, dividend projections, or discounted cash flows. In addition, a penny stock is like hidden knowledge; an investor who has an interest in a certain stock often feels special, because he knows something that the others don't know. If he talks about his investment, people will listen, because it is something they haven't heard about.

A penny stock lacks liquidity. This is why a lot of experts don't recommend buying this kind of stock. However, it is also very volatile, meaning that the price may experience wild fluctuations, creating a lot of opportunities to profit quickly. An inexperienced investor may continuously buy shares of the penny stock because the price continuously goes up. He doesn't realize that he is one of the people who drive up the price. In case he intends to sell his shares, he soon realizes that no one wants to buy the stock anymore. An investor decides to invest in a certain penny stock because he believes that this company is the next Microsoft or Walmart. He fails to recognize that these companies, which started from humble beginnings, offered shares to the public when they have grown large already. These companies opted for IPOs due to their desire to expand the business.

Actually, these investing traps can be avoided if the investor thinks of himself as the owner of the penny stock company. He has to take his emotions out from the investment equation in order to make a realistic and correct decision. Liquidity isn't even a problem if the penny stock company continues to grow.

Considerations in Buying a Penny Stock

A lot of traditional investors have become rich due to having invested in high-quality stocks; but only a few, if any, have become rich from penny stock investing. The power of compounding consistent gains from high-quality stocks is the single factor responsible for the enormous wealth of these traditional investors. Their chosen companies continuously increase their profits and offer high returns for the investors' money. Dividends are often distributed to shareholders, and investors continuously buy shares to increase their earnings.

On the other hand, an investor in a penny stock company can't increase his shares because of liquidity problems. If he continues to buy, he will cause the price of the share to increase. The penny stock is inefficient; therefore, an investor has to buy at higher costs for every transaction. These costs reduce any profit that may be earned from his investment. In fact, he may even lose money because of these frictional costs.

Types of Penny Stock Scams

Inexperienced investors often fall into the hands of penny stock scammers deceiving them to invest in cheap and worthless stock. Most of the time, traders lose money after investing in such scams. As a beginner, you need to be aware of all these scams, which are detailed below (Reynolds, 2018).

Reverse merger - At times, a private company will collaborate with a public company for them to be a publicly traded firm not having to pass through the stress of a more traditional method. This kind of step results in the company changing its earnings and inflating the prices of its stock. Though, we do have some legitimate reverse mergers; determining a genuine one can be done simply by reviewing the business' history and picking out speckled activities in its merger

Pump-and-dump schemes - There is a common scam where stock promoters oftentimes get investors' interest in an unknown stock, leading the novice to buy the shares. Then, the moment the stock gets to a given inflated price, the fraudsters will sell off shares, thereby dumping the stock at huge profits. With this act, traders end up in a high and dry situation. Often, this strategy is spread via free penny stock newsletters in which the publishers have been paid to include overrated and unpromising stocks. In case you come across any of such newsletters, get more details on their site and get to know the initiator.

Short-and-distort - This scam is used to make profits. Shorting works when stocks are borrowed by investors and then sold immediately in an open market at a higher price, anticipating that the company's stock will fall; by then, though, they can scoop up the shares they have sold at a lesser price. After this, they give these borrowed shares back to the owners. Some frauds of penny stock usually short-sell a stock and see that there's a fall in the stock by the dissemination of rumors that are untrue about the company. Short sellers make a lot from their fraudulent strategy, while investors end up on the losing side.

Guru scam - There are several fake ads, and unfortunately, people fall victim to them easily. Often, these ads will talk about ways they became successful by using a special secret to eventually earn enough for things such as lakefront houses, glitzy, boats, and cars, etc. For a small amount, these so-called "experts" will promise to share their secret with you. Please make sure you trash any email you receive from someone promising to make you rich.

Avoiding Scams

There is so much manipulation in the penny stock market, including fraud and chicanery. There is then a need for investors to know that this kind of act is not the dominant situation of micro-caps and penny stocks. Is there a way for a serious trader to avoid getting into the hands of fraudulent penny stock promoters? Take a look below at some suggestions that might help you.

Determine the credibility of the company - The success of any organization depends solely on the leadership, and this is also true for penny stock companies. You will never see a top-rated manager in charge of a penny stock company. Moreover, you should go through the track record of the management to review successes or failures of the directors and executives and also to see if there exists any general issues or legal issues.

Differentiate between research and promotion - Promoters often employ writers of newsletters to formulate a dishonest story about their stock. They mostly come up with a compelling story for investors in penny stock through the use of outlandish projections, hyperbole, and in some scenarios, a deliberate misrepresentation. As a penny stock trader, you must be able to differentiate between stock promotion and true equity research. You will be able to conclude if it's an advertisement by finding out if the writer was paid to write when you read the "disclosures" section.

Quality of disclosure - A company that provides more disclosure is an indication of its high level of corporate transparency. By investing in a company that you know little or nothing about or in stock that you are advised by the OTC to be careful of, you are putting yourself in a danger zone. A penny stock company that has been involved in suspicious promotional activities like spam emails or ones that have a case of fraudulent activity at hand could earn this kind of stigma.

Chapter 14: Tips and Tricks

Penny stock trading is a risky venture, but with the right information in hand and good guidance, you should be able to avoid the risks and dance around the manholes that litter the road to penny stock success.

Here are some tips that can help you to avoid falling into a schemer's trap and ensure that you receive a good profit in every transaction:

- Refrain from believing stories. The world of penny stock trading and investment is full of people whose main goal is to lure unwitting investors to fall into their deceitful scams and schemes. One way of doing so is by spreading stories across the internet that tell of individuals who made it big in penny stocks by doing this and that or visiting sites here and there. Most of the time, these stories are sent through emails and posted on social networking sites, which are platforms that can reach a lot of people efficiently in a short period of time. If ever you encounter these stories in your email or in forums, it's best to ignore them.

- Focus on good penny stocks only. It is recommended that you put your focus in penny stocks that will surely give you profits. Look at how the stock's earnings grow. Make sure that they are consistent and make 52-week highs. They should also have good earnings breakout and trade in volumes of at least 100,000 shares.

- Lengthen your search time. Stocks that consistently appear in the listings of exchanges are more likely to be consistent performers also. This will help you avoid falling for stocks with only short bursts of luck.

- Pay no heed to tips. Like stories, tips on penny stocks abound the internet. Mostly, these tips are about when to sell and what penny stocks to sell, and they're usually delivered to people through their emails or distributed through penny stock newsletters.

- Always look for disclaimers. In connection with the previous paragraph, one way to avoid getting fooled by tips is to look at the disclaimer portion of the newsletter that contained the tip. There's actually nothing wrong with penny stock newsletters by themselves. In fact, they can serve as ways for small, growing companies to gain publicity. The problem with them is that newsletter publishers are paid to give these tips and spotlight a company's stock. However, most of the time, they also print good information about how a company is doing despite their very poor performance. To avoid getting fooled, you should read the disclaimers that are printed in the newsletters, which are usually found in the bottom section. Disclaimers are required by the Securities Exchange Commission to be included in newsletters, and it's there that the real purpose of the tip is indicated.

- Get your hands off of fast-growing stocks quickly. For an investor who has just started trading in penny stocks, getting your hands on stocks with a large and fast growth that can reach around 25 percent is absolutely amazing. Usually, beginners tend to be amazed too much and want to reach a higher return. However, veteran penny stock traders recommend letting go of these kinds of stocks quickly. For one reason, you should grab the chance of benefiting from the stock when it's at its highest performance. Another reason is that stocks with good performance within only just days are more likely to have been subjected to the pumping and dumping scheme.

- There are sources that say that shorting penny stocks is a good way to earn more profit. However, shorting penny stocks is best left to the more experienced and professional penny stocks traders and investors. The problem with penny stock shorting is that penny stocks are unpredictable, which can lead you to lose large sums of money instead of gaining profit. Another point is that it's quite hard to look for penny stocks to short.

- Know what stocks to buy. Buying the wrong kinds of stocks will not help you gain any profit, but will bring you loss instead. Experts recommend buying stocks which trade equal to, or more than, 100,000 shares per day. Investing in shares that trade in high volumes will make things easier for you when you want to get them off your hands. The importance of research again enters the picture here. You must know the volume of the shares traded and the volume of the dollars.

- Avoid trading big. Although you need to invest in stocks that trade in high volume for each day, you should also avoid trading at least 10 percent of that stock's daily trading volume. For example, for a stock that trades 100,000 share volumes, you can buy 10,000 shares.

There is a large number of outright lies and misleading information out there concerning penny stocks. Now that you have invested your time into learning how to be successful in penny stock investments, below are some helpful tips to remember as you venture forward into successfully becoming financially free by wisely trading in penny stocks:

Invest in your education - It can be easy to get overly confident when you have a few good trades under your belt, especially if you're new at trading in penny stocks. You won't ever really know it all, and that's why it's so important to make the furthering of your penny stock education such a high priority. It can also be very beneficial for you to seek out the investors who you think have achieved what you would like to achieve in penny stocks and then learn everything you possibly can from them. If you are lucky, you will get in contact with a seasoned penny stock trader who will share their knowledge and findings with you and help you to become a stronger and more informed trader.

Remember that only about 5-10 percent of investors out there consistently make a profit. It also may be a good idea just to ignore what traders happen to say in chat rooms, on message boards, and on the trader social networks. Most traders will tell you that they are making consistent, good money with the sole purpose of trying to sell you something. This is extremely common when it comes to penny stocks, which means that it would be a good idea for you to choose your mentor(s) wisely. One way to identify a legitimate mentor is by seeing if they are completely transparent. Ask for your mentor's records of trades, as well as tax statements showing their profits. If that mentor hesitates or retreats, so should you.

Use a journal to keep track of your trades - As a beginning penny stock investor, it would be in your best interest to start a trading journal that includes the moves you have made, which size positions that you decided to take, and if you had a profit or loss on that trade. Your trade diary will end up teaching you a lot about trading and about yourself as an investor. This simple but valuable resource will help you to become consistently profitable. The most successful traders around are very methodical; they don't make plays on just a whim. Successful traders take their past actions into consideration and then utilize their experiences in order to better their odds at making successful trades in the future. The information concerning the trades you have made in the past will be extremely useful when honing your skills as a penny stock trader.

Give back to your community - Just like anyone else, traders tend to get caught up in the day to day activities. Traders bury themselves in their work, and it can be difficult to pay attention to anything that isn't making them money after a while. That is just not what life's about, though. Make the time to get some of your hard-earned money together, and use that money to impact just one family in your community. It can be really humbling to see someone gushing over simple, inexpensive new clothes, a washing machine, or a gift card for a grocery store. This will change your view of money. There is nothing like it in the entire world.

Have respect for risk - You should respect the fact that risk is a huge (if not the biggest) part of trading penny stocks. Things can change very quickly when trading penny stocks. A penny stock that you may think is on the rise can actually go south in mere moments, and vice versa. One of the biggest reasons that penny stocks are so risky is because most of the companies that issue them do not meet the SEC filing requirements. Actually, the bottom line here is that you simply do not know what you may be in for with penny stocks. The risk in penny stocks is inherent. You may not be able to fight it, but you can make a choice to respect it. Make sure that the position you take is not big enough to affect the stock's price.

Don't believe everything you hear - In fact, you should rarely believe what you hear about penny stocks. By this point in the book, that statement should sound pretty redundant. People who promote penny stocks are really quick to try and sell you grandiose stories about extremely exciting companies that are about to blow up and forever change our world with their magical new products. These are, of course, lies and hype. Penny stock companies are not usually legitimate companies; if they were legitimate companies, they would be traded on the AMEX or the NYSE and not priced like common lottery tickets. In all actuality, about 99 percent of every penny stock company will ultimately fail, so the odds of you catching the mere 1 percent that does grow is very slim. Do not believe all that you hear about penny stock trading, and discover the truth for yourself. Those companies may all be scammers, schemers, and thieves, but that does not necessarily mean that you can't use them right back in order to make a profit.

Adjust your profit expectations - Another huge piece of hype that you will often encounter with penny stock promoters is about how fast your investment will grow. While it's possible for a penny stock to go from $1 per share to $10 per share, it is unrealistic to try to make more than about $0.75. Don't get greedy. It's great if you make more than that, but keep in mind that by keeping your trades small, you are keeping your losses small, as well. Practicing this will result in you making a lot of money in the long run. If you're always going after big wins, you will end up forcing trades that really aren't there. This is the type of mistake that will push you out of the game before you ever get a chance to play.

Take care of yourself - Finally, make sure you are taking care of yourself while you're working so hard at finding financial freedom. It's really easy to get so wrapped up in stocks and trading that you forget to take care of yourself. This is very easy to let happen. Keep in mind that you really have nothing if not your health. It can be difficult to remember to eat a healthy meal and get some exercise when you are so busy watching charts all day long and then researching all night, but it is so very important. You will end up being a much better trader if you're in good health, and you will also be able to live longer and enjoy more of the benefits of your success if you take good care of yourself. Get rid of the bad habits now before you're set in a bad stock routine. Focus on staying healthy, so your good health is there to support you all throughout your long, successful career.

Chapter 15: How to Find the Right Help

If it's hard to find good help these days, then it's exceptionally hard to find good help and advice in the world of stock trading - and it's excruciatingly difficult to find good help with penny stock investing. The main problem is that the massive clutter of nonsense and scammers makes getting sound advice like finding a needle in a haystack. In this chapter, you'll learn some tricks to locate credible sources of advice as you pursue your fortune in penny stock investing.

Screen Your Advice and Advisors

Penny stock investors must have screening criteria. Otherwise, the sheer quantity of penny stocks on the market may baffle you; you simply can't research them all. The challenge lies in the presence of many individuals who want to offer advice and, unfortunately, not all of them have your best interest at heart. Here are some indicators that you can look for when you're wondering whether a stock advisor, TV personality, broker, or some combination of all of the above has your best interests at heart.

The media superstar - Stock experts are often seeking fame and an audience. While being able to muster up good stock picks can definitely help an expert gain credibility, there are sometimes other attributes that factor into whether a stockbroker eventually appears on television, such as that person's charisma, sense of humor, and all around personality. If you want to check a TV personality's actual competency as an investment advisor, investigate their track record. Have the stocks the advisor has recommended performed well over time, or are they in the position they're in merely because they're sure to draw good ratings?

The fragile ego - Some investment advisors hate being wrong and continue to insist that a stock is undervalued for years on end, regardless of the evidence. Spot these personalities, and learn how to distinguish between what may actually be sound advice and what's merely the product of the advisor's insistence on his own infallibility.

The sociopath - There is a particular class of investors who are unsettlingly common on the penny stock scene that don't really care at all about whether or not the advice they provide is legitimate, profitable, or even based in reality. They believe that stocks exist in an essentially chaotic universe, and the only role of the broker is to encourage transactions and collect commissions. These individuals often don't even enjoy their jobs. They are chronically difficult to reach, reluctant to provide information, and quick to pull the authority card, wanting you to trust them for no reason other than that they're the purported "experts."

Look for a Verifiable Track Record

Brokers, advisors, or other stock experts who are serious about supplying good advice are proud of what they've accomplished for their clients. They want to show you their statistics and proven ability to read the market.

In the penny stock world, these brokers and advisors stand out, because it's easy to contact and communicate with them. They don't hide behind a shadowy brand that changes every year after the company ruins its reputation by giving out bad advice.

You want to see a track record that spans at least a year, if not substantially longer. Spend some time verifying that the picks and successes reported are accurate and not just made up. One way to verify the accuracy of an advisor's pick sheet is to follow his picks for a time and then check to make sure that the picks he made are the same as those reported on his track record.

Skepticism is good, but at some point, you're going to have to trust someone, or you're not going to go anywhere. Always be ready to establish the difference between the two archetypes of a bad stock analyst and a good one who's on a bit of a cold streak. At some point, it's just going to come down to trust; you must trust the person who's helping you invest your money. Your challenge is to cultivate trust with someone based on a series of rational evaluation points, including criteria that go beyond how well a person dresses, his golf score, or his political affiliation.

Conclusion

You should now have the foundational knowledge needed to enter the world of penny stock trading. The lessons that you've learned in this book can only be used to the greatest effect when you set time and be patient about making intelligent trades based on what you've learned. Regardless of the trading style that you adopt, whether that is day trading or value trading, you must be aware of the total trading volume and liquidity for every company that you invest in. To be a successful day trader, you need to dedicate an entire day to trading, making at least four bets in a single day. If you go down this path, you will be relying on pattern recognition, volatility, and strong liquidity to earn you a steady and consistent profit.

If you decide that you're more tuned to value trading, then you know that you'll be relying on research and investing in companies that have either an underlying patent or asset that isn't reflected in their market cap. In addition to these details, you will need suitable liquidity to sell stock once the price has been adjusted. How you research and find the valuable assets of these smaller companies is going to depend on the sector you are most interested in researching.

Stick with what you know; if you work in technology, focus on penny stocks related to tech. If you work in any specific sector of the economy, focus on companies with backgrounds that you can understand and fit into the grander economy. It's not that you are waiting for these companies to suddenly make millions, but rather, you will understand their underlying assets and know when the market capitalization does not accurately reflect the value of the company.

Regardless of the trading strategy that you decide to invoke, please make a trade log and use it diligently. It's also recommended that you use this trade log to do one week of fake trading - that is, one week where you make trades and log them in your notebook. Use this practice week and focus on why you chose the stocks that you did. Also, try to determine what mistakes, if any, you have made. For day traders, mistakes commonly come down to improperly predicting market liquidity (not able to sell their holdings). For value traders, a common mistake is overvaluing an asset. Make sure that you have a proper assessment of a company if you believe their holdings are above their market capitalization. Both strategies require practice, and you will get better with this in time.

If you enjoyed this book or received value from it in any way, then I'd like to ask you for a favor: would you be kind enough to leave a review for this book on Amazon? It'd be greatly appreciated!

References

Basenese, L. (2017). Decoding the Cryptic "Pink Sheets." Retrieved from https://www.wallstreetdaily.com/2017/05/15/decoding-cryptic-pink-sheets/

Beers, B. (2018). Introducing pink sheets: the OTC market. Retrieved from https://www.investopedia.com/articles/fundamental-analysis/08/pink-sheets-ottcb.asp

Hayes, A. (2013). Stocks Basics: What Are Stocks?. Retrieved from https://www.investopedia.com/university/stocks/stocks1.asp

How To Avoid Penny Stock Scams | MyPennyStocksHub.com. (2017). *MyPennyStocksHub.com.* Retrieved 9 May 2019, from https://mypennystockshub.com/avoid-penny-stock-scams/

Leeds, P. (2019). 6 Proven Financial Ratios Reveal Winning Penny Stocks. Retrieved from https://www.thebalance.com/penny-stock-proven-ratios-2637035

Leeds, P. (2019). The Best Investors Share These 6 Personality Traits. Retrieved from https://www.thebalance.com/investor-personality-traits-3867158

Lewis, M. (2019). How to Pick and Trade Penny Stocks. Retrieved from https://www.wikihow.com/Pick-and-Trade-Penny-Stocks

LIOUDIS, N. (2019). The Difference Between Stock Trades on Pink Sheets and the OTCBB. Retrieved from https://www.investopedia.com/ask/answers/what-does-it-mean-when-stock-trades-pink-sheets-or-otcbb/

Metcalf, T. (2019). Why Do Companies Sell Stocks?. Retrieved from https://smallbusiness.chron.com/companies-sell-stocks-59896.html

Murphy, C. (2018). How to invest in penny stocks for beginners. Retrieved from https://www.investopedia.com/articles/investing/091114/how-invest-penny-stocks.asp

MURPHY, C. (2019). A Review of Pink Sheet Stocks and How Investors Can Trade Them. Retrieved from https://www.investopedia.com/terms/p/pinksh eets.asp

Murphy, C. (2019). How to Find and Invest in Penny Stocks (ADAT, ANAD). Retrieved from https://www.investopedia.com/updates/how-to-invest-in-penny-stocks/

Murphy, C. (2019). How to Find and Invest in Penny Stocks (ADAT, ANAD). Retrieved from https://www.investopedia.com/updates/how-to-invest-in-penny-stocks/

Reynolds, C. (2018). Entrepreneurs, Be Careful to Avoid Penny Stock Scams | The Startup Magazine. Retrieved from http://thestartupmag.com/common-penny-stock-scams-look/

Staff, M. (2016). *What Is a Penny Stock? -- The Motley Fool. The Motley Fool.* Retrieved 8 May 2019, from https://www.fool.com/knowledge-center/what-is-a-penny-stock.aspx

Technical Analysis and Penny Stocks. (2019). *Extraordinaryinvestor.com.* Retrieved 9 May 2019, from https://www.extraordinaryinvestor.com/technic al-analysis.html

Trading Strategy. (2019). *Investopedia.* Retrieved 9 May 2019, from https://www.investopedia.com/trading-strategy-4427764

What are Penny Stocks and How Do They Work? - Wall Street Survivor. (2019). *Wall Street Survivor.* Retrieved 9 May 2019, from https://www.wallstreetsurvivor.com/starter-guides/what-are-penny-stocks-how-they-work/

Day Trading for Beginners

Want to be a Day Trader? Learn How to Trade for a Living and Discover These Powerful Day Trading Tips and Strategies in 2019

Bill Sykes

Timothy Gibbs

executed to present accurate, up to date, and reliable, complete information. No warranties of any kind are declared or implied. Readers acknowledge that the author is not engaging in the rendering of legal, financial, medical, or professional advice. The content within this book has been derived from various sources. Please consult a licensed professional before attempting any techniques outlined in this book.

By reading this document, the reader agrees that under no circumstances is the author responsible for any losses, direct or indirect, which are incurred as a result of the use of information contained within this document, including, but not limited to, — errors, omissions, or inaccuracies.

Table of Contents

Introduction

Any successful trader will tell you that day trading is a lot like riding a roller coaster. Though fun and exciting, it sometimes depletes your hope and takes away your will to continue. There are moments you will be extraordinarily happy, but in others, you will feel powerless. What you should know is that these low moments should not get to your head and make you panic or even quit. As in every journey you begin in life, you should be keen on how you address adversities since no one promised that there won't be hard times along the way. It is at these times that you should look into the stories of successful traders and see how they have managed to overcome such times.

Successful trading is an art and a science. Most of its aspects are those of business like any other. You obviously need to look out for the market signals, obtain as much information about the market as you can, and maintain a focus of getting a competitive edge in all markets that you participate in. Sooner or later, you'll learn that the same lessons that drive the most successful trading firms are the same lessons that drive their trading each day. Once you get it right from the beginning, every day for you will be a winning day.

In today's information age, you are bound to hear a lot about day trading from the media outlets. The complexity and variety of these voices can make it hard for you to separate the truth from the myths and misconceptions. Yet, to be a successful trader, you must get the facts right in all aspects! Some of the most common misconceptions that you need to avoid include:

Day trading is a hoax: The entire day trading business is thought of as a business of the chosen few who live off of new traders' gullibility by promoting the stock to drive their prices. Whilst there truly is a pump and dump scheme in which self-serving stock promoters drive up prices, sell, and leave the buyers staggering, this is just a small phenomenon within the entire occupation. In fact, there are always unethical dealers in every type of business who sell counterfeit products and mislead the buyers. The trick is about learning to identify and avoid such unethical traders and pursue your activities successfully. Most of the naysayers who lose their money in day trading and blame it on the occupation fail to understand that this is due to their lack of appropriate knowledge and misinformation. This doesn't make day trading a hoax.

The get-rich-quickly mentality: Rumour has it that placing a few stocks is your gate path to financial success. Truly, there are some outliers in the scene who record substantial success within a short period, but this doesn't always happen. Just as in any other business, you'll probably experience various ups and downs, and it all depends on how resilient and willing you are to learn from your mistakes. In fact, those who work their way up there through plenty of hurdles have better risk management skills, and their trading prowess is enhanced by the day.

The "must-get-rich using the basics" mentality: In reference to the above point, continuous learning exposes you to an oasis of knowledge you could never have imagined. Furthermore, the trading market is constantly changing and learning places you on the top of the trends to eventually make you the most profitable. Essentially, you will need to respond to the market changes through continuous learning. You will eventually become obsolete if you don't keep up with training.

You need huge sums of money to be profitable in the market: One of the rumors that keep people off the trading scene is that those who have made it are those who began with a lot of money. This would mean acquiring a big trading account and placing big trade positions. This is just not true. In fact, you can have a lot of money when you begin to trade and lose all of it if you don't know how to handle the market. Day trading is one of the professions you can consider as a "small business" option. Your job is to concentrate on building up your trading skills before you can think of investing a lot of your money.

Most outrageously, rumor has it that you don't need to be trained to day trade: While you technically don't need a certificate for your training, assuming that you need no education to engage in trading is one of the most common myths in day trading. Learning about the basics is important, but it's the real-life training that exposes you to aspects such as the best strategies and identifying patterns and finding a framework that works for you that matter. Saying you don't need training is setting yourself up for failure.

You can make massive amounts in a single trade: Well, true as it is, making such a dubious statement makes it look like this happens all the time, while it is certainly not the case. In fact, when you're just a beginner, perhaps with a small account, chances of such immediate massive profits are rare. The truth is that, similar to any other business, you will have to identify a workable strategy to make the wisest investment, without taking too much or too little risk.

That day trading compares to gambling is simply a myth. This is the stereotype used by the masses that do not trade or have dived into the trading scene before without good skills and failed terribly. They view trading as a gambling machine that only lets you win once, then eats away your money every other time. The truth is that trading can be like gambling if you allow it. You would allow it to be by failing to train and master the best skills.

That said, remember that you can ultimately achieve financial success through day trading, using consistent efforts and strategic trading. Entering the day trade profession is not a process to be taken lightly. There are the basic requirements for entering the trade, and there are the critical requisites that you have to observe for you to make it in day trading. For instance, you must be able to apply a workable strategy, get a lot of practice, know about the capital requirements, consider goals that you want to achieve and their constraints, choose a broker, and be in the right mental state. This book guides you through the most profound aspects of day trading.

Section 1: Day Trading Benefits and the Requisites

Chapter 1: Why Day Trading is a Profession to Consider

Reasons Why People Pursue Day Trading

The truth is, trading can be disheartening at times. Even the top achievers have some losing periods, so never be too hard on yourself. It is always good to learn about focusing on the positive side of something, lest you miss an opportunity that could mean everything to your life. Whether you are a full-time day trader or starting out part-time, there are evident reasons why you should actually engage in trading. The following offers a list of some of these reasons:

Trading gives you financial freedom: One of the most obvious reasons people want to become day traders is to improve their finances, and they think it is possible in this field. Trading gives you a chance to not just cater to personal and simple bills, but to be able to live comfortably from anywhere in the world. You have the freedom to purchase not based on what you can afford, but on what you actually want.

Trading improves your mental toughness: Clearly, day traders are people who have chosen to not follow the masses and what seems acceptable by the majority of society. They have chosen to see the world for what it really is and are ready to challenge the status quo that trading is only for the chosen elite few. That's what mentally tough people do. They have the mindset of a winner and are always ready to face a situation for what it really is, believing it's going to pay off if they stick to the journey with consistent efforts.

Trading gives you flexibility as you escape the usually 9-5 day grind: What's better than earning big and being flexible? Most of the white collar jobs that pay well require you to stay in the office from morning to evening. Day trading is among the few professions where you earn enormously from the comfort of your home or any location in the world. You can make a schedule to travel or go on vacation without having to worry about missing work. Also, it saves you from having to wake up, drive to your job, and work for 40 or more hours per week.

It makes you more knowledgeable - you gain a better understanding of the world: In trading, you are exposed to the conditions of various economies of the world. By playing around with currencies and exchange rates between countries, you remain updated about the world at all times, much more than people who do not trade. You can even identify a place to travel or relocate to by learning about its currency value.

Trading has a leveled playing field: To be a day-trader, you don't have to present a certificate to anyone to show your education level. Whether you are a college dropout or university graduate, all it takes are most of the soft skills you already know, such as diligence and commitment. In his study on the profitability of day trading, Ryu (2012) observes that most of the successful traders in the world have no formal education. Through these skills, you gain a better understanding of yourself, and you can calmly and tactfully handle all other situations around you.

Trading equips you with life-enriching skills: Life in the modern world has become increasingly demanding. People are under the pressure of meeting the various demands from their personal and work domains. The modern lifestyle has increased our chances to mold our lives the way we want by giving us a lot of opportunities and material possessions. To make our lives better, we are expected to have some crucial skills that can help us through various hurdles in our day-to-day life. These include:

Critical thinking and problem solving: While participating in the market, you take the other marketers as a single lot and attempt to figure out what they are thinking, so you can gain a competitive edge. It is through anticipating the steps of others that you can call in your shots in the trade market. These skills are not only applicable in trading but are useful in all other domains of life. You find an opportunity, think critically through it, and know how to solve a challenge.

Risk management: Trading has been a training ground for people to manage risks better since it is all about risk management. Just like the SEALs who undergo hectic training to become the best in the game, traders undergo a rough risk management training where they have to know just how much is acceptable and at what time. To be a successful trader, you have to establish the point in the market with the potential of giving you the highest ROI. Unlike in gambling where you gamble all day long, say in a casino, with your chances of winning anything is almost close to zero, day trading gives you a chance to maximize your wins all day long. This is done through proper management of your positions by being calculative about your risks. Therefore, risk management is a fundamental aspect of trading, which differentiates it from gambling.

Failure management: One of the best skills of the most successful people whose success stories we read about is failure management. They understand that failure is part of the journey, and it's what adds up to your experience. Trading exposes you to various wins and losses, and it is usually in the moments of failure that you are expected to remain mostly positive.

You learn your strengths and weaknesses: Whether it's making decisions quickly, giving up easily, or being organized, trading will sooner or later expose these traits within you. This will help you realize a part of your psychology you may have never known about. It also helps you utilize your strengths to the best and take steps to address your weaknesses.

Introspectiveness: Trading forces you to master the skill of carefully analyzing your life to learn about the things you did well and those that you did not do well, so you can improve your chances of success in the long run. This is a skill that most people struggle with, and they do not realize that some qualities are hidden under their misguided outlook of themselves.

Objectivity: To make it in trading, you are forced to always be objective. Objectivity is the pillar that keeps us from being bias from in our judgment, and we need this value to be able to trade effectively. Once we master this skill, we are able to keep away from poor judgments, and we cannot easily get frustrated in any area of our lives.

Why day trading is better than buying and holding

Most people are conflicted between buying and holding (investing) versus day trading since the two appear to be at odds with each other. Yet the ultimate goal of every investor is to buy low and sell high. Day trading is the riskiest form of stock trading since it involves rapidly buying and selling stock to maximize on the small price changes within a day. Technically, stock trading is all about deciding beforehand on the percentage decrease you are expecting to buy and deciding beforehand the percentage increase you want to sell at. There is a fair share of risk that exists in day trading since the price of a stock may not go as you want in the timeframe anticipated.

Conversely, the buying and holding model of investment is one in which the investor buys and keeps an investment for an extensive amount of time, waiting for the value to rise. Its risk is determined by the organization's long-term prospects. Its potential risk is found if the company does not take the direction earlier anticipated and based on the price the investor bought it at.

What is outstanding about day trading is that it offers you a chance to benefit from your efforts. It enhances your autonomy and helps you become a more experienced person every day. Buying and holding for a long period of time means that you are relying on the efforts of others (a company) for you to benefit. Your profits are determined by their long term outcome. You have a passive role in the investment since you identify appropriate funds or securities and hold them up for a long time. In day trading, you have an active role since you monitor the market every day to maximize the best buying and selling times. Day trading gives you the chance to have a full-time job while buying and holding is like keeping your money in a relatively safe place, waiting for it to mature.

Besides, day trading isn't about perfection, since you can purchase stocks that recuperate support mark in capacity when you sell while buying and holding requires you to be absolutely right about a company's success. In day trading, you get quick feedback which transforms you into a better trader every day, and you can spot your woes quickly by studying charts.

Even so, day trading allows you to enjoy your money as it comes rather having to wait for an endgame that never comes by buying and holding. Day trading, as mentioned earlier, gives you the financial freedom to spend your money when you desire.

Ways to make money in the market

As highlighted earlier, a day trader has to ensure that all amounts of the specific securities are closed by the time the market is closing for the day. This means that a trader who wants to be successful must be speculative and exit a day's trade tactfully before being caught up in unimaginable risks of negative gaps in prices between two days. There are various ways through which you can make money in the day trade market, provided the trader is sound and understands just how to go about it. It can be rough because of the fast-paced action, but the necessary tools and knowledge lead to success.

For instance, successful day traders focus on establishing stocks with high betas, which refers to the condition of how fast a stock's price can go up in the market. This entails identifying the companies whose business is doing really well. Since day trading refers to trading on positions on only one day, as a trader you ought to identify the stocks that can move up and down fast, provided you are able to capture the movement and know when to execute the buy orders and when to execute the sell orders.

Also, day traders seek to identify penny stocks, which refers to the small companies' stocks, which basically have a worth of fewer than 5 dollars per share. Regardless of their size, these stocks carry a high-profit potential with them. Rather than awaiting the big companies' stocks that may not have that high of a propensity to changing in a day, a wise trader goes for the penny stocks and exits the trade in the evening with a good intraday profit.

Further, day traders increasingly embrace binary options to trade, which is done by entering a position and betting that its value will increase even though they do not own the stocks. Through the binary options, you choose a security and set the duration of time that you are going to hold the position. It offers returns in a short time, and even though you bet that the value of the security will rise, its fall does not affect you since you still make money from the market volatility using proper timing strategies.

News playing is also a basic way of acting on your position in the market. Most successful day traders rely on major news announcements to buy or sell stocks. The movement of prices triggered by such announcements is quite significant for a day trader, and the success of a trader depends on how much they had indulged in the market based on rumors which always circulate before the actual news announcements. Furthermore, traders make money through artificial intelligence, which allows technical analysis on a real-time basis and gives traders substantial knowledge about market conditions.

The reason why most people do not go for day trading or indulge in it and fail is simply that they don't have time to engage in the trade that much. Yet extensive research is what day trading entails to be able to spot the penny stocks and high beta stocks, and know exactly how to leverage them.

Summary of the rest of the book

Of course, there is no universal answer to the right time or the right way that one should be trading to reap good fruits. There are various traders out there who engage in the stock market at different levels. Some take it as a part-time gig, while others trade for a living. Day trading is not as simple as sitting down, accessing the internet, and staring at your computer screen. It requires enormous efforts that are not even guaranteed to pay off. However, even with this reality check into day trading, you can always set realistic expectations and use the right tools to achieve your goals. This is what the rest of the book is dedicated to.

It discusses the basics of day trading, the essential information you need as a beginner, the most popular and workable strategies that successful traders have always used, and the daily tips you can leverage for success. It helps you to distinguish between the best platforms and strategies that beginners use from those that suit the veterans. Also, it shows you the cost requirements for each of the commonly used platforms to ensure that the platforms you use fit your budget.

Further, it offers insight on the appropriate amount of risk that you, as a day trader, should take depending on your experience, knowledge, and the platform that you are using. It shows you the best tips and techniques that the most successful traders have used to give you a competitive edge while you engage in day trading. The common mistakes that the average or losing traders commit are explored throughout to help you omit them and prevent you from becoming the 89% of day traders who lose in the game. It also shows you the kind of mentality to avoid while day trading and the one you should embrace for your benefit instead.

Finally, it shows you why day trading is the best form of trading for you, especially if you are looking for a job rather than just making an investment and waiting for long durations. While other forms of trading are also worthwhile and they have had a great success record, the rest of the book focuses on day trading and shows you why you should select it.

Chapter 2: The Basics of Day Trading

Obviously, the first thing that traders want to know is how much money they can make from trading. Most of us have heard that day trader get a lot of money from this profession. True to this, there is plenty of profits to be earned from day trading. It is quite obvious that some traders will still need an additional job on top of day trading every month, but others can attain a comfortable lifestyle based on day trading alone. How much money you make as a trader is mainly determined by various factors including the amount of money you begin with, how much training you've invested in, the market in which you trade, your personality, and even the volatility of the market. This chapter takes you through the fundamental aspects that you are sure to need while in the day trading market.

Day trading terminology

Learning about the trading lingo offers you a secret code to the significant day trading ideas. The following is a checklist of the most significant and trading-unique terms that you should be aware of, and which are used throughout the rest of the book.

- Initial public offering (IPO): Used to refer to a firm selling a particular set of shares in the market

- Float: The number of shares available for trading from a company

- Leverage rate: The rate at which the platform you use multiplies your deposit to enhance your trading power

- Profit/loss ratio: The measure of the likelihood of a platform to generate profit as compared to a loss

- Entry and exit points: The points at which you buy and sell your position, respectively

- The Bid: The price at which a broker buys a security from a trader

- The Ask: The price the broker sells the security at

- Spread: The variance between the buying and selling price of a security by a broker

- Liquidity: identifies as the ease of a stock to be purchased and sold in the market devoid of major price effects.

- Market makers: the determinants of buy and sell orders as well as facilitating liquidity.

- Resistance level: the point at which the position holders subsumes the buyers in the market and therefore diminishes the chances of stock price rising.

- Support level: Contrasts with the resistance level. It is the point at which buyers override the position holders, diminishing the chances of stock prices diminishing.

- Breakout level: the level beyond a security's preceding resistance point.

- Trend: the inherent direction that the price of a stock assumes. A trend can be upwards or downwards.

These terms are applicable throughout day trading to understand the general information, charts, strategy, platforms, and patterns of trading.

Personality traits for successful traders

Discipline: Good traders have taken the market to be like their workplace. They understand that discipline is core to achieving good results. It is not just about getting a strategy and assuming that all is set for trading. The markets expose you to infinite chances to trade, and yet there is only a short time that is right for you to trade. There are only a few seconds in which your chances of success in a day are optimal. Therefore, there is only a short time of actual trading. Now, discipline lets you give those few moments your maximum concentration. Should you lack discipline, you will always be distracted during the best times for you to trade. Such people are the naysayers who spread rumors that they spend the whole day on the computer trading and they only incur losses. Yet it is during the most crucial moments that they were distracted. At a time when social media has become part of daily life for most of us, it is easy to get distracted in the world of the internet and lose sight of your stops for the day.

A good trader is disciplined and follows their schedule, and they are able to act instantaneously when trading opportunities occur.

Adaptability: In the trading market, there are hardly two days that are similar. Today there is high volatility, but tomorrow the volatility might be low. If you strictly follow an example as if it were an exam that you are about to sit for, you are bound to fail. You need to learn to be flexible and take each day as it comes. You need to be able to implement suitable strategies for all types of market conditions and know exactly which strategy fits which condition. A good trader is one who acts real-time, knows when to step aside and watch, and when to dive right in and trade. Failure to become adaptable is one way of setting yourself up for failure.

Patience: Now we know that trading is just like starting a business. You do not expect to begin making lump sums right when you first begin. It is only in a few cases that these exceptional gains do occur for a new trader. Being successful takes a lot of patience and consistent efforts as you wait for success. But basically, day trading entails a lot of waiting. Furthermore, we already know that there are bad days, even for the very experienced traders. You need to have the patience of waiting for tomorrow, and even if tomorrow doesn't work, the next day might. Also, you need to learn to wait for the great market entering times, lest you enter too early or too late. In day trading, patience goes hand in hand with discipline, since patience allows you to wait for the time you should enter the market and discipline ensures that you are actually set to enter the market without hesitation. Typically, patience is among the greatest trading personality traits.

Forward thinking: You can't be dwelling on the past if you are a day trader. While it is paramount to use historical data to make trading decisions, you must be able to apply the information in the present day and time. You cannot buy a security at a particular price and then ignore all the market price data that changes within 10 minutes. You must be like a chess player - one who is already planning their next move tactfully based on what the opponent, in this case, the market, does, and also is able to anticipate the opponent's response to that. You keep considering the various scenarios that may play out in order to be able to implement a plan under the different scenarios.

Practice forward thinking by considering what needs to happen for you to enter a market, and what might happen when you're there; for instance, if the prices go up or down fast against you or the prices do not move, consider how you should react in each scenario. Trading is all about knowing that each step you take brings a particular result, and being equipped with the ability to foretell.

Mental toughness: As mentioned in the reasons you should trade section, day trading in so many ways forces you to be mentally tough. But we know that people quit trading all the time, saying that it is not their thing, it is something for the elite few, they don't seem to be getting it, and all sorts of negative things. This is because they have refused to be mentally tough. Day trading requires you to be mentally tough. Mentally tough individuals never quit. They never give in to pressure no matter how competitive the playing ground is. They never allow the failure of one day to discourage them from continuing with the journey. In fact, they take failure as a good chance to learn and become smarter. They are thick skinned and are always ready to take any blows the trading market may throw at them. Most importantly, they are smart and curious enough to know the most appropriate risks that they should take. Making it in day trading requires you to understand that there are losing days, but they should not discourage you. It requires you to remain positive under all circumstances, and losses shouldn't deter your judgment since this will most definitely lead to more failures, and you will eventually quit having not explored your optimal potential.

Independence: Independence goes hand in hand with forward thinking. While you get some help from your mentors and books initially, day trading requires you to eventually become independent using the knowledge you have accumulated.

Finally, as a trader, there is the need to be open-minded, persistent, and decisive. You need to expect any kind of result when you trade, but you have to be consistent with your efforts despite having a loss as your result. Most importantly, you need to be decisive so that you can promptly act upon the trading opportunities when they arise.

How day trading differs from other types of trading

The most popular trading model that any newbie in the trading scene will be introduced to is buying and holding. The trader buys stocks and holds them, and the investment increases in value over a long period of time. Usually, the long-term wait is met by positive results which could even be augmented through dividends and reinvesting the profits. While some traders go for the buy and hold approach, others prefer to enter and exit the market on the same day, while still others prefer to use other approaches that outdo the former.

Thus, besides the buy and hold approach, other approaches include:

Position trading: This is a trading approach in which the traders are free to utilize both long and short term trading techniques, as they anticipate gaining from longer-term trends than those of day trading. Basically, position trading takes a span that ranges from months to years. Decisions to trade are made based on weekly and monthly price market results. While it resembles the buying and holding approach, traders in this method are not restricted to long-term only.

Swing trading: This is an approach which follows a generally short-term path since positions are held for days or weeks. Traders using this approach anticipate gaining from short-term pricing fluctuations. What mostly determines when the trader's exit is if the scheduled time is up, when a target is reached, or when the market is fluctuating contrary to the trader's expectations. This approach suits traders who are not able to be active in all trading sessions, since it does not require you to always be there. Therefore, this approach differs from day trading because even though it operates in the short term, positions can go for days without exiting the market.

Scalp trading: This is a method of trading that involves a shorter span than that of day trading. Traders buy and sell actively within seconds and minutes. It follows the business sales strategy, which reduces the selling price to make more sales because every position gives a low margin return. As such, traders in this market often buy various positions to accumulate the little profit gains obtained from each position. Additionally, they seek the lowest trading commissions lest all their profits are taken away in the commissions.

High-Frequency Trading (HFT): This trading technique entails high-frequency trades. It is perhaps the riskiest, most complex, and involved style of trading, which demands speed and attention on a 24-hour basis. Traders using this technique rely on analyzing multiple markets concurrently for profits. Successful traders in this segment are able to evaluate their composite and trademarked systems of trading. Usually, a beginner, perhaps working from home, is usually not competitive in this market. This trading approach differs from day trading since day trading follows a one market approach.

Essentially, day trading differs from all these trading mechanisms because of the holding period of the stocks bought. Remember that trading mainly entails buying low and selling high. Also, remember that day trading entails entering and exiting the market within the same day. Day trading is often like a full-time job, where you have to identify and ensure that all requisites are in order. Any disruptions of the working space can make traders miss the intraday price fluctuations, and hence miss their best trading opportunities. However, it is not as complex, intensive, or risky as scalp trading, which takes less trading spans and stricter conditions.

The most commonly used platforms for day trading

When you are a newbie or a veteran who has realized they need a change, you might get confused when choosing a strategy, platform, and market to enter in day trading. However, you may have a rough idea of what you want in a platform, for instance. It is a no brainer that you want premium research, low costs, a comprehensive platform, and innovative tools for trading. There are various brokers for trading out there, with every platform trying to attract as many traders as possible. The most commonly used platforms include:

Trade station: This platform is number one when it comes to trading technology through its web-based technique. It is actually the ultimate go-to option for many future investors and active traders. It equips traders with information gathering capabilities through access to a large database. Studies and charts that have been accumulated over a long period of time are available in this platform. Furthermore, these studies can easily be adjusted to fit user specifications using the platform's easy coding language.

Interactive Brokers: With its ability to cater to active trade, Interactive Brokers is generally preferred among day traders. While the platform has no allowance for newbies, it sure has hotkeys and special orders for placing any kind of trade. It also has margins ranging from low to high to cater to traders of all levels of risk tolerance. That said, IB offers the lowest commissions in the industry, and thus, it is common in the institutional community day trading.

Ameritrade: This platform is popular for its variety of tools which help traders in their day to day activities. It offers access to analysis of earnings, charts, and even backtesting. Traders are able to analyze stocks on a real-time basis and share layouts of their workspaces. Also, this platform gives access to above-average commissions and services. It is useful for anyone ranging from active and experienced traders to newbies.

Charles Schwab: This platform has progressively created a positive image in the trading scene through its delivery of high-quality customer service. It has a wide range of features that makes its interaction with the trader easy and worthwhile. It also has a lot of Exchange Trade Funds (ETFs) without high commissions. It allows access to a wide research base, and a trader far from lacks any information they need. However, this platform has high trade commissions that any trader wants to consider before committing.

Lightspeed: This is one of the most favorable platforms for beginners. It allows one to trade with simply the click of a button. It allows a high level of personalization, whereby you can put as many as four modules allowing you to access and join different pieces of information suitable for your trading strategy. You can also make a shortcut key to take you directly to the page you want to keep monitoring. However, the platform has a price that many newbies may not be comfortable with, but it also has demos that one can try before committing to the fees.

Ally Invest: This is another one of the go-to platforms for active traders because of its good charting, analytical tools, and even researching offered for free. Also, it has low commissions, and the account has no minimum, giving the trader a chance to plan for their money no matter the amount. However, Ally has been discredited on various occasions for the lack of branches that can offer traders a wide range of alternatives, and the lack of mutual funds for transaction-fee.

Of course, there are many more platforms, including eOption and Fidelity, but these are less popular. In fact, Interactive Brokers and Trade Station are the most popular platforms. Nerdwallet provides a comprehensive review of these platforms to give traders an easy chance of getting their options right when choosing a platform. Those that meet the criteria of flexibility, standard fee, and access to information are most notably Interactive Brokers, Trade Station, and Lightspeed.

What is there to be traded: The main day trading markets

The stock market, Forex, and futures are all major markets in day trading. Others, such as options, are prevalent as well. Options, however, is most suitable for Swing traders who have their positions for weeks, not an active day trader.

The following is a brief overview of each:

Stock market: This is perhaps the most popular market that crosses the mind when one thinks about trading. This market allows ETFs and shares of companies to be traded under various opportunities, which include spread betting. This opportunity, for instance, allows you to gain even if the prices may be falling. Positions in this market are best attained at news release or financial reports, and from studying the practical signs. Further, all positions are exited at the end of each day at a particular time. There has to be an equity balance of at least 25,000 dollars. The implication of this to new traders is that they should begin by setting aside 30,000 dollars to trade.

Forex: Now, Forex is the largest market across the globe. It is highly accessible and allows trading for the whole day. It appeals to day traders because of its massive volume. It contains multiple opportunities for trading with high liquidity, which makes the opening and closing of positions relatively quick.

What is more appealing even for beginners is that they can start with capital as low as 100 dollars, although about 1000 dollars is the ideal recommended amount. The mainstay of this market is that one currency is exchanged for another. In this exchange, there is the term called currency pair, which entails the amount that, say, the US dollar is exchanged for another, say, Canadian dollar.

That said, every trading platform has its own requirements for Forex trading, and this is the point where a trader thinking to enter the Forex trade should be most careful. One should make demos to their friend to practice and learn. Profits in this market are earned from speculating how the price of one currency will move relative to another.

Futures: As its name suggests, Futures is a market which mainly focuses on future prices. A buyer and a seller agree to buy or sell a particular amount of a commodity or security at a later date. Day traders benefit from the intraday price fluctuations between the duration of the contract during the day. Futures requires less capital than stocks, but more capital than Forex. With about 3,500 dollars you can trade in Futures, where you can get Futures contracts such as S & P Emini. Different contracts give rise to different official market hours. The trick for a day trader is to keep tabs on the particular contract's official hours to know the right time to exit a market.

Also, specific day trading platforms have different requirements for Futures trading, and this should be an important factor for consideration.

Binary Options: Although less popular, this is perhaps the simplest market in which a trader knows in advance the timing and the returns of a successful position. This sector is seemingly booming, and regulations are changing. Remember that laws surrounding a market are a major consideration when you're thinking of getting into trading. Another factor to consider while trading in this market is if the asset you are trading will rise or drop in value. Understanding these dynamics is not difficult, considering the potential outcome is known beforehand. Binary options offer a unique day trading experience and can even contribute to traders' portfolio of the day.

Cryptocurrencies: Cryptocurrencies have become the talk of the day when it comes to trading. It is a market that has attracted many investors and became a great source of finances in the recent past, with the most popular currencies being Bitcoin and Ethereum. There are minimal entry barriers, and the market is relatively easy to trade, even for beginners.

Commodities: This market simply entails the trading of foodstuffs, minerals, and even oil.

Risk in Day Trading

Risk management is among the fundamental lessons learned in trading. You must learn how to manage your money because, after all, it is not worth it to trade if you'll run broke after your first month in the venture. The most successful traders are those who know how to manage the different types of risks prevalent in day trading, with the greatest being the financial risk.

Financial risk: As the mother of all risks in day trading, traders must be careful about the volatility of the market prices, in which fluctuations can make one lose terribly. It is hard to benefit when a market moves in the negative direction by a large margin. Furthermore, there are few opportunities being preyed upon by too many traders. In cases such as this, it's always best to be careful whenever entering trading, and also entering a position on a particular day. Especially for newbies, it is recommended that they do not place huge amounts of cash into a single trade since this can discourage them from going on. Market information is paramount in avoiding financial risk.

Capital risk: There are various upfront costs associated with trading, including the software, infrastructure, and news services. There are other ongoing expenses in every platform, including commissions or ECN, interests, charting packages, as well as communication charges. You don't want to indulge in a venture where you will lose all the money you've invested. Also, you don't want to engage in a platform where all you'll be doing is paying for the ongoing expenses without really getting the value for your money.

Mental risk: Trading is perhaps the most addictive form of gambling, and with a trader's intelligence being enhanced day by day, they are much more likely to get addicted. One might wonder, why not be on their trading spot all the time and earn a lot of cash, provided they are good at it? It may look interesting, and you may be tempted to think that it is good for you, but in the long run, being addicted to trading exposes you to adverse mental risk. After all, the main aim of day trading is for you to have the financial freedom to do other things. If you do not take time off, when will you ever enjoy your money? Remember that too much work without play always makes one a dull person. You should control how much trading you do in a day, or how much space trading occupies in your mind. Do not invest in a venture that will give you financial freedom but a lifetime of mental bondage.

Types of orders in Day Trading

While placing a trade order seems as simple as clicking a "buy" or a "sell" button when it's time to do so, executing orders requires maximum attention to the various types of orders and knowing exactly what to do every time you are in the market. Each of the order serves a significant purpose.

The following is a checklist of trade orders that you should pay attention to in order to avoid slipping and losing:

Market order: This is perhaps the simplest in the trading market. It has a buying and a selling option. Usually, the trader has no control over the buying or selling price of the market order. The market gives you the prevailing price, and that is what you get. It is preferable at times when traders are in need of entering or exiting positions, but can be dangerous since you may buy at the ask price and sell at the bid price, or experience a large negative difference. The ask price is the one that sellers that are willing to sell to you have, and the bid price is the one that the willing buyers place.

Limit order: Likewise, there is a buy and sell limit order. It is a directive to purchase or give away a position at a specific price, different from the current price in the market. It gives allowance to the traders to trade at a preferable price, be it buying or selling. A buy limit order, for instance, allows a buyer to set a limit beyond which they can't buy shares. For instance, if the current price of a stock is 10 dollars, a trader may choose to set a limit of 8 dollars, and only when the price of the willing sellers hits 8 or below can the trader execute the order. A sell limit order, on the other hand, allows the trader to set a limit below which they can't sell an order to prevent them from making losses. A limit order is more preferable to market order when the trader has a lot of time to wait for the order, but the market order is considered more efficient just when the trader wants to execute orders quickly.

Stop order: This is a buy or sell order which is designed to help prevent losses for the investor. It is generally considered useful for long positions, but can also serve as stop-losses for short positions. A buy stop order, for instance, is one that is placed above the prevailing market price; hence, the order is executed at or above that stop price. Once the stop is reached, a buy stop order becomes more or less like the market order since the trader is given any price, and now they can stop before the prices move too contrary to their expectations. A sell stop order can be leveraged to exit a long trading position. Orders are filled when the price is at or below the stop point. Upon reaching the sell stop, the order is executed at the amount buyers are willing to give, just like in a market order, preventing impending losses when the prices are moving against the trader.

The major limitation with stop orders is that one cannot be sure of the buying or selling price they will receive. For that reason, there is the stop-limit order as described below.

Stop-limit order: This directive is almost comparable with the one above (stop), only that it has a boundary which prevents it from acting like the market order once the stop is reached. Clearly, it has the features of both the stop and the limit order. In this order, the trader sets two price points, the stop, and the limit price. It begins as a stop order, but upon reaching the stop, it turns into a limiting value directive. It gives the trader a degree of security to exit the positions if they suspect any impending losses and also allows them to set the price at which they prefer to buy or sell stocks.

Trailing stop order: This order has many similarities with the stop order, only that the stop order has a specific price that it targets for the order to be executed, while the trailing stop order allows a trader to set their preferred change in the prevailing prices. Traders use it to exit short positions, even though it is generally considered appropriate for long positions.

Chapter 3: Beginner's Day Trading Essential Information

Essential Tools

Infrastructure: Day trading is just like any other profession that requires infrastructure to enable it to run. Technology has made trading easy because traders have access to most of the equipment they need, which includes computers or laptops, modems, routers, mobile phone with internet connectivity, and great communication capability. Also, traders need some specialized software to keep tabs on every activity going on in the market all day long.

The active traders who have made day trading their full-time job acquire Electronic Communication Networks (ECN) such as SelectNet and Instinet to keep up with all the market activities. Having this software exempts traders from having to pay a fee for every trade to the brokers since they can solely access all information concerning their position. These ECNs are normally free but to join and use any, membership must be approved. They prefer this to get ECN capabilities to monitor the market. Alternatively, some traders, especially those who trade occasionally, use online brokerage accounts, whose major drawback is that it incurs more costs.

Such infrastructure requires some dollars every month. However, it is important to note that using the brokerage approach incurs you more costs and exposes you to the risk of getting delayed information. Yet in day trading, it is the little expense details that determine the difference between success and failure in becoming profitable.

Capital

The principles of day trading are applicable for all markets, including stock, commodities, and options, but the capital requirements vary for each market. As mentioned, and even as a basic rule of nature, you need capital for you to engage in trade. Hence, if you are thinking of starting up, you must set aside capital to start and be a reasonable risk taker, lest you lose it all.

Be sure to have your initial capital outlay get you somewhere concerning your trading goals.

Some of the capital requirements reflect in commissions for the Direct Access Brokers. Commissions are computed on the basis of the volume of shares being traded. Whenever getting in and out of a position, you have to consider the corresponding commission charges. Some brokers ask for high commissions, while others are considered cheaper.

Other costs are incurred in the spread, which refers to the difference between the prices at which quick buyers get securities and the prices at which quick sellers sell their securities. Essentially, a trader must have the capital to be able to take bids. Also, as discussed in the infrastructure section above, all traders need market information, and they must be able to pay for it to access.

Information

Information is perhaps the single most significant tool that you need in day trading. Remember that you are relying on every slight price movement for you to make a move.

Whilst you are not really concerned with the intrinsic value of the companies whose stock you are trading on, you are definitely concerned with how these stocks interplay with others in the market.

Using special software, internet connectivity, and computers, day traders are able to perform technical analysis and compare historical price movements with the current to make a decision. They need to access charts and to also know how to interpret those chartings to their benefit.

Time commitment

As earlier mentioned, day trading is one of the trading options that can easily become a full-time job. To benefit from this trading, you have to be sure that you can commit up to 10 hours per day in the market, either trading or preparing to trade. You definitely need to maintain your focus on the market conditions to identify any short-term opportunities. You must research for the most recent news and ongoing news stories, including regulations and earnings reports that can potentially impact your profitability.

The right personality

Personality matters a lot when it comes to day trading. As mentioned earlier, a day trader is assured of benefiting in the long run if they are disciplined, consistent with their efforts, patient, and even tough-minded. Day trading is not for the faint-hearted. One has to be ready to embrace any results and move on to try what the next day has to offer. Also, one has to realize that profits do not come by the first time of trading. It takes time and effort to accumulate experience and trade like a pro.

A day in the life of a Day Trader: What traders normally do every day

Just like in any other business, mistakes keep happening in day trading. These include errors as simple as clicking on the wrong tab, say buy instead of sell, or placing a wrong position. Other errors come forth when the trader is bombarded with information surrounding the trade, which further causes panic. In this connection, it is paramount to have a proper schedule for pre, during, and post-trade to minimize the chances of errors. Active day traders begin their day following a plan that they intend to maintain for the whole day. Although every trade is different, the following is a checklist of what should be in your daily plan:

Pre-trade:

- Check the economic calendar

Any big events in the economy can potentially affect your trade because the economy influences the prices in the market. The wise traders avoid being in trade at the time surrounding high impact economic events since anything can happen. The market typically opens at 9:30 a.m. ET. Hence, a wise trader catches up with any events that happened overnight or are coming up in the day that could affect their trade before this time. To see economic events, check the DailyFX economic calendar for Forex trade, Bloomberg for stocks, and the Yahoo! Finance earnings Calendar for individual company stocks to ensure the company has no major announcements or significant earning changes in that day. Since most of the traders participate in Forex and Futures markets, which are "around-the-clock" markets, traders can expect price rises before the market fully opens at 9:30 a.m. ET.

- Launching the workstation

After checking and taking note of what the analysts have to say, day traders then head on to their workstation and launch the platform. A wise trader checks if the platform is working seamlessly by ensuring that quotes are streaming in smoothly from the brokers. Since there is an interplay of various technological devices and software involved here, traders spend a few moments checking that everything is functioning properly.

- Be sure to trade in the correct account

It is possible for a day trader to have a great trading day and realize in the evening that they have been trading in a simulated account instead of the real account with real capital. A beginner especially should be very cautious, since most will have the simulated account. Also, for a market such as Futures, be sure to trade with the highest volume contract and check to see the ones whose deadlines are over.

- Note down significant texts

It is good to note down any scheduled high impact news releases as a constant reminder. In fact, you should include it in your chart at the approximate time it is bound to happen. It is entirely human nature to become too indulged in trade and end up forgetting such significant events.

- Checking strategies

Check the automated orders such as stop orders and stop limit orders to ensure they are set correctly, since failure to do this may give you some of the most unwanted results. If you are using a robot to trade, ensure that all settings are correct to avoid mishaps. You already know by now that even if you are trading manually, you can have some automated orders as well; hence, this is a necessary step.

- Check to position

This is especially a critical step for traders who use default position size. Errors could include an extra zero added to or removed from the actual position, which leads to a messed up trading session. Also, note your account balance to ensure that your market entry point and any stop order that you may set are well covered. Also, be sure that when positioning, you do it correctly to minimize the potential risk. Keep in mind the most amount of risk that you want to take in a particular day.

- Self-reminder

It is good to set a few moments to go through the situations under which you've made mistakes in the past. This helps you to avoid committing the mistakes again if such situations arise again

- Scanning the market for potential opportunities

When you are all set, everything is working properly, and you are mentally prepared to handle the day, hover over the market to identify the potential opportunities to trade. You can use the technical indicators option on the chart in your market for easy establishment of what's happening. Some traders have acquired market scanning software which identifies positions which meet their targets.

Conducting this assessment guides you on how to enter the market and start trading. In days with a high volatility tendency, you would expect a higher profit margin than when the volatility is stringent.

Early trading

The first few minutes of trading are technically volatile, so you want to give the market some time to balance and avoid being rudely stopped out of a position you may set. Traders then practice the waiting game at this moment until intuition can tell them to go ahead, based on their plans, experience, and observation of prevailing market price movement. In very short holding periods, which also means less profit expected, timing must be carefully done to jump in and trade during any opportunity. Remember that seconds make a huge difference in trading.

Now, this is the time you submit orders to the market, either in the state of market price orders or stop limit orders or any other depending on your goals. Whilst some traders prefer to enter simultaneous positions, others prefer to wait until one position closes to enter another.

In the time towards lunch is when traders become extra vigilant to check if their positions have reached the target, since the period after lunch is normally less eventful. High volatility and volume of trade gradually diminish towards midday. Essentially, therefore, the successful day traders are highly active during the morning and late-morning sessions.

Second wind

This represents the period after lunch to the time the market closes at 4 p.m. ET. Institutional traders come back from lunch hour and activity resumes, allowing traders a chance to look out for some more opportunities.

Traders continue monitoring their positions taken in the morning phase and now since they all have to close before 4pm. They are very alert to jump into any opportunity once their targets are reached before the close of the market. Also, traders rarely enter a position past their own limit time, say 3 or 3:30 p.m., to allow time for exiting properly without exposing themselves to losing risks.

As 4pm draws nearer, traders close the remaining positions and cancel orders that have not been filled. Leaving any open orders can cause huge losses, since they may automatically get filled without the notice of the traders.

This is just another day at the office, where you leave having broken even, experienced a loss, or gained a profit. To the successful and enthusiastic traders, the results of the day do not really matter. They look forward to what happens tomorrow and the accumulated events over time.

Post-market time

After closing the markets, traders review their day's activities, noting down what went well and what didn't, what worked and what failed, and their mistakes during the day. This helps them to note what can be improved for the sake of tomorrow. The more organized traders maintain a journal where they note down every trade and all its details, including whether it was a success or a loss. It is important to note that a journal provides a good framework for a trader hoping to elevate their trading efforts. It is also a good motivator to actually see that you have made some wins, and you can surely win again. Traders also go through financial news to get a review of the day's activity and plan for the next day. Finally, the trader shuts down their workstation and gets time off to rejuvenate and refresh for the next day.

Ideally, most of the time of a day trader's day is spent studying and seeking to understand the market and enhance their skills using simulations. Almost all traders had experienced a time when they traded for $1000 when they actually meant to trade for $100, but all this is part of a trader's development. A proper daily schedule that is well followed is what leads to success eventually for a beginner.

Formulating achievable goals and understanding common constraints

Having learned what day trading entails and the daily activities of a trader, you would think that perhaps pulling out an excel sheet and listing how much money you need to make each day to reach your goals is the way to go. In fact, this is the case for most traders. They cannot be blamed, because our society has taught us from our childhood that when you grow up, you work for a fixed amount of time for a particular amount of pay. However, one of the greatest lessons you learn as a trader is that the trading market does not really care about your daily or weekly or even monthly targets.

Day trading is complex, and setting a subjective goal does not really work. That said, I think that attempting to make profits, since this is the ultimate goal of every trader, without clear goals is like starting a journey without knowing the destination. Therefore, despite the complexity, you have to make (realistic) goals as a trader.

The first thing you should get off your mind is the employee's perception of work, where you think you ought to earn a certain amount after working for a certain amount of time. This mentality will have you placing trades even when conditions are not favorable as you try to get ahold of targets. This will frustrate you.

Second, when setting the goal per trade, try as much as possible to be realistic by matching your targets with the market conditions. Remember that setting realistic goals increases your chances of winning, and it is often the small wins that motivate you to keep going.

Also, relate your fixed goals per trade to the amount of risk that you have taken. For instance, setting a profit goal of about 30,000 dollars if you risked about 10,000 dollars is pretty reasonable. Over time and through a chain of trades, you are likely to get 3 times your capital investment and lower losses. Remember that you must account for losses. Since it is not good to over-focus on the negative side, the losses, it is good to consider them in your goal.

Also, relate your goal to the amount of volatility in the market. Volatility describes the number of price fluctuations in the market. High volatility translates into an equally big profit or loss margin. In low volatility conditions, the profit margin is likely to be low, and so is the loss margin. If you are sure of your strategy, timing, and position, you can set a higher goal in higher volatility, only you ought to be keen on the price movements.

Your goal should relate to the strategy that you are using and the platform. Every platform has different rules and techniques for trading. Based on the platform you operate on, you should be able to set a reasonable goal. If you aren't careful, you might set unreasonable targets that your brokerage platform may not produce.

Another tip to consider when setting trading goals is your mental status. Psychological issues inhibit clear thinking and prevent one from executing their technical trading strategy properly.

What differentiates between amateur traders and veteran consistent traders when it comes to making goals per trade is the factors considered when setting a target. Take it as a rule of thumb to refrain from looking for a quick fix, but instead work through your journey the right way. It is recommended that you use a simulation program to help guide you on how to set reasonable goals for each trade

(Abdolmohammadi & Sultan, 2002). By observing your various outcomes from the strategies used in the simulation account, you are able to determine the potential amount of profit you can make from a trade. Also, be sure to use the simulation strategy in a demo account to be sure about your decisions.

Maintain a journal where you record your goals in the past, say, 2 months, against what you actually achieved. If you notice an improvement trend in your results, know that you are on the right track and that you need to implement the efforts you have been using consistently. Day trading is technically meant to be more risk-averse compared to other forms of trading since stops and profits are discovered in short, quick spans. Success in day trading goals depends on the ability of a single trader to execute orders sensibly when chances arise. You should strive as much as you can to focus on the process and not the results, to learn the plan that works for you and has probably worked for your mentors, and to be careful in analyzing the prevailing market conditions.

Keeping your emotions under control in day trading

Trading can be such a hugely emotional experience. One moment you are gaining, the next you are losing terribly. Day trading is fast paced, and there are many different kinds of orders to execute. If one is not careful, they may end up making their trading decisions based on emotions and not facts. Yet this is among the most detrimental things you can do in day trading. Also, the lack of a balance in emotions makes you become frustrated and quit sooner.

Humans are not by any means technical calculators, and sometimes our moves often become misplaced. Yet day trading has been proven to be a large cash machine if well utilized. The aspect of attracting profitability and sustaining the course requires a stable steering wheel, which is why you should be sure to leave emotions far from the trading station. It means being able to maximize your gains, minimize losses, and maintain mental fortitude to have strategies for both ways. The emotionally stable traders are always strategic, disciplined, and motivated, and they aren't simply gambling while in the market. They make conscious decisions to be as rational as possible. Gambling is what most people do while in trading, where they make decisions based on their emotions and cross their fingers instead of relying on their brain.

That said, emotional times will arise, be it in moments of victory or moments of losses. Your emotions will become involved at times. However, it is by being able to silence the inner monologue that you will attain stability on the ground. Doing so will not only earn you a sense of satisfaction in your job, but it will also mean that you are on track to getting higher profits. Rely on analytics alone and not feelings!

Factors to be considered when beginning to trade

There are various crucial factors for consideration for a beginner as they begin to trade. These include choosing platforms, strategies, and styles.

To identify the best platform for you to trade in, you should seek to understand the necessary conditions needed for you to succeed. For instance, Lightspeed is the platform with the highest potential to customize, Trade Station has the best tools for trading, and Interactive Brokers has the fairest costs for traders to maximize gains.

The most essential attribute of a day trading platform is the speed through which searching for information and the implementation of orders are done. Also, a good platform is one which offers a standard fee that does not change after a month or two. There are platforms which are made seemingly attractive by the promos, and it is easy for a trader to fall for the usually appealing promos which fade in a short while and leave traders frustrated. Also, a good platform should be able to access stocks from various places in the world and not be limited to just one country. If you opt for one that does not have further options, you are limiting your chances to benefit. Further, a good platform should be easy to use and easy to integrate with the services you are using.

Also, when choosing the ideal broker, you need to consider the speed of execution, in which you're sure the platform you settle for does not restrict you from getting the price you want when you need it. Cost minimization is also paramount for a day trader since you will most definitely be entering various positions and you need the lowest possible commission rates and fees. Furthermore, be sure that your broker is properly regulated and they are legally obliged to care for your finances. Your broker also needs to be able to offer you support whenever you require it since you can be sure of needing assistance from time to time. Thus, the platform needs to have strong customer support. Your ideal leverage and margins should also be present in the chosen platform. As explored in *the various day trading platforms* section above, you should carefully choose that which suits your overall plan, and which maximizes your utility.

You ought to keep in mind that in the trading market, there is nothing that comes for free. In fact, you might want to assume that a platform with lower trading costs translates into less quality, fewer tools, ease of use, and mobile phone unfriendliness. In any case, you should be able to have around or more than $25,000 to assume a normal trading pattern.

Also, factors to be considered when selecting the style of trading that suits you include the amount of time that you can devote to trading, your risk forbearance levels, your level of experience, the size of your account, and your personality. Are you really patient? Are you a fast learner? Are you generally tough-minded? All these are factors for consideration which allow you to have a positive trading experience, and help you benefit from trading greatly.

Section 2: Strategies

For most people, strategies are used in businesses to give business operations a sense of direction. However, most people ignore the fact that strategies are an important part of our everyday lives. They enable you to live your life in order and achieve even the simplest of goals. Basically, any journey undertaken without a strategy does not have an actual blueprint for addressing the various elements of the journey. The significance of workable strategies cannot be underestimated when it comes to day trading. They form the framework under which the market can be studied, and traders leverage the most lucrative chances of making profits. In all day trading strategies, there is a need for in-depth technical analysis to establish the patterns of the price movements through charts and the different indicators for different strategies. The basic tenet of a day trading strategy is that emotions should be out of the strategy development process. Every strategy chosen should be based on facts, and there are various factors to be considered when choosing any strategy.

Chapter 4: The Candlestick Strategy

Originally established by Muhenisa Homma in the 18th century, the Japanese candlestick strategy has been in the trading scene for a long time. It was originally used by the Japanese rice merchants for market analysis, to help them predict and achieve trading power. Since then, it has passed the test of time and was reintroduced into the financial market scene 3 decades ago by Steve Nison. This way, the strategy became a standard analysis tool for the financial market. Should it have been fake, it would have become obsolete long ago, but it is significant now more than ever. To understand how exactly you can use the candlestick strategy for your benefit in your day trading endeavor, I believe it is paramount to understand its usage since its inception.

Muhenisa used candlesticks for charting and tracking the contracts for rice. Whilst everyone else was taking the same approach, Muhenisa took an emotional tactic to analyze the greed, fear, and the herd mentality, which prevented most people from joining the trade due to the widespread norms. Muhenisa sought to embrace the trade risk and benefit from it early enough. By observing the behavior of his counterparts, the masses, Muhenisa earned himself a competitive advantage since he was able to manipulate those behaviors. He did this by tracing the opening and closing prices as well as the low points and high points of the day. By placing the traces on a chart, he was able to perform a critical analysis of a day's market. The graphic representation of the columns that looked like candlesticks led to the development of the name "candlestick strategy."

Ideally, Muhenisa proved that there could be order in a market that looked so complex and chaotic. He formed an insightful basis of why prices behaved the way they did in the market. The consistent patterns became his framework for his future success in the market. Reports indicate that he made massively profitable trades.

The 1989 remaking of the candlestick strategy by Steve Nison was what brought the framework to the Western World. More traders joining the scene embraced the strategy. It has been described as a significant winning tool for day traders alongside technical analysis knowledge. As a beginner, it is easy to get lost in the variety of technical indicators in the scene, but adopting a minimalist approach is recommended. You only have to master about 2 or 3 indicators and understand them. You should have an indicator for trending and for ranging.

Going forward, a candlestick chart is used for technical analysis by the active traders. A candle can represent one minute, day, week, or even months' worth of trading action.

Each candle has a different pattern depending on the trend of the market. For instance, a green candle indicates that the traders are in control of the trade since the market opens at low prices and close on high prices, and it is also called a bullish candle. A red candle, on the other hand, represents the situation where the traders are price takers since the market opens on high prices and closes on low prices, and it is also known as a bearish candle.

Also, a morning/evening star candle is one which represents the points of reversal of a trend. They are made from long, small, and a third long bearish or bullish candle. Also, there is a rising/falling wedge which describes a candlestick formation that has extended durations. Traders use them to establish the continuation of a longer-term trend. Finally, a Doji candle is one which signals consolidation or impending breakout.

What traders are advised to pay attention to are the indicators of changes in trends in the market stock and the movement for each candle.

Patterns of candlestick strategy that work

Some of the seemingly crazy names used in the chart were developed by Muhenisa as he sought a way to make sense of the patterns. He wanted to link the tag of war between traders in the market by making a visual concept of the chart. The hanging man, the Harami, the Evening star, Doji, and the abandoned baby were the names he gave to the various high and low points of a typical trading day as indicated by his chart. Even though some have been translated into English because of its widespread use in the 21st century, the same pattern of high and low points remain.

Candlestick patterns do not all work equally. Some patterns have been de-popularized by the portfolio managers who use algorithms to alter the functioning of the patterns. They use technical software to take advantage of traders seeking high-odds outcomes in the bearish and bullish models. Yet based on the conventional way of working, traders can study the various tradable patterns that continue to arise. That said, the following are a few patterns that work:

The three line strike: In this pattern, three downward trend candles are engulfed by a reversal pattern with three lines. After the engulfing three candles, the fourth bar opens in a lower position but reverses in a much higher position than the first series candle. This pattern has proven a high level of accuracy through the reversals.

Two black gapping: In an uptrend with a prominent top and a gap down that has two bars with weaker low, the 2 black gapping appears right after it. This pattern shows the potential of a deteriorating downward trend through more lowering of prices. The accuracy of this pattern is above average, and it is something that day traders want to look out for.

3 black crows: This is a reversal pattern which happens close to the highest high of an uptrend.

It has 3 bars which record lower lows, and it is a signal that the downward trend will continue deeper. It has an above average accuracy that traders watching out for momentum plays may be trapped inside it.

The evening star: This is a bearish pattern that begins with a tall candle which records a new high in an upward trend. The next bar records a higher point, and it produces a narrow pattern of the candlesticks since new buyers do not appear at this point. The pattern is completed by a third bar, which indicates that the downward trend will continue even further. This pattern has also had a fair share of accuracy, and it is a pattern that any day trader wants to look out for.

The Abandoned baby: This is a bullish reversal pattern that usually is at the bottom of the low of a downward trend. The next is a Doji candlestick that shortens the market gap. It is followed by a bullish gap as the third bar, which completes the pattern and helps to indicate that the increase in prices will most probably rise higher in an upward trend. This pattern has had a high degree of accuracy, and it has helped various traders.

The major variation from the main candlestick strategy is the engulfing candlestick strategy. It allows the trader to get into trending moves whilst the momentum picks up. Similar to the simple candlestick technique, the engulfing candlestick has both the bearish and bullish patterns. An engulfing bullish (green) candle is one whose body of the up candle totally wraps over the body of the prior down candle. On the other hand, a bearish (red) engulfing candle is one whose wide part of the down candle totally encloses the wide part of the up candle. The wide parts are ones which indicate the close and opening of the trade. A large down candle followed by a larger up candle indicates that the direction has shifted significantly. This trend creates a powerful strategy of trading, having predicted the right direction.

The best way of working with the engulfing candle strategy is by using it together with a trend. After establishing the dominant trend, then you can tell the right direction to adapt when trading. There are two main types of trends, an upward and a downward trend. The former occurs when the price advancing waves are bigger than the price pullback waves, making the market pricing progress. The latter occurs when the pullback waves are stronger than the advancing waves, which makes the overall process pullback more. Assuming long positions during an uptrend is advised while short positions are advised for downward trends. However, if no trend is observed, using this strategy is setting yourself up for failure.

Once the trend is established, the pullback should be observed, which allows you to get the opportunity to trade. A pullback should relate to the candle pattern, either bullish or bearish. Be sure to apply a stop loss order to prevent losses, since it is not always guaranteed that the trend will go on uninterrupted.

Benefits

The advantages of using candlestick strategy are that it offers you a competitive edge in the market, gives you strong buy and sell signals, and it is relatively easy to use. It makes the study of the current state of the market and the direction of price substantially easier. The market behavior elements that this strategy helps to identify are breakouts, consolidation, trend continuation, and trend reversal. Furthermore, the candlestick chart is visually appealing and easy to identify all trends and patterns.

Limitations

The major weaknesses of this strategy include that the candlestick looks different on every time frame. Most traders experience difficulty executing orders when using this strategy because although it is perfectly formed, the candlestick always looks different for every time frame that the trader uses. Traders would have to assume one timeframe to be able to follow this strategy for their benefit. Also, risk management, when using this strategy, can be somewhat difficult. Even if one places a stop order at the candle's low and enters on its high, how long the candle is going to be is highly unpredictable. If the candle closes beforehand or long overdue, then your risk-reward becomes substantially impacted. Nonetheless, these candles have been considered a sluggish indicator since traders will most likely execute a trade at the end of a candle, and other participants may need to move prices to benefit; hence limiting your chances of profiting.

Chapter 5: The Trend (Momentum) Strategy

Trading is all about momentum. Finding the momentum is among the first things new traders learn. The only way to make profits in any trade is when the prices are moving, i.e., when there is momentum. Different stocks move in different percentages at different times, but there is always a movement in the stock. Fong, Tai, and Si (2011) estimate that there will always be a stock moving at 20-30 percent, although sometimes it is more than that. Now, the trick that traders use to profit from trading is identifying the indicators that these movements share. For a momentum day trading strategy, the basic feature to look for is a moving stock. Further, the trader needs a float of shares, strong charts, high relative numbers, and to look out for any relevant news and reports, which act as a fundamental catalyst. Momentum trading is all about purchasing securities that indicate an upward price trend movement or short-term securities with a downward trend. Traders who use this strategy rely on the fact that whenever a momentum is established, chances are that it will continue. Whilst this shouldn't be the case in a market, historical records prove that this happens. Stocks that begin to rise tend to keep the trend for a long time, while those that are performing poorly deteriorate in the poor performance for a lengthy time.

Technical analysis is used to tell about the potential price of shares. Usually, the emotionally driven traders fall prey to traders using this strategy, since they trade based on the poor decisions of others.

Financial experts and economists explained the validity of the momentum strategy based on the efficient-market theory for a long time (Fischel, 1978). Common conclusions include that traders using this strategy take advantage of the weaknesses of other traders, including disposition, over or under reaction effect. Also, it is established that this strategy is especially fruitful for high-risk takers.

History of Momentum trading

Richard Driehaus, George Seaman, and HM Gartley were the first people to put momentum trading into practice back in the 1920s and '30s. They used this technique to manage their capital based on the ideology that a trader could earn more money by buying high and selling even much higher. They contrasted this approach to the popular ideology of buying underpriced securities and awaiting their prices to escalate. The basic value sought from this strategy was fast moving stocks that would allow reinvestment of the money earned into new stocks rather than holding down capital awaiting markets to determine when the stocks can be sold. The basic tenets of this strategy were, however, applicable as early as the 1700s by the great economist David Ricardo. He used this strategy to accumulate profits by purchasing stocks with a strong performing trend. Although its use began long ago, not much of the early history has been written about this strategy due to the scarcity of writing material prior to the 20th century.

The late 19th century is when the strategy's technical analysis gained momentum, and the great traders led by Richard Driehaus coined the trend following by introducing the basic elements behind the psychological cause and effect which could allow traders to observe the behaviors of their counterparts. What was and is still required for this strategy to work is entering positions on the basis of the movement, to hold onto these positions whilst observing the movement and to liquidate these positions on the same basis. The renowned traders in history argued that they held onto positions while they watched their profits rise.

Technical analysis tools

Successful execution of the momentum strategy depends on getting ahold of the main momentum. Technically, momentum trading entails buying recent winner stocks and selling recent loser stocks. It requires strict risk management tools to handle the overcrowding, volatility, and the hidden traps that may come in the way of profit attainment.

Therefore, a marketer has to know the main indicators to benefit from trend following:

- Trend line: It is the primary tool for measuring price movements. It connects two points of prices on a price chart. A line that is going up indicates a positive movement of the price, and traders are expected to leverage this to buy. On the flip side, a line that goes down indicates a negative movement, and this shows the trader that they can sell their securities.

- Stochastic oscillator: This a tool which analyses the pattern of closing prices of assets. A positive trend is identified by a closing price that goes near the high point, while a negative trend is identified by a closing price going near the low point.

- Moving average: This is a point which allows momentum traders to refrain from giving in to random price fluctuations. Price moving beyond this point shows that an upward trend is prevalent, and below this point, a negative trend is present.

Also, some of the rules that accompany the use of this strategy include:

Selection of security: When you are trading, you want to be sure that your strategy aligns with the type of security you trade on. In this strategy, traders are advised to select liquid securities because of their short-term nature and to avoid risks. Securities such as leveraged may not be accurate since they have a complex fund construction that may not give proper tracking. It is good to select those that trade high amounts of shares per day and have high floats, even though low floats can be leveraged when there are emotional reactions from other market players.

Risk management: Now, we know that risk management is among the basics of day trading. However, the simplified nature of trend following may lead to traders' poor judgment and decision making, leading to adverse failures. Some of the things you should not do include exiting a position late after saturation point, entering a position before a momentum forms since there may not be a momentum later, after all; leaving an open position overnight due to the occurrences of the night that might turn the momentum to your opposite direction, leading to losses; and if you are not alert to exit the trade immediately the momentum begins to take a reverse gear.

Managing positions: Position coordination is paramount when it comes to trend following because these momentums carry with them wide ask and bid spreads. This means that for you to gain maximum profits, momentum has to move far in your favor. The period for holding the securities should be carefully decided because staying in positions for long exposes you to greater risk. Whilst the position should be long enough to allow you to benefit, it should also be reasonable enough for you to avoid risks.

Exiting trade: As mentioned, it is paramount to exit a trade whenever you suspect the trend is about to take a reverse gear, although the basic key in this strategy is waiting for a reasonable amount of time as the trend moves higher. Now, it is important to exit your position whenever the price moves rapidly into an overextended state since this signals potential changes in the trend.

The variations from the main strategy

Absolute momentum: This is the technique in which the price of a stock is compared against its price in the previous period. The trader will most definitely enter a position using stocks that show a positive movement in prices.

Relative momentum: This is the situation where the price of a stock is compared with other stocks within the market. Usually, momentum traders will choose to trade with the stock that is performing stronger than others.

Advantages

One good thing about this strategy is that traders are not concerned about the performance of a company since it is a short-term strategy.

Also, it gives high profits over a short amount of time. At times, a trend may have prices shoot rapidly over your intended holding period, and there is the potential of making even up to 50% returns on your invested capital. Also, it performs much better than other basic trading techniques, since factors such as time, asset class, and geographical location do not really matter. Using this strategy, you are able to maximize on the volatility of the market, since you look for securities that have an upward moving trend. Also, it is relatively easy to use and worthwhile, as its history has proven its workability.

Disadvantages

The major limitation and the reason why this strategy has been overly criticized is that it contains with it high risks for the periods when it just doesn't work. Just the way a momentum gets better by the day, if a stock you are trading on gets a bad momentum, then you are on the losing edge.

Also, this strategy is arguably expensive because the high turnover on stocks usually incurs high fees. Furthermore, this strategy consumes a lot of the trader's time in waiting for momentum to form and also waiting for the highest potential of the momentum once it forms. Nonetheless, this strategy is market sensitive since momentum forms when prices are rising. A downward trend does not favor this strategy.

The mainstay of the momentum/trend following strategy is to not be the trader on the side that is taken advantage of. There are various traders being controlled by emotions, no matter how many times they are told that emotional responses are an enemy in the trading scene. If you are controlled by emotions, you can't be a good momentum trader, since other momentum traders who are alert will take advantage of your emotional decisions.

Furthermore, various traders are practicing this strategy on a professional level, thus as an individual trader, perhaps working from home, it may not work for you. You may lag behind and become overtaken by the professionals who have mastered the art of getting news and reacting to it instantly. Technically, failure to act right on time in this strategy leads to overall losses.

Chapter 6: The ABCD Pattern

THE ABCD pattern is an indicator that detects the rhythm of the market movements, helping traders to know when to enter and exit positions. It is a part of the harmonic group of patterns alongside others such as cipher patterns and Gartley. It is interchangeably used for AB=CD. It is one of the simplest patterns to identify on a trading chart.

As its basic chart indicates, the ABCD pattern indicates a price action that begins at point A moving in a new direction, then reaches point B and makes a swing, retracting down to level C, then resumes the same length of the leg created by AB, up to point D. When the AB leg equals the CD leg, a price reversal from CD is expected. This gives a confirmation to traders that they can rely on the pattern to enter positions right after the reverse of the CD price move.

History

The ABCD pattern is a relatively new strategy as compared to others discussed above. It can be traced to the teachings of the founder of Harmonic Trader.com. He is known as Scott. M Carney and he established the Harmonic trade approach in the 1990s. His idea was to develop a system of the recognition of price patterns, which has been popular in the past two decades. Whilst there are other conventional chart patterns that are great powers in identifying market trends, the ABCD has also proven its great potential in understanding and leveraging the volatility of the market.

Types of ABCD Patterns

Bearish ABCD

A bearish pattern is one in which the pattern begins with a low price that climbs up, then takes a swing to drop. The bearish line AB is reversed by BC, which then reaches CD. Notably, point D goes beyond the first point created by B. Such a pattern indicates that price swings will continue to take place.

Bullish ABCD

For a bullish pattern, the first price point is at a higher point (A) to the point where the first swing takes place (B); hence the pattern that forms is one in which the prices go down then rise. In a bullish chart, the CD leg goes at a much lower point than that created at B initially. However, a price reversal at point D is expected, and this means prices are rising.

Rules for trading with the ABC pattern

The unique chart for the ABCD pattern implies that there is a unique set of rules for trading with it:

Entry point: The first thing that a trader does when entering a position is to confirm the validity of their strategy. Therefore, to confirm that the ABCD pattern is really valid, you have to identify two reversals parallel to each other and of equal length. If these features are present in the chart, then you are set to enter a position at the point when the CD leg takes a reverse. Also, you should be keen to follow the direction of the price move that is counter and not parallel to the CD leg. Hence, you should be keen on establishing whether it is a bearish or bullish pattern since for either of them you enter in a different direction from the other.

Stop loss. Now, we know the significance for stop-loss orders, since despite how accurate you are in entering a position, there is always the probability of the market taking a wrong move, contrary to your expectation. Hence, it is always safe to include a stop loss order to be more prepared to evade loss. For the ABCD pattern, the appropriate stop loss position is the point above the extreme formed at the end of the extreme CD leg. Noteworthy is that the trade entry point and the stop loss point are very close to each other since the trade is entered at the beginning of a new trend.

Take profit. In the ABCD pattern, the minimum target for any position that you assume should be a move which equals the CD leg length. In this case, since you enter the market at the point where the CD move began reversing, the price move that comes after this reversal of trend should reach 100 percent retracement of CD, or in simpler terms, it should equal CD in length. However, as a trader, you definitely want to maximize profits, and it is always good to remain open to maximization. Therefore, since a length which equals CD is the minimum profit point, the length could extend further, and by keeping your trade open, you could catch higher profits.

For the tactical traders, they wait until the price move attains the minimum target and close about 50 percent of their trade and keep the rest trying to catch the profits from the continuing trend. This is a way of spreading risks and at the same time making the most out of a single trade. While awaiting the maximum price, a trader should always keep their eyes open for any emerging news and chart patterns that could indicate a potential shift of direction. If there is enough evidence that the trend could take a negative turn and affect your trade, you should act promptly to close even the remaining 50 percent and avoid impending losses.

Essentially, the ABCD pattern is the foundation of all other charts and patterns in the market, since they all follow price movements from a particular starting point to another.

Advantages

The fact that the entry point and the stop loss point are very close to each other means for the trader that there is a great win-loss ratio. Once you get it right when entering a position, you can rest assured of worthwhile returns. The major thing you do is look out for when to exit a portion of your position and leave the rest in the market awaiting even greater profits. Also, this strategy allows the trader to know the risk and reward ratios beforehand, and the trader gets a good view of what to expect.

Disadvantages

There are various problems associated with the use of the ABC pattern. These include the fact that this strategy is subjective to the kind of harmonic leg that traders want to pursue. It's been mentioned from the beginning that subjective decisions always lead to poor results. For instance, any market consists of several impulse legs, and using subjectivity to select the one that you want is always going to result in a loss. Whilst the basis of this strategy is choosing the leg that coincides with the resistance structure, it is always challenging to choose the optimal leg amidst several legs.

Also, traders using this strategy expect that the market will see and respond to the patterns in their head, yet we know that the market never cares about your profitability or loss. You are on your own, and the market cannot change to your exact expectations. It only responds to the purchase and sale aspects.

Also, this strategy is more common in range markets, which may make a trader lose out on trending markets. It usually does not follow the trend, but goes against the trend, making the trader cut their trades often times. Nonetheless, in a range market, it is not always that you will get a harmonic pattern to leverage, and waiting to identify the right harmonic leg for you to invest wastes a lot of your opportunities in other stocks.

Enjoying this book so far? I'd love it for you to share your thoughts and post a quick review on Amazon!

Chapter 7: Reversal Trading

In finance, market reversal identifies as the situation in which the value of a stock goes back to the point it was at the beginning of the trading period. The prices in the market take a turn into the opposite direction.

Therefore, reversal trading is the change in the direction of an asset's price. A reversal occurs in either direction, either downward or upward depending on the direction, the price had assumed.

Reversals often occur intraday, weekly, monthly, or even in a year, and they usually happen in quick paces. They are used by different traders differently based on their position duration. An intraday reversal is basically relevant to a day trader. A trend that is upwards is technically characterized by stronger high swings and weaker low swings, but if it reverses into a downward trend, the high swings are normally less strong than the low swings.

Indicators such as moving averages assist in identifying the possibility of a reversal. After setting the moving average, if the price is continuously moving above it, then the trend is continuing to move up, but if the price is moving below the moving average, then there is a likelihood of a reversal. Also, a trend-line that indicates the stronger highs that an upward trend makes is used in the case that if the prices get below the trend-line, then a reversal is likely to happen.

There are various reasons as to why reversals occur in the market, but the major reason will always be the forces of supply and demand, which are known as the major price determinants. Further, the forces of demand and supply are determined by a variety of factors in the market, including the adjustment of trade policy by the economic planners as they try to grow their economy or even as a result of changes in interest rates. Such factors act as catalysts that determine how traders indulge in the market, which further determines the direction of the prices of stocks.

History

The model of reversal trading is as old as the trading history since it is intertwined with the price action concept. Technically, price action entails an analysis of the price movements with the aim of identifying proper position entry and exit points. It is usually not concerned about the actual performance of a security but takes into consideration its price movements. It is all about the actions of the price of a security.

This strategy has withstood the test of time since various credible authors have written and highlighted various benefits of this form of trading. Most of them base their sentiments on the real case scenario in the market and offer valuable insights to traders. They accredit it to various wins in the trading history.

For instance, Mark Fisher, in his *The Logical Trader*, discusses credible techniques for analyzing the market volatility and its potential high and low points. Fisher discusses ways of identifying the potential price changes to act on a position. He gives rise to variations of the basic trend reversal strategy, with the most relevant being the sushi roll. As its name suggests, this technique was discovered by a group of traders over the lunch hour. This technique is explained using a five-bar scenario, whereby the first 5 bars have weaker highs and lows, while the remaining 5 have stronger highs and lows. The last 5 usually engulf the first 5 in a bearish kind of pattern. If it is present in an upward trend, the sushi roll indicates a strategic long position selling, while in a downward trend, it indicates a potential reversal of price trend. The major drawback with this variation strategy is that the ability to capture this pattern is limited because the sushi roll must have 10 bars. This is unlike the engulfing bearish strategy, which normally has two bars and is easy to spot in a chart.

Another strategy variation is the outside reversal strategy, which is basically the sushi roll but that which uses data daily from Monday to Friday. It is even harder to achieve since it requires that the first five days in the week record lower highs and lows, while in the second week the five days record an outside engulfing with weaker lows and higher highs.

Advantages

It is among the best strategies to leverage to identify the strongest price trends. It is a simple strategy to follow, and you don't necessarily have to use indicators for you to see a trade signal. The price is the major indicator. In fact, most traders who try to introduce other external indicators often beat themselves in their own game. This is especially the case for the traders who think that indicators have to be used without actually serving a real function. Further, it has relatively high profitability, since it is all about getting a reversal pattern, and it is given that all price trends eventually reverse at some point. It is in the reversal trading that huge gains are found. Even though it has higher risks than simple strategies such as the trending technique, the higher the risk in reversal trading, the greater the returns. It only requires a disciplined trading model that is able to handle the risk involved.

Disadvantages

One major drawback of using this strategy is that it is difficult for the trader to establish whether price changes are minor and stay abreast of all the noise in the market. Most often, reversals are fast-paced, and traders fail to recognize them beforehand and act quickly to avoid losses. This happens even while indicators are rightfully placed, and it is often beyond the control of the trader.

Further, the market often has fake signals that a reversal is possible. Prices may go totally below the indicator, which means that there is a reversal, but it may resume immediately to the prior trend. Even if the reversal resumes its initial trend, the traders have already experienced their fair share of losses if they had not withdrawn from their positions.

Overall, the key elements of reversal trading include that traders attempt to exit positions in which a reversal is possible, or when the reversal is happening to avoid losses. It basically shows that the price of an asset has changed from increasing or decreasing in the opposite direction. Usually, the price changes that matter are the high margin ones, and the small changes in prices, also known as consolidations or pullbacks, do not have much effect on the trade.

Whilst a reversal is a total change in the price direction of an asset, a pullback is usually a countermove that does not necessarily reverse the price direction. Pullbacks are the situations which create stronger lows in the upward trend, and a reversal does not occur until the prices go below the indicator, say, trend-line, that the trader is watching. One thing to be keen on is that reversals often begin as potential pullbacks, and before you know it, it has started, and it is too late for you to act.

Finally, reversals are a must in the trading scene. No price takes a particular direction for the rest of its trading time. At some point, a reversal is expected. Therefore, the sooner one understands these reversals, the better it is for them as traders.

Chapter 8: The Scalping Strategy

It is among the most common strategies in the trading sphere. Traders rely on this broad strategy to benefit from little changes in prices. It fits users who have great position exit strategies. It also requires traders to make several trades in a day to make a profit. Also, it requires a proper technical analysis on a real-time basis since it basically refers to the mechanism of holding positions for the shortest time possible. Failure to capture the position and trend of the prices of the stock you are trading in could cause massive losses, which eliminate other various small gains you may have accumulated.

This strategy is based on the ideology that any stock completes the first phase of the movement, after which some stocks do advance further, while others do not. Therefore, a scalping trader focuses on the number of trading results and not the size of the wins. This strategy contrasts directly with the *let your profits run* perspective. The latter identifies as the situation where traders focus on optimizing the wins by increasing the winning margin while letting some other trades reverse. Thus, while some traders win through about half of their overall trades in a period on a long time frame because the wins are usually larger than the fails, the scalping trader has a potential of winning much more trades than they lose, although the wins are in small sizes.

Also, scalping can be used independently or can be used together with other day trading strategies. If it used independently, the trader enters several positions in a day and uses very short timed charts since the duration of the trading time frame is limited. The trader ought to have access to high functioning analysis systems and execute orders automatically. Most scalpers use the Direct Access Trading approach to get real-time information.

When used together with other strategies, the scalp strategy will come in as a supplement. Traders who focus on longer trends such as the ones discussed above can utilize the scalping strategy while awaiting their long trends to form. The trader enters in the longer time frame trade, and whilst it takes form, one enters into other tiny positions in the form of scalping.

Variations

There are a few variations to the main scalping technique. One is market making, which describes the condition where the scalp trader concurrently places bids and offers for a particular security. This strategy works for stocks that cause the least volatility in the market, and it is usually technical for a trader to compete with the market makers by being a bid and offer maker.

The second variation is when the trader buys several shares and looks out for a very small change in prices, usually a change as small as a few cents. This strategy requires highly liquid stock that is able to record changes in prices in quick successions.

The third is the scalp trading that looks almost like the traditional trading methods. A trader holds a position for any amount of shares as soon as the first signal is evident.

Fourth is the 1-minute scalping technique, which is perhaps the most popular technique in the scalping strategy. It was developed by a man called Paul Rotter when he placed various buy and sell orders frequently and made millions out of it. It particularly entails setting the chart on a one-minute timeframe.

Scalping techniques

That said, scalping is not the easiest strategy for beginners or inexperienced people, as it involves fast decision making and monitoring positions constantly, but there are some techniques that traders can use to benefit from scalping.

Order execution: A beginner would have to master the art of fast execution since a delay wipes out any accumulated profits. Order execution has to be accurate to make up for the limited profit margin per position.

Frequency and costs: This factor comes in the right from when the trader is choosing the brokerage firm, to when they are making trade decisions in every trading timeframe. Buying and selling stocks in the market accrues many commissions, which in turn have great impacts on the trader's profit share. Some platforms do not provide for scalping, and some charge a commission that may not be worthwhile when scalping.

Trading: The secret to all trading techniques is the ability to spot trends. This is even more important for scalping. Understanding the market price movement can place scalpers on the competitive edge since they do no stay in the position for very long and can benefit while the market is experiencing a slight boom.

Trading sides: The key to maximizing profits in scalping is balancing the long and short trades, but a scalper should especially maximize trading confidently in buying on the side.

Analysis: Now, we know that technical analysis is paramount for every trading strategy. To handle the high-frequency trades in day trading, traders should learn to analyze the market situation carefully and gain a competitive edge in the highly competitive environment. This is especially the case for scalping. You don't want to place your trades on a downtrend no matter how small the loss margin. You need to be careful to be able to gain as many small profits as possible.

Volume: In scalping, the high volume trades are often the most liquid, which is a good thing for the scalping strategy.

Advantages

The major benefit of the scalping strategy is that it limits the amount of exposure to the risk of a trader since one places small trades at small margins. Also, it increases the chances of winning, since making small moves is easily achievable. For traders focusing on big wins, there would have to be factored in the market influencing the actions of the traders heavily and hence increase market volatility. Further, a trader will always have something to do in the market, because even when the market looks relatively quiet, there are still small moves to be made.

Also, scalping comes off as a risk management technique in any trading system, since small trades can be taken within a major one to spread risks.

Disadvantages

The scalping strategy can be a disadvantage because of the fact that a trader needs a large deposit to be able to enter various positions. Usually, amateurs may not make much from it because they cannot leverage the market information like their dealer counterparts. Also, this strategy demands top-notch quality in mathematical skills, instincts, and automatic reaction to take advantage of the most lucrative chances. Additionally, it is time-consuming and may drain you mentally because of having to monitor the various positions that you have.

Overall, the primary goal of scalping is leveraging the sudden changes in the market and executing various orders in a quick manner. Since there are small gains obtained from each trade, you are expected as a trader to use above average leverages. The stop-loss order is highly workable in this strategy, so you can leverage these to avoid great losses. Even though it is the least risk intensive strategy, there is a need to have a profitable and solid strategy to use to gain the most out of it. Finally, it is certain that all traders enter the market to gain the maximum profits out of the trade. Remember that the scalping strategy gives small profits; thus, you have to work extra hard and enter as many lucrative positions as possible.

Chapter 9: Daily Pivots

Pivot points have for a long time been used by traders to determine the resistance levels of trades and provide critical support. The range-bound traders who maximize their trade on stocks that operate in price channels use the pivot points to establish the best position to enter and to identify the best breakout positions. They are useful for intraday trading, which has high-frequency trades. Prices tend to react to these pivot points, and they automatically set themselves up every day automatically.

There are various charting software programs in which the indicator can be customized. While some of these programs may allow you to have weekly or monthly pivot points, they are set on an ideal basis of one day.

The pivot point, also known as the average price level, is obtained by integrating the previous day's close, and the high and low points of the market as a function. This value is then divided by 3 to give out 3 support and resistance levels.

A wide range between these values leads to bigger distances between levels, and a smaller range gives a lower distance between levels. However, it is important to note that not all levels appear at the same time on the chart.

Once created, pivot points are the leading indicators to establishing the best turning point in the market, for identifying stop loss order positions, take-profit positions, and for entry or exit points.

Advantage

Pivot points are widely used in the day trading scene, although they were widely used in stocks and futures markets as well. The major advantage of pivot trading is that traders can use the pivot points as major indicators for getting ahead of the market. The position of the pivot is the central level on which every move within this strategy is evaluated. If a certain stock is trading beyond the pivot line, then there is a likelihood of the market trend for the day is bullish, although this does not mean that the trend can't take a reverse and trade below the pivot line. When there is minimal volatility in the market, the price of stocks revolves around the pivot line

Limitation

The major drawback for pivot points is their sensitivity to time zones. They are limited to the closing prices of London or New York's time. If a trader is using a different timeframe, then they have to be keen on the previous day's closing prices based on the strategy's basic time-zone. This drawback has often cost many traders because they plot different pivot points from the real situation in the market.

History

Similar to most other strategies, technological devices were not born by the time the pivot trading strategy was discovered. This strategy was discovered back in the day when traders need a way of keeping up with the relativity of market prices of stocks. This technique was born out of a mathematical equation. By taking the highs, lows, and closing of the previous marketing period, traders were able to find a framework for finding the 3 support and 3 resistance levels, as mentioned above. Traders depicted a reversal tendency when prices moved towards these levels, and if reversals did not occur, the traders would go ahead and look for the trade breakouts from the market prices.

Pivot points techniques

Gauging probabilities: Traders use pivot points to estimate the potential of the direction of the price being self-sustaining. There are certain estimates that seem to occur concerning how the price is likely to close the trading during the day below or above the levels. Although they are rough estimations, they often guide the trader in assuming a particular position when a certain estimate hits.

Stop losses: Pivot points are as well used as stop-loss orders, whereby a reversal is expected at some point. The stop loss level is normally the one above or below the reversal point in the case of a short trade and a long trade respectively.

Profit targets: The long term readings on a pivot chart indicator are used as a directive on how to take profits. Should the direction of the price move take a reverse, the trader is offered a good chance to exit their positions in an optimum manner and also to buy other stocks at a good price.

Breakouts: Whilst for most traders, arguably, high volatility is what guides their trading activity, the pivot point strategy equips a trader with the ability to spot support and resistance levels even when there is minimal volatility in the market. Each of these levels offers a chance for a day trader to enter positions in a highly liquid market since, after all, they do not hold these positions for longer than a day. The only drawback about using pivot points as breakouts indicators is that they tend to be more accurate for longer-term durations, say weekly or monthly durations.

Reversals: Although they happen less commonly than the breakouts, reversals are good indicators of prices going upwards or downwards. If the price is at a support level, then it is considered to have gone down, while if it is playing at the resistance level, it is considered to have gone up. It is always good for a trader to be sure that such an opportunity of buying low and selling high will occur before they can assume a particular direction.

Overall, pivot points are significant for viewing the likely resistance and support levels in the market. This helps traders to approximate the points where prices can overturn or consolidate. They are appropriate for day traders and can be leveraged using a combination of analysis tools and indicators that inform decisions.

Final thoughts about strategies

Whether you go for the automated strategies, the beginner strategies, or the advanced strategies, there are some basic components that every strategy should have. These include volume, volatility, and liquidity. Every strategy should be able to show you how much given security has been traded over a certain timeframe. This is, in day trading, referred to as the daily average trading volume, which tells you how much traders are interested in the asset. This can give you insights into whether or not there is a likelihood of good performance with the security. A high volume definitely indicates that traders are highly interested in the asset. Second, a good strategy should allow you to see your potential range of profits, based on market volatility. High volatility, as aforementioned, means that the prices can move quickly down and they can also shoot high, making the profit/loss margin potentially high. Also, a good strategy will allow you to trade on the stocks you find most liquid without limitations. Such stocks could include natural gas and oil.

Note that for the extensive learning on the strategy you decide to settle on, you can leverage videos and texts to increase your chances of understanding the content. Clearly, every strategy discussed above is suitable for different traders at different times. Once you identify yourself as an individual, you can establish the best trading strategy that suits you. Finally, being consistent with your strategy and making the best out of it is what it takes for success.

Section 3: Completing Your Trade

Chapter 10: Building a Watch List

In this context, a watch list is a list of stocks that you would prefer to trade, or rather those that fit your trading approach. You may term it as a list of securities being monitored for investing opportunities or potential trading. There are thousands of issues in each stock market, for instance, US stock exchanges list more than eight thousand issues. However, traders concentrate on a fraction of the securities. It can be agreed that identifying the most suitable stocks is challenging and requires a skilled trader. Exposing yourself to various aspects related to establishing favorable securities will play an important role. The first requirement for having a good watchlist is understating the modern stock market environment. You should understand how various sectors respond to catalyst overtime and how various levels of capitalization affect price development.

Importance of building a watchlist

As mentioned, there are numerous stocks listed in various stock markets such as Nasdaq and NYSE - to total is estimated to be more than eight thousand. Truthfully, it would be a challenge to keep up with that high of a number of stocks. Even the highly educated, experienced, and those with access to much information would find it difficult to keep up. Having a watchlist will help you identify potential trades that meet your trading strategy or criteria.

It is a reliable tool to use, regardless of the trading approach you use. It means that you have narrowed down to specific stocks or securities to observe attentively. Identifying suitable security requires more information, or rather reading beyond the promotion and message board. Lack of preparation has been identified as the key reason why more than 90% of traders lose money. Thus, a watchlist filters a number of stocks that you will focus on when trading. Thus, it will help shape your concentration and focus, which are essential aspects when it comes to trading.

When you are focused on a certain number of stocks and securities, it makes you ready so that you can quickly react if and when a trade's signal triggers. it is important to know that stocks can trigger trade signals simultaneously, and if you delay, there is a risk of missing entries or exiting. You can look at a watch list as a tool to prepare you ahead of time and a weapon to curb delays in the case of signals. In focusing on a few stocks, it is possible to capture and anticipate moves early enough. Another advantage is that a strong watchlist enables you to diversify your opportunities when trading. The mistake that most traders make is spreading too thin with many stocks and impulse jumping to any trigger. It results in revenge trading, impulse trading, and over-trading.

How to build a stock list

When you are seeking to build a stock list, you will need to keep in mind various considerations. One of these is to note that you are looking for stocks that meet your trading strategy or criteria. Also, it is important to consider the amount of time that you will be dedicating to trading and observing the financial markets. If trading is part-time, it is recommendable that you keep things simple by having a list of 50 to 100 issues to observe, track, and trade every day. If you are a committed trader or a professional, you can have a primary database that contains between 300 to 500 stocks.

Trading screens are important components in stock trading. As a trader, you have to decide on the number of trading screens and the form of stock charts that they display. The general rule points out that a trading screen can hold twenty-five to seventy-five stocks depending on market depth windows, news tickers, scanners, and space that charts take. You can choose to dedicate a given screen to tickers which show percentage change, net change, and last price.

We noted that you need to know the stocks that meet your trading criteria. It means that you will keep in mind the following things about a stock before including it in your watchlist.

Company details

You will need to know what the company is, what it does, and/or its market portfolio and market reputation. Although trading is different from buy and hold stock investing, it is important that you be conversant with the company aspects.

Stock analysis

The stock analysis involves fundamental analysis and technical analysis, all relating to searching for information about a given stock. The traditional stock analysis involves learning the history of stock trading. When doing fundamental analysis, it will entail learning about the business and its environment. The essential tools when doing fundamental analysis include the overall financial position documents as well as Securities and Exchange Commission filings. Most people avoid fundamental analysis on the notion that it is tiresome and time-consuming. However, you can greatly benefit from the information it provides. In doing technical analysis, it will require you to know the recognizable patterns, current price trend, and historical price movement of stocks. When analyzing, you should look at the stock with the biggest percentage gains from the previous day. It should be followed by looking at chart breakouts.

Interesting and most suitable stocks to choose are earning winners and contract winners. The advantage of identifying which stocks fall in the noted classifications is that one does not need to comprehend complex financial statements. For instance, you can search for stock spike, which is simple to identify. When looking for contract winners, you can search for the press release of small companies that are signing deals with big companies. If the deal is legit, then there will be a spike in its stock price. Also, trading volumes are good indicators of a possibly good stock. As a trader, you should stay away from a company whose stock has fallen by a significant percentage, such as 50 percent in a day.

At this point, you have equipped yourself with important information about potential stocks that you can trade. To avoid spreading yourself too thin, it would be good to limit yourself to five to ten stocks. It should begin with the strong to the weak market sectors. Also, you have to ensure that each of the stocks included in the watchlist has potential trade triggers, ensuring that you have planned the trade triggers ahead of time. This is why you considered the stock in your watchlist. Prior planning will entail having the legwork done in the pre-market to ensure that you will be ready when a given trigger forms. We noted that a trigger is that which determines whether you will buy or sell a given stock. Experts in the market describe a suitable stock as "shovel ready." The implication in this is that you can immediately take a given action on a stock when an indicator triggers.

Also, we noted that a watchlist entails those stocks that fit your trading strategies. You should actualize this by ensuring that you are honest with your trading style. Take, for instance, an intraday scalper. For such a person, the most suitable stocks will be those that follow through and have good momentum and volatility. Also, those stocks that are gapping on a catalyst event or on the news are best suited for such traders. How will you carry out good scalping? The best way to do this will be by implementing shorter time frame charts. A swing trader will focus on different things. These include targeting less volatile and slow moving stocks because they allow for longer holding periods.

Other important considerations are liquidity and volume. While you may wonder why you should bother with these aspects, it is important to note that volume to a certain degree ensures liquidity, while liquidity supersedes price. A good or tradable stock is that which meets both conditions, as they prevent you from being disadvantaged. You should avoid a stock that has no volume. In doing so, you are proving to be selective to the best opportunities. In doing this, you will have to ensure that you do not waste time on mundane prospects.

The other trick is to set alerts for intraday and swing trades. It is not as complex as it sounds, because most charting programs and trading platforms allow the users to set alerts. It has proven to be a reliable technology because constant monitoring of stocks could be tiresome. You can set alerts depending on indicator triggers or price. However, ensure that you separate swing trade alerts from day trading alerts. The essence of alerts is that they allow you to maximize your focus when needed.

When you have implemented the noted guidelines and familiarize yourself with trading, you will realize that you are well versed with information. With time, you will see that your watchlist is growing large. At this point, having multiple and diverse watchlists categorized differently is beneficial. The categories may include long-term investment stocks, sector plays, swing plays, and short-term stocks.

Chapter 11: Paying Attention to the Market Until the Trade is Completed

Self-sabotage has been established as one of the major drawbacks for a trader. As aforementioned, it is usually the errors that traders commit, which lead to losses, and not the method that they are using. However, most traders want to pick a method and run it in the market without efficient coordination, yet still, blame it on the method when they fail. One of the best ways through which you can avoid sabotaging yourself while trading is being keen on the market until the trade is over.

One of the biggest and longest-running traders in history, Peter Bandt, compared day trading to a marathon race. The main focus of a marathoner is getting to the finish line. Marathoners do not lose their focus until they get to the finish line and the ones who give in to distractions along the way, or listen to people's comments, or even doubt themselves never win.

The reason why day trading is compared to a marathon race is that its positions are short-lived, yet entail a very eventful time period. How well you maintain your focus on your set time periods for holding a certain position determines your performance in the trade. Focus maintenance most often is the distinguishing factor between winners and losers in day trading, just as is the case in the marathon race.

Some of the ways through which you can maintain your attention while day trading is:

- Make small and manageable watchlists: Truth be told, you are bound to have too many items on your watchlist, which will make it hard for you to remember them all at various points in our trading times. At times, there are too many active and ripe stocks for you to trade, and you may get confused in the midst of creating your intraday trading goals. Typically, no one wants to miss out on any hot plans in the market. However, when you want too much, you end up losing it all. We are all human, and our concentration is bound to get lost when we are trying to handle too much. Therefore, indicate the items that you want to focus on in a day, so you are assured of not losing focus once you enter a trade. There is still tomorrow, and you can try different options. After all, each day brings with it unique fortunes.

- Use a few technical indicators: Whilst indicators are among the crucial requisites for success, they can be harmful if not well used. Using a lot of them denies you the opportunity to maintain your focus on the trade, since all the time you will be shifting from one indicator to another trying to capture what you are supposed to do for each indicator. In the midst of this, you might lose concentration or just get exhausted and lose your focus.

- Define your trading style wisely. Whenever you set out on a journey, you have to know what you need. You have to know how you are going to handle anything that might come your way while trading. Most importantly, you must have a blueprint that you follow in your trading journey. In a market characterized by many players, platforms, strategies, and techniques, you have to define your style really wisely, lest you won't be able to pay attention to one trade that you enter. This is discussed in detail in the minimalism approach section below. It is built on the perception that most often, more does not mean better. A simple style can allow you to focus until your trade is over.

- Avoid the noise in the market: As already mentioned, most of the messages you get are pure noise while in the trading market. Everyone in the trading scene can start a rumor, under or over-analyze a small issue, and it can come up in your way, making you lose your focus. However, be sure to follow your intuition and model without getting distracted from your trade until it is over. When you are focused, you know how to distinguish between messages that are valuable for your trade and those that are not. You will ignore all rumors and follow your trading plan.

- Eliminate any distractions: Just like in any other job, distractions are a major threat to maintaining your focus on a trade until it is over. As aforementioned, we are living in a world full of distractions, especially those brought by the technological communication devices, with social media being a major distractor. Having the power to avoid being distracted while you have an ongoing trade is critical to your success. It is not easy to multitask and have a sustainable focus. It is not easy to keep browsing your social media platforms and still be able to give your ongoing trade the focus it needs.

Chapter 12: Day Trading Tips for Success

Day trading is considered to be among the most hyped yet misunderstood styles of trading. People often confess to hearing a lot of myths and misconceptions surrounding the practice, and it is worth identifying credible tips concerning what it takes. As stated, day trading involves the purchase and sale of stock within the same day. A position held overnight and longer is not considered to be day trading. Among the tips that significantly help achieve success include:

Identify Key Entry and Exit Points

In the trading spectrum, there is usually the price at which a person enters a trade. The point is usually referred to as the entry point, and it is considered best if it is backed up by a research-based strategy. The entry point is typically similar for all traders and is usually at the point at which the stocks are their low points.

As is common with shares, the par value changes in accordance with many factors. There are different ways through which one can identify key entry and exit points:

- Using the pivot point, support, and resistance strategy. The pivot points are usually calculated using the open, high, low, and amounts at which the stocks closed during the previous day. The pivot point usually uses a short-term time frame as well as a standard pivot point to calculate the points. To begin, one can open a one-minute OHLC (open, high, low, and close)[1] bar chart from the specific market and add the daily pivot points. Once open, one then waits for the price to move towards a pivot point, indicating the highs as they proceed. One is then supposed to wait for the price to touch the pivot point, which means that the price is trading at the pivot point price. This is the point at which one should trade at, buying shares from the companies which they wish to.

- The next point is usually waiting for the trade to exit. This usually involves waiting for the price to trade at the targeted price as well as the stop loss. The pivot point usually changes after a very short time and can take anywhere from a few minutes to several hours for one to reach their target. Depending on the market being traded, the target time is not defined, though knowledgeable day traders are usually able to discern and predict the most likely times for the trade to exit.
- Lastly, repeat the steps as many times as possible, until either the daily profit target is reached or until the market is no longer active.

Avoid Hitting and Running

To succeed in day trading, hit and running must be avoided at all costs. The approach usually involves a person entering the market at its high, then exiting when it declines. The people who use this strategy are usually interested in making sudden huge profits and, typically, take immense risks using the strategy. These people focus on what they consider to be "sure bets," placing a huge amount of money on stock while at its lowest and selling when it attains the highest point in the day. The traders never concentrate on particular stocks and shares, but rather determine the stocks which they would want to deal with in the morning.

The biggest disadvantage with this strategy is that it restricts the traders from growing in their trading craft. Hit and run traders always attempt to play it safe and do not really follow the tenets of trading as they should. Therefore, they do not advance to the real trading scenario, which teaches people a lot of the skills necessary to earn immense profits. Also, sticking to specific markets may enable traders to be able to learn all they can about specific companies, thus enabling them to be able to predict expected changes when certain events occur. In such a case, the traders are better suited to organize their finances and plan towards devising strategies that would enable them to make the maximum profits.

Limit Losses

One of the basic rules that supersede all others in the quest to excel in day trading is limiting losses. As is known, day trading is a game of probability, where there is always the possibility of making profits as well as making losses in equal measure. Despite the fact that sometimes it is impossible to prevent losses, there are a number of strategies that can be used to improve the chances of success while significantly reducing the chances of accruing losses.

The first step towards limiting losses is analyzing and determining the expected returns on all of the trades that one is considering. Calculating the expected returns of all of the trades that are being considered enables one to compare the results and choose the ones that promise and offer the most opportunity for profit. The formula that is normally widely used in the calculation of expected returns is:

Expected Return = [(gains probability) x (The take Profit % investment Gain)] + [(loss probability) x (Ending Stop Loss % Loss)][2]

Another vital way through which trading losses can be managed is through the strict management of the risks possible on individual trades. A good rule is that a good trader should refrain from risking more than 1% of their balance in one trade. An example is a situation where one has $10,000 in their trading account. To manage their risk, they should not risk more than $100 in a single trade. It is always worth noting that one can have extremely bad days in trading, and investing minimally ensures that they never have to lose everything on a bad day.

Creating a daily stopping point is also vital for risk management. A good trader always knows when to invest and when to stop. When a trader is coming up with the daily trading strategies, they must always decide how much they can afford to risk each day and the point at which they must stop. For instance, a person can decide that they will always stop when they lose a certain percentage of their investment, say 3%. Some people also decide to stop when they lose a certain number of times in a row. Most traders assert that when they decide to stop based on their average profits, the overall amount that they can afford to lose always grows significantly over time. Skills develop significantly using such strategies.

Also, creating limit orders helps to keep losses at a minimum. Using limit orders is also considered to be a great strategy of limiting losses in day trading. The limits are mostly used for buying and selling. Buy limits only purchase stocks which are below the limit price and sell limits only sell stocks when they are above the limit prices. The best way to limit losses is always to create a plan and stick to it. Day traders must always be very vigilant and stick to their orders to benefit.

Starting Small

Day trading, when done right, is one of the best ways through which people can invest and gain financial freedom. Most of the successful day traders whose investments run into millions assert that one of the strategies they used is starting small. Regardless of the amount that one has, they can put in into an investment and start earning. Currently, it is possible to begin investing with as low as $100. When the traders combine other aspects such as being open to learning as well as learning as much as they can about the trading process, they can enjoy wins that accumulate over time.

When one is just starting out, it is always imperative to diversify investments so as to ensure that they do not lose their initial income. Small day traders are usually advised to focus on small yet reliable profits. The small hits always have the capability of adding up to much bigger gains over time. As the profits increase over time, one is then in a position to take much bigger risks and consequently pool in more money for individual trades.

Willingness to learn

Just like any other craft, day trading has distinct strategies and procedures that help improve chances of success. Experts assert that people exempt from studying do not have what it takes to be profitable traders. There are very many practices and new modes of operations that come up each and every day, which improve the chances of success for traders. Learning about the new and emerging modes of operations is beneficial since it keeps the traders on the forefront of the credible trends as realized with the changes in the trading patterns. Willingness to learn entails being humble and acknowledging that there are things you don't know. With such a mentality, one can be open to learning, as well as devise strategies which will help them grow over time. There are experts who have been in the game for a long time and can give invaluable advice to aspiring listeners. One cannot grow without listening to advice from experts, hence the need for a willingness to learn.

In addition to the expert advice, the traders need to learn that different events affect the values of shares significantly. There is usually the need to learn how to discern events that affect the trading prices from the onset. For instance, whenever scandals hit a certain company, its share values drop significantly. With proper discernment, the traders can be able to predict which shares will regain their value as well as those who cannot recover under any cost. The traders are then better suited to purchase the stocks which will recover since they will make an undoubted profit. For the stocks which are likely to decline, even more, the traders should keep off their purchase. Traders who are willing to learn about discernment are able to make the right decision during all transactions.

Risk only what you can afford to lose

One of the smartest pieces of advice that new day traders must acknowledge is that one should only trade with the money which they can afford to lose. As is known, there is always the possibility of gaining as well as an equal chance of losing. Trading may go sour, and a person is always likely to lose all of the investment that they made. Therefore, it is immensely wise to only trade with what you can afford to lose. There are numerous cases of people falling into depression and even bankruptcy due to losing some of their livelihoods when they risk money that they need for their livelihood.

When investors know how much is at stake, they may end up confused and full of anxiety, which prevents them from making sober decisions. Some of the traders put the entire amounts in one share, consequently leading to a total loss when deals do not go through. Such huge losses are, in most cases, irrecoverable, and the result is undue depression and a life full of misery. Breaking up the money into a number of share investments increases the chances of gaining and leads to small losses when the inevitable occurs. As has been stated in the previous section, minimizing losses is imperative and a must for any trader who wishes to continue succeeding in the trading process.

Be realistic

Unrealistic expectations are one of the causes of failure in day trading. While the major goal of trading remains to be able to make profits, there are instances where traders may have unrealistic expectations. The fact that many people have become millionaires while trading does not mean that a person is bound to get rich overnight. Trading is usually a process, and sometimes, huge gains are the sole result of good luck. Therefore, it is not definite that a person will enjoy huge benefits at a go, and some people actually wait several years before they are able to make a substantial income.

Usually, the first step towards setting realistic goals is analyzing the statistics. In any business and any amount tradeable, there are always people who have traded before, leaving behind a trail of achievements as well as possible gains and losses. When the day traders study statistics, they are able to determine the extent to which they can achieve certain milestones as well as the potential losses for some investments. The data available is in the millions, and one only needs to log in to various databases and get the results that they would want.

The next step involves testing the mettle in a real life day trading sector. Currently, there are very many online platforms which have stock simulators and virtual trading platforms. The site involves simulators which act as they would in a real trading platform. Potential day traders should first use the simulators, to get a feel for what they would achieve were they trading in a real platform. Through such simulators, the traders can then be able to make estimates regarding what they can earn and achieve in the real world, which enables them to set credible and realistic expectations.

Finally, as one grows into the real trading arena, they should track their progress periodically. In most cases, the traders are usually likely to identify strategies which work for them, and which enable them to have a successful run. When such strategies prove to be continuously beneficial to the trader, they can adopt them in future cases and be able to realistically determine the expected returns.

Timing the Trades

Trading is just like any other activity. There is always the best and the worst time to conduct it. Experienced traders know that there are certain days of the week as well as times of the day when it is considered to be the best time for trading. Some of the vital times which are considered to be ideal in trading include:

- Opening hours, which is the best time to buy stocks. The hour after the market opens is considered to be a highly volatile time since the buyers and sellers are reacting at this time. Established traders assert that the first 15-60 minutes are the best time to buy and sell stocks. The volatility that occurs in the accompanying hours is particularly challenging for new traders, and losses are increased.
- Established traders also assert that Mondays are the best time to buy most of the stocks. There is a well-documented tendency known as the "Monday-effect," which proves that most stocks drop on Mondays. Therefore, this remains to be the best

time to buy such stocks since one increases the chances of selling them at a higher price.

- Fridays are considered to be the best day to sell stocks. Contrary to the Monday-effect, Fridays are usually the time when most of the people desire to unload the stocks that they bought throughout the week. Usually, most companies do not trade on weekends. Therefore, Fridays remain the last trading day of the week, and many brokers choose to sell on the same date.

Discipline

Just like any other craft, discipline is of the essence. Most day traders perform the trading tasks on a full-time basis, thereby making it one of their permanent sources of income. When the traders are immensely disciplined, they are able to go on with their trading practices unabated. Typically, traders are not restricted to certain companies and commodities but are able to trade thousands of products every single day.

Discipline also extends to following the day plans and strategies laid out. When the traders are able to follow strict guidelines and policies, they are able to prevent incurring losses by ensuring that they follow their safe methods of operation. Most importantly, traders require the discipline to be able to do nothing when there are no opportunities and be on high alert for potential opportunities. When the latter occurs, discipline is required to act instantaneously and keep a sober mind to ensure that the chances of losses are minimized.

Trading Plan

A trading plan is imperative to any business and any trading setup. As is commonly said, "failing to plan is planning to fail." Established traders assert that there are only two choices in their craft: either following a trading plan methodically or failing. Some of the tips which help in the creation of suitable plans include:

- Disaster avoidance. Trading is a business and must be treated as such. There are very specific elements that enable a person to be able to succeed in the craft. For instance, reading books, charting a program, and opening a brokerage account are not really plans.

A plan is a determination of what amounts will be put up in a certain sector, the trading strategies to be used, as well as knowing when to exit. The trading plans should be followed systematically and updated as one gains trading knowledge.

- A skill assessment must precede the preparation of a plan. Most distinguished traders normally test their skills out on paper before attempting to use them in the real world, so that they can have confidence knowing that the strategies actually work. Trading in the market is usually a matter of giving and take. Often, the traders operate on probabilities and are unsure about the outcome. When paper skills are confirmed, the traders are then able to operate comfortably in the real world.

- A good plan must always have a set risk level. Depending on a person's trading style, the risk level may range from a small percentage to a relatively high margin. By nature, some people are better risk takers than others. Therefore, one should identify the length to which they can go so as to be able to set their limits. You may also find that in some situations, you're willing to risk more than in others. Ensure you're always making logical and thought out decisions that are not based in emotion.

Chapter 13: Learning to Begin Day Trading with a Minimalist Approach

When all is said and done, it all boils down to what you do with your trading space. Trying to chew too much never proved beneficial for anyone, and neither did cooking too many pots at a go. Most traders struggle with trying to do too much at once. Absorbing too much information at once, understanding all trading concepts at once, trying out too many strategies at once, trading in too many platforms at once, or even entering way too many positions at once. Yet the quantity of what you do never matter over the quality of how you do it. It is in this connection that the concept of minimalists approaches to day trading crop up.

So what is minimalism, anyway? In general terms, minimalism can be described as the condition in which you intentionally acquire and only lead your life with the things you really need. Its basic tenets are intentionality, simplicity, and drive. It is your intentionality that makes you endorse the things that are most valuable to you while removing every other thing that distracts you from your purpose. The most successful people have one thing in common: they embarked on their journey, whether in sports, in business, or in any other area of their life, with a lot of focus and staying purpose-driven. Therefore, day trading is not exclusive to the minimalist approach.

In trading, a minimalist strategy is one in which you focus on those one or two things that work for you in the trading scene and growing your potential to trade day by day. It is about eliminating all the noise and maintaining your focus on perfecting a few skills that will help you edge the competition.

For traders, it takes quite an extensive time before you can really figure out what mistakes you've been making that do not necessarily have to do with your trading method but stem from the emotional mistakes that we can all agree have led us into errors at some point in our lives.

You need to ask yourself as a trader, the role that the clutter in your everyday charts plays in your failure to make it big. Just like our materialistic nature leads us into purchasing and acquiring things that we do not necessarily need but which arguably makes us feel fulfilled, the craze of learning how to trade drives you into making unthought-out moves that fill your plate with *"crap."* The idea of having too many indicators and analytical tools, for instance, will obscure your judgment about a certain trade day.

The benefits of minimalism

Clarity of the mind: We already mentioned that the pillars of minimalism include clarity. Truth is, the connection between all the things that we try out, and our mental and emotional health is just magical. That magical feeling that you get when you clear that junk drawer in your kitchen is the same you should expect to feel when you cease employing way too many tactics in the trading scene. Remember that emotional state is core in making trade moves. Since minimalism gives you a chance to be clear about everything on your table, you should embrace this approach.

Too much monitoring of way too many prices moves stresses you and, eventually, you become unproductive.

Freedom: At the beginning of this guide, we saw that day trading is meant to be a form of financial freedom, and actually freedom to spend that money. It is not in any way meant to tie you down on a 24/7 basis. Yet it is so easy for day trading to hold you down every other time if you try tackling too many things at a go. Even the most successful traders in history never employed too many strategies at one time. In fact, almost all trading strategies were discovered by a different person. This is because when one discovered one approach, they focused on it and made it work on all levels. This way, you have time for trading and attending to your personal life.

Self-confidence: Since having a few indicators and trades in a day allows you to study them and learn every trick about them, this enhances your confidence in going about your trade, and you can be assured of making sound trading decisions. You begin to feel good about your overall life, which is an unexpected advantage of living with fewer things.

Purpose enhancement: When you are clear of the unnecessary things that you don't have to do in trading, a clear sense of purpose and goal achievement happens to you. You become motivated to trade on a daily basis because you have a clear direction, and there are not many alternatives confusing you. Having a few commitments motivates you to achieve them and see where you get with them. You can set daily milestones, look forward to achieving them, and then actually achieve them. Achieving the little milestones allows you to keep fetching wider profits progressively, handling each day at a time.

How to incorporate minimalism in your day trading approach

Now that we've seen the benefits of minimalism, the following is a checklist of some basic ways, you can incorporate the strategy in your daily trading strategy.

- Always start your day with a clean price chart. Do not dwell on trading robots for analysis, since these may obscure your trading day's judgment. Being able to start on a clean note calms your mind, and you will be able to focus when analyzing the market.

- Concentrate on the simple price action strategies. Be sure to choose the simplest method of studying price movements, because this makes everything much easier than trying to look complicated like the trade gurus.
- Do not spend all your time analyzing the market every day. Rather, concentrate on creating quality analysis times that will give you a few workable signals.
- Do not engage in too many markets in a day. Instead, concentrate on enhancing your focus on the major markets, and this will ensure that you handle the markets like a winner.
- Refrain from the idea of fancy trading tools such as fancy computers or desks. As far as the minimalist approach is concerned, these are just added stresses that you are adding to your list. The best thing for you to do is actually buy what you can afford and not fill your working station with clutter in the name of being fashionable. Ensure that your trading station is clean and simple. You

don't need 100 books on trading sitting around you for you to look serious. Bring minimalism to your surroundings as much as possible.

- Most importantly, eliminate any unnecessary things from your life that may be causing stress for you. Learn to cut off toxic and unnecessary relationships, do not indulge in day trading along with several other small businesses in the notion of income diversification unless you have a trusted person taking care of your business, and do not have too much of a social media presence that might expose you to all kinds of rumors that may deter your thinking.

The key to making it big eventually is taking baby steps and being keen on every milestone that you arrive at every time. Before you can totally fix your feet on the ground, be sure to trade on about 3 stocks in a typical day and earn the most out of it. It is always better to start small and do really well on a few securities than be on the losing edge with many, whilst not learning anything at all. Minimalism is simply a secret code to living a happier and more fulfilling life in whatever you are doing. The basic idea here is to minimize what you put down on charts and maximize on a few tactics that work for you. Remember, the greatest failure in day trading does not come from the method you employ to trade. It mostly comes from the errors that you make while trading. Most traders are quick to assume that a method just did not work when really they did not take time to learn about the method and focus on trading fully with it. They simply learned about too many methods and added too many indicators as they think the gurus do, and they ended up beating themselves up. The thing is, a lot is not better than a little!

Chapter 14: Avoiding the Herd Mentality

Also, popularly referred to as the mob or the pack mentality, the herd mentality is a condition that describes how people are influenced by others in their decision-making process. Rather than their decisions being based on a rational idea, they are based on emotions because of the mob influence. Due to its increasing impacts in most people's lives and given its detrimental impacts to an individual's goals and purpose in life, the concept of the herd mentality has become increasingly studied as the experts and social psychologists attempt to create awareness among people.

The paradox of it all is that as a trader, you have all the reasons to get carried away by the herd mentality. As aforementioned, it is the herd mentality which prevented the masses of people in the Japanese rice trade from embracing the candlestick mentality. Muhenisa, who belonged to the small percentage of people that did not entertain this kind of mentality, leveraged the trading space and received many benefits out of it. We cannot deny that there will always be the masses who dictate what individuals do, and there are always those individuals who will follow the masses. In fact, the herd mentality is a strong force amongst our social lives, since all new fashion and norms are dictated on the societal level by the masses. It is hard to resist. However, it is this mentality that holds you back from joining the trading trend early enough.

Most often, it is usually the traders who go against the wave of the masses who make the most out of trading. The herd mentality lies to people and says that it is yet too early and unacceptable to buy stocks, and most people feel afraid of taking risks, and they settle with those sentiments. These people then miss out on lucrative opportunities of booming markets. In fact, most people fear day trading because the masses have it that day trading is all about losing your money and that it is a profession for the chosen few. They fail to embrace the goodness of day trading. Besides, the herd mentality is what makes most traders commit mistakes and end up losing their money, because they believe in rumors and execute orders in the market, which are wrongly led. One of the most recent detrimental impacts of the herd mentality is the 2008 housing bubble, which led to a crisis. It led to huge negative impacts from which economies are still struggling to recover. Every participant saw that the boom was bound to collapse, but because of the herd mentality, they continued being speculative and placed a lot of their cash in the market. You probably have come across news about the 2008 financial crisis even if you have not been a fan of news or economic trends since this topic has made headlines ever since. You know what happened. People lost huge amounts of money. Financial institutions collapsed, and money circulation was greatly interrupted. Those who might have been clever enough had exited the market and were safer with few or no losses, more than the masses who only decided to look at one side of the coin and thought the trend wouldn't change. Fast forward to know, and we know that successful trading calls for careful assessment of the market conditions, based on facts and not emotions. Being on the opposite side of this mentality helps you focus on what you can do to rock it in the market. It allows you to manipulate the vulnerability of others, which accrues from their herd mentality.

The average investor uses emotions to make decisions. They rely heavily on social trends. They manage positions based on the rumors going around and do not wait for the release of official reports or news to be informed in their next move. If all people in the market are interested in a particular stock, then most of the traders are likely to move in the same direction. Needless to mention, you should avoid the mob mentality if you really want to benefit from day trading. So many rumors and trends can arise in a single trading day and affect your judgment and decision making. But as one of the world's most prominent traders, Warren Buffett, would argue, you should be acquisitive when others are drawing back and draw back when others are overly acquisitive. Be sure to follow facts when making decisions and be your own master in the game. Do not be a slave to the herd mentality! You can do it!

Chapter 15: Reflecting on the Lessons Learned from Trading

When reflecting on the lessons learned from trading, it is important to note that the market has changed in the course of the years. As such, most of the tricks that traders used ten years ago may not be effective in the current industry setting. For instance, more than ten years ago you would have called in your buys and sell orders to your broker. This is not done anymore. People engaging in trading today meet a completely changed game. It is true that trading could be deceiving, and the best way to face the market is to be equipped with information, experiences, and lessons from those who have traded for a long time. The following are some of the lessons to learn from:

It pays to be a defensive-minded trader. A credible trader, Warren Buffett, developed a unique and famous quote. It states that a trader should have it as a basic principle to always strive to not lose money and to never forget this rule. The cautioning message in this rule is that as a new trader, one should not only focus on making money but rather try as much as possible to protect their money. The use of a defensive approach entails trading when your trading criteria have been met, not only when the market conditions are favorable. What you ought to know is that the goals of trading are not to lose money, but to make money.

The other key point of defensive trading is to preserve your trading capital. The implication of this is that as a trader, you will be able to maximize when an easy opportunity arises. This approach means having as much money as possible when an easy target or stork emerges. It means that a good trader will preserve their capital for an easy trade setup. These easy targets tend to have high probability price action signals that are obvious. Risk management is an important aspect of trading, and when you have properly considered its aspects as a trader, you will not be disappointed if you took a confluent and strong trading signal, but it failed.

Your last trade results should not affect your next trade. It is important to understand that results from your last trade have no effect on the next trade. It means as a trader, you should not be influenced by the last trade when making the next. You should know that every single trade you take is unique and different from the previous one. Although they may appear the same, it is important to note that the surrounding market context will be different. To affirm this, know that winners and losers are random when trading. For instance, if you make 100 trades in a year, you may end up with 50 losses and 50 wins, but the fact is the pattern is totally random. Or you could buy 5 losses followed by 1 winner followed by 7 more losers, and follow that with 30 winners. Noting this, the main question is - how will you handle the random nature of losses and wins?

The implication in this is that if you have decided to become a trader, be dedicated, confident, and a perpetual risk taker. These, among other qualities, will be key aspects in ensuring that any single trade will not distract you. If you let the results influence you, it will hinder you from realizing the real nature of trading. However, you need to be extra careful after a big winner. It is human nature to become over-confident and excited after a major winner or overly-fearful after a losing trade. Getting overconfident lures you into taking uncalculated and risky trading moves. The bad thing with this is that you may end up making losses. Trading through the influence of emotions can lead to wiping out your account in a day. So, it is important even after a big win to remain calm and make rational decisions.

Doing less trading activities could bring more: trading is not about doing too much, and most people who fall for this mindset are the new traders. However, it does not mean that conducting good research or watching the charts is wrong. Having a low-frequency trading approach has been accredited by the most successful traders. It may be debated with some pointing that this is a wrong lesson. What it means is a good trader should be able to filter the good trade signals from the bad rather than just jumping into action. You can do this by reading the footprint of the market. It will help in realizing the good stocks worth risking your money on. The mindset here is being cautious of the money you worked hard to earn.

Know where you are coming from before beginning to trade: As you have come to know in a trading business, you are the boss, and there is no authority above you. As such, quality of discipline and being able to hold yourself accountable are important. If you know that you are not self-controlled or disciplined enough, it is important that you develop these qualities first. You should know that exiting the market is harder than entry. A good trader removes himself from the trade exit process as much as possible. You should note that most traders exit the market based on emotion. In most cases, it results in large losses or small losses. It is true that it is harder to exit the market when it is favorable. The best course of action is to exit the market when it is in your favor instead of when it is cashing back against you because you will end up losing.

Master your trading strategy: while most people assume that they understand how to use the trading platform as per their trading strategy, this is not the case. You will find it a difficult trade when you have not adequately mastered your trading strategy. Look at it as trying to fly a plane while you have no training nor prior experience. Practicing your trading strategy will help you to get used to it as well as learn the most suitable tricks. You have to commit and master your trading strategy before the actual trading begins. Also, having one trading method is more helpful than having different trading methods. An additional component to this is having mastered your money management. You will do this by not increasing your trading amount until you see consistent success.

Master yourself: An excellent trader is the one who has already mastered themselves. As a trader, it is important to deal with the emotional or mental weaknesses that you have, because failure to do so will make it difficult for you to make money. Most traders fail to realize that success comes from going on a personal journey and conquering the pitfalls. You will do this by checking your ego. As a trader, being confident is an important quality, but being over-confident could be harmful. Overconfidence is also a weakness even to the greatest traders, which makes them make poor trading decisions. The aspect of over-confidence results from making several good winning trades.

Be disciplined: A good trader is a disciplined person. You may question the essence of discipline in trading. The element of being disciplined means that even after making a huge win, you will not do anything out of the ordinary. It is normal to feel wonderful or ecstatic after winning. But you should continue to trade as per your plan. As a strategic trader, your plan should provide for what to do after winning trades. An undisciplined trader, when they close a nice winner, tends to jump into the market and make another trade. Unfortunately, this turns out to be a mistake in most cases.

Employing confluence: In the context of trading, confluence entails numerous supporting factors lining up to support the trades. The modern trading platforms have mechanical trading systems that have strict rules that they have to follow. The advantage with this system is it helps to eliminate human error. However, the best way to do this will require writing your trading plan well. You must have and adhere to a given trend, signal, and level agreement. For a beginning trader, a system like a robot trader has mechanical advantages. It will help you to build and improve discipline and confidence with your trading strategy.

Conclusion

Day trading is one of the most popular professions whose potential is overlooked. Most people consider day trading to be a profession where people just gamble or look to luck for their earnings. In fact, day traders are considered unethical. Most see it as a thing for the elite few who utilize mind games to take money from the naive players in the market. Yet day trading is just a unique profession, but with all the rules and principles of a typical profession. Profits in day trading are earned through every individual trader's efforts and tactics.

As discussed above, there are various reasons why you should indulge in day trading, including the fact that it gives you financial freedom, gives you a better overview of the world, it has a leveled playing field for all players, and it has life-enriching skills such as mental toughness and risk management. As a trader, you are forced to become the master of your own trade and get ahold of the best strategies to maximize your profitability. There are various strategies to be leveraged to make day trading work, and they all cater to different kinds of traders. Your day trading style is largely determined by factors such as capital availability, experience, and knowledge of the market.

Further, the basic start-up tools for a trader are relatively affordable, and it gives you the pleasure of working from the comfort of your home office or anywhere else. One of the most important things as a day trader is for you to ignore the herd mentality and not let it come between you and your trading intentions. Most people have failed because of over speculation or under speculation. Decisions in day trading require facts and not emotions; hence, you have to be stable emotionally and avoid being influenced by baseless rumors. Also, in day trading, you have to know how much risk you can take based on your qualifications and the nature of the market. The good news is that day trading is not something for the elite few. It is for everyone. You can become part of it, and you can attain big wins. Once in the market, your alertness, readiness, and consistency determine your victory or failure in the long-run. Just believe that you can do it and you will!

If you enjoyed this book or received value from it in any way, then I'd like to ask you for a favor: would you be kind enough to leave a review for this book on Amazon? It'd be greatly appreciated!

References

Abdolmohammadi, M., & Sultan, J. (2002). Ethical reasoning and the use of insider information in stock trading. Journal of Business Ethics, 37(2), 165-173.

Fischel, D. R. (1978). Efficient capital market theory, the market for corporate control, and the regulation of cash tender offers. Tex. L. Rev., 57, 1.

Fong, S., Tai, J., & Si, Y. W. (2011). Trend Following Algorithms for Technical Trading in Stock Market. Journal of Emerging Technologies in Web Intelligence, 3(2).

NerdWallet-Make all the right money moves. Retrieved from https://www.nerdwallet.com/

Ryu, D. (2012). The profitability of day trading: An empirical study using high-quality data. *Investment Analysts Journal, 41*(75), 43-54.

Forex Trading for Beginners

What Everybody Ought to Know
About the Day Trading Business,
How to Understand the Forex
Market, Scalping Strategies, and the
Secret of Making Money Online

Bill Sykes, Timothy Gibbs

Table of Contents

Chapter 4 - The Mindset of a Winner: What They Do and How They Do It

You Are Not Other Forex Traders
The Blame Game
Track Record
Risk Within Your Limits
News is Facts, Not Prediction
No Plan. No Trade.
When You Are Starting, Forget Fundamental Analysis

Emotional Wreck
Step 1: Be Disciplined
Step 2: Change Your Beliefs
Step 3: Evaluate Your Mistakes
Step 4: Write Down the Consequences
Step 5: Create an Action Plan
Step 6: Master Your Stress and Confusion

Commonly Used Platforms for Day Trading
TD Ameritrade
Fidelity Investments
IG
CMC Markets
FOREX.com
City Index
XTB

Determining a Position Size and the Importance of Using a Formula
Step 1: Establish Your Account Risk
Step 2: Find Out Your Pip Risk
Step 3: Get Ready to Determine Your Position Size

Chapter 7 - Your Plan of Action: Crafting Your Battle Plan

Introduction

Imagine being part of the most liquid market in the world.

How liquid? We are talking about a market that trades in currency worth $5,100,000,000,000. That's 5 trillion dollars by the way[1].

Now, maybe that number doesn't sound all that exciting. After all, if you had to combine the number of transactions taking place around the world, then perhaps 5 trillion isn't such a large number. At some point, that number will be reached anyways.

But what if you realized that the above mentioned 5 trillion dollars is the currency traded in one day.

Yes, just a single day.

Applying basic math, we are looking at $1,861,500,000,000,000 worth of transactions taking place in a year. Which is why more and more people are jumping on the Forex bandwagon, hoping to take even an infinitesimal portion of the amount traded in a day. Think about it this way, even if you thought that perhaps you might aim for a small percentage of that amount, maybe just 0.001%. You don't want to be greedy here. Let's take it slow.

That still gives you $51,000,000.

That is still a huge amount. That is big money. And that is one of the reasons why Forex has been growing recently.

At one point, Forex was the realm of the "big shots". We are talking about global banks, multinational corporations, hedge funds, and wealthy investors. It seemed like a private club that was meant only for the elite.

But the liquidity of the market combined with the rise in internet technologies changed all that. That is why you can see tens of thousands of traders from around the world who have joined in on the challenges and excitement of trading in the Forex market. With the increase in accessibility (using trading apps for example) and the ability to get started with as little as $25, the allure of Forex is too hard to resist.

But the Forex market is not all about simply deciding to invest a bit of money, waiting for a year or two, taking out the cash, buying your own private island, building a castle, and retiring to sip mojitos and watch The Avengers reruns on a 100-inch screen.

You can't just think that by aiming for 0.001% of the currencies traded in a single day and investing a small bit of money, everything will simply happen on its own.

There is more to it than that. You need to be smart. You need to be patient. You need to be precise. And these are not just random things added here to inflate the importance and challenges of Forex. They are what you should be aiming to become.

Take for example the story of the financial analyst at a Canadian pharmacy[2]. He tried to bet big on a volatile market but ended up losing all his life savings.

But within all the stories spreading about Forex, there are numerous successes as well.

Think of the story of Bill Lipschutz. He made hundreds of millions of dollars in profits in the 1980s at an Fx department. The best part? He had no prior experience in trading with currencies. None. Zip. Nada.

Even if you have previous experience with the Forex market, it does not mean that you are ready to face the unexpected situations that crop up. After all, Forex is highly predictable. In fact, Bill Lipschutz (the trader we just mentioned in the example above) says that the key to becoming a successful trader is trying to make money when you are right probably 20 or 30 percent of the time.

Try and put that into perspective and imagine why one of the most successful traders in the world believes that you will be right a rather low percentage of the time. His statement is not an indication of the intelligence of the traders. He is not saying that you are too dumb to do anything right.

Rather, he is talking about the severe unpredictability of the Forex market. He is talking about being prepared and having the right knowledge to figure out what to do in any situation.

And that is what you have here with you.

You hold in your hands a compendium of knowledge that helps you better understand the Forex market.

You are going to learn more about the Forex market, what it is, and why it has seen an explosion of growth in recent years. You are going to understand how to get into a winning mindset and the things you should avoid in order to have a rational and logical state of mind (very important when you are trading).

We will then look at the different ways that you can tackle trading, how to begin your trading journey, and how to form a strong battle plan.

We are also going to look at some of the tools that traders use to stay ahead of the game.

We are going to make your foray into Forex a smooth process.

However, this comes with a caveat.

Remember that at the end of the day, you will be making the tough choices. There are no get-rich-quick tactics in Forex trading. It all depends on your actions. Of course, this book will help you navigate many of the complexities of the Fx market, but in the end, you will be the one taking charge of your trading.

Which is why, one of the biggest pieces of advice that you should stick to is that you should never, ever, EVER make assumptions about a trade without having all the information or knowledge about the market. In the world of Forex, more is always welcome. And by more, we are referring to more information. You see, information is the currency you use before you even begin working on the actual currency. It might not seem that obvious in the beginning. You might be trading on small amounts and the losses might look like lessons. But as you increase your trades, you are going to find out that the risk increases exponentially.

Zig Ziglar, the popular salesman and motivational speaker is quoted aptly, "The best time to do something significant is between yesterday and tomorrow."

That is why it is never too late to learn something and develop yourself.

This book will help you learn, understand, and navigate the world of Forex.

Welcome to Forex Trading for Beginners.

Chapter 1: Welcome to Forex Exchange Trading!

What is Forex?

The term "Forex" is often shortened to "FX", but the word itself is also an abbreviated version of two words "FOReign EXchange".

Forex is a global trading market that provides a platform for businesses, banks, public entities, corporations, and private investors to exchange certain currencies. This exchange allows the parties to either make commercial transactions or merely speculate on the currencies.

Now, this might remind you of another form of market, the Stock market. But the two function in entirely different ways. For one, Forex deals with currencies. Secondly, stock markets have a fixed schedule that they adhere to. On the other hand, Forex is open to the public 24 hours a day for 5 days a week.

Forex begins its activities at 5 p.m. on Sunday, Eastern Time, and then closes the market at 4 p.m. on Friday (ET). This allows people to trade from anywhere in the world, no matter what time zones they follow. This degree of market availability is possible because there are always markets that are open around the globe. Additionally, gone are the days when traders have to be physically present at a certain venue to conduct their trades. Today, you simply have to boot up your internet or your mobile app, select your trading portal, and conduct your activities.

Forex does have a few "main markets" or centers where the majority of the action takes place. These markets are located in Sydney, London, Zurich, China, New York, Toyko, and

Frankfurt. But again, you do not have to be there physically to conduct your trades.

When you are performing a transaction in the Forex market, then you are doing two things simultaneously:

1. You are buying one currency.

2. You are selling another currency.

In other words, currencies are traded in pairs and if you open a Forex platform, then you might notice currencies labeled as GBP/USD (which is short for pound sterling/U.S. dollar) or USD/CAD (U.S. dollar/Canadian dollar) to cite a few examples.

When dealing with pairs, you have two components to focus on. The first is the base currency, which is the first currency in the pair. The second component is the counter currency, which is the second. Let us take one of the examples of currencies we just mentioned above.

In the GBP/USD pair, GBP is the base currency and USD is the counter currency or quote currency.

When you trade, you are typically doing it under the idea that the value of the currency you are buying increases when compared to the value of the currency you are selling. If this happens, then you typically sell the position and make a profit.

Why Trading Forex is Better Than Other Options

There are three main reasons why Forex is better than choosing other avenues for trading, be it stocks, bitcoin, or even options. We have already explored one of the options, so let us start with that.

Forex is Highly Liquid

The stock market trades in roughly $10 billion in volumes in a single day. But what is that compared for Forex? In fact, that does not even amount to 1% of the total trades carried out per day in the Fx market.

Better Information

Forget Tyco. Forget Enron. Forget all the other companies that provide you with information about companies, bitcoins, or markets. When you work with Forex, you are not dealing with the knowledge provided to you by a few entities. You are looking at the strengths and trends of an entire economy. An economy at such a scale will have multiple reports surrounding it. This means you get more accurate information about your trades.

Closing

Other markets have to close at the end of the day. Not Forex. This gives you flexibility when it comes to trading. You can choose when and how you would like to trade.

These are just some of the reasons why you should venture into Forex. We are going to look at a lot more further below.

Why Forex?

At the core of Forex, you are dealing with currency trading. And at the core of that currency trading, you have speculation about the values of currencies.

Hold on, you say.

Speculation? You ask. Didn't you tell me not to assume anything? Now you are telling me to go ahead and speculate?

Of course, you are going to speculate. But before we get to that, let us cover some of the basics first.

Currency trading is speculation. It is as simple as that. You are using what knowledge and information you have to make a profit by buying currencies. It is like buying stocks or any other financial security; you make a transaction and hope to make a profitable return on it. However, in the Forex market, the securities you are dealing with concern the currencies of nations.

But in the world of Forex, speculation is not based on blind assumptions. It is not even gambling (even though some people might think that it is so). When you gamble or make a guess, you are playing with your money even though you know that the odds are against you. You just hope that, given time, lady luck will smile at you with teeth so white that you could use them as floodlights. Typically, when you invest, you are aiming to minimize the risks and maximize the return over a certain period of time (usually months or years). In Forex, you are maximizing returns over a short period of time (usually minutes, hours, or days). This involves speculating (or also known as "active trading" in the Forex world) where you adopt calculated financial risks in order to gain a profit.

And there you have the keyword that comes into play when describing Forex: calculated. You are not just sitting blindly twiddling your thumbs hoping to make it rich. You are going to read the trends, understand the shifts, and even use the latest news to make calculated risks.

The best way to understand your actions is by taking the example of a business. If you are the owner of a business, then you are going to be making calculated risks. Should you increase the available stock that you have? Do you want to hire more employees? Should you think about expanding your business or opening a branch in another location? Do you need to spend heavily on big marketing campaigns?

You may never be certain about the outcomes of any of those decisions. But you do make choices based on the information you have. For example, you notice that there is a demand for your products in another state. After conducting a market survey, you decide that it would be profitable for you to have a branch in that state. You immediately open up another business.

But what if you are not receiving profits that way you had expected? What are you going to do then? Are you going to pack up and call it quits? Or will you try some other tactics to attract customers to your business?

It is the same with Forex. When you speculate, you are making decisions about your investment based on the information you have with you.

This is why not many people realize before venturing into Forex that they need to be equipped with a certain frame of mind and skill set (thankfully, you have this book).

- You need to be dedicated. You can invest in the Forex market and ignore it for a few days, but then you must return to it to make a few changes.

- You need to have financial and technological resources. Even though you can start small, you are not going to last long if all you have is lunch money. When it comes to technological resources, you need to make sure that you have a steady access to the internet and the trading platform.

- You need to have financial discipline. You do not need to have a finance degree. Rather, you should be capable of understanding trends and numbers.

- You need to be emotionally strong. Things do not always go your way. But some of the biggest successes in Forex happen because people do not get emotional over their trades. They figure out ways to bounce back.

- You need to have the perseverance to always seek out new information, new ways to manage your risk, and look for new opportunities.

- Finally, you should be a sponge, able to absorb knowledge about the politics, economics, and market situations of a particular country. That means it is time to renew your newspaper subscriptions.

Why Choose Forex Over Other Options?

We just looked at the fact that Forex gives you a 24-hour market to work with. But what other benefits can we get by choosing Forex over other forms of security investments options?

Let us look into some benefits here.

Low Transaction Costs

For short-term traders, the Forex market is the best place to trade because of the low transaction cost. This is because of the over-the-counter structure that people can take advantage of. How is that possible? Well, you can use a purely electronic marketplace where you can interact directly with the market maker. This removes the need for any middlemen.

Let us take the example of an equity trader. Let us say that this trader has placed around 30 trades a day. For these trades, he has to pay around $20 in commission fees. Because of this, the trader then has to pay up to $600 simply as transaction costs every single day. This not only becomes a rather hefty investment, but it curbs profits and in some cases, creates losses. In an equity transaction, there are several people involved and this is why you usually end up paying a high transaction cost.

The Forex market is decentralized. There are no clearinghouses or exchanges. This means you do not have to spend unnecessarily on transaction fees.

Both The Bear and The Bull Are Profitable

The terms "bear" and "bull" are used to describe how markets are performing. This means they gauge whether a market is appreciating or depreciating in value and also describe investor sentiments about a market.

When the term "bull market" is used, it is referring to a market that is improving. In such scenarios, investors are optimistic about the fact that there will be an upward trend in the market for quite some time. The reason the word "bull" is used is because a bull typically attacks by lifting its horns up to sheesh-kebab its helpless victims.

On the other hand, the term "bear market" is used to describe a market in decline. When that happens, investors are pessimistic about the market's future. The word "bear" is used because a bear typically swipes down to attack.

When working on any other options other than Forex, you are going to be paying attention to market sentiments. It matters when you want to aim for a profitable return. In a Forex market, you do not have to worry whether the market is bull or bear because you are always buying one currency and selling another. This is why even a bear market is an opportunity.

Low Chances of Errors in Online Trades

When you are trading with currency, it generally involves a three-step process. You place your trade on the platform, the dealing desk at the Forex market executes your order (usually automatically), and then the trader receives the order confirmation logged onto his station. All of these steps are completed in a matter of a few seconds.

Now let us compare this with other trading options that have around five steps to complete your transaction. If you are the client, then you will be typically calling your broker to place a particular order. The broker then sends your order to the trading floor, where a specialist is responsible for matching the orders (this is done because there are many other brokers who might be competing for the same trade). Finally, the specialist confirms the order, and you receive a confirmation notification on your platform. As you can see, this is a pretty long process and the chances of something going wrong or human error taking over increases exponentially with each step.

Information is Key

We explored this point earlier but let us see what this means in more detail.

When you are dealing with currencies, you can analyze the countries. For example, do you want to discover the growth rate of countries? Then you should be looking at their GDP. Want to know about levels of production in a country? Then check out their industrial production data. By analyzing all of these facts, you get a picture of how a country is performing. This means that you can choose to invest in the currency of that country. There is an incredible amount of data released about a country, much more detailed and copious than the information about a company. This data cannot be falsified or adulterated. Everything is clear-cut for you to understand.

The Forex Market and How it Works

To better understand Forex, you need to know that the market involves a Forex quote, which is essentially the price of one currency in terms of another (because currencies are always traded in pairs). This means that one unit of the base currency matches the exchange rate of the quote currency.

Let us take an example. If you are dealing with EUR/USD and the trading value is at 1.13122, then it simply means that the price of 1 euro (which is the base currency) in dollars (which is the quote currency) is 1.13122 dollars.

We are going to look more into the basics of Forex in the next chapter, but for now, the idea of how the currency pairs are matched will help you understand future concepts.

Who Participates in the Forex Market?

When you examine it broadly, then there are 5 main participants in the Forex market. Most others can be placed in any of the 5 categories mentioned below.

Banks

One can say that banks are the major participants in the market. After all, we are dealing with currencies and their value is how commercial banks can assist with the nation's fiscal policies. At any given point in time, there are an average of 150 banks from around the world performing transactions in the Forex market.

It is important to know that banks do not only conduct transactions in the market on behalf of their customers but also on their own behalf with the sole aim of earning profits.

However, there is another group of banks that also participate in the Forex market: central banks. These banks have a direct impact on the Forex market because whatever policies or movements occur in the central banks, traders will pick up on that to check what is happening with the currencies they are trading. Additionally, central banks can also directly intervene in the market, leading to drastic shifts in currency values. For example, a central bank can use some of the reserves of its foreign and domestic currency reserves in order to buy foreign currencies in the market, thus influencing their value.

Brokers

Brokers are people who help arrange trades between two or multiple dealers. They constantly monitor the currency rates and fluctuations so that they can offer some of the best avenues of investment for their clients. Brokers do not invest their own money. They are simply people who arrange for transactions to take place.

Multinational Corporations

When MNCs deal with international operations, they make use of the Forex market. This happens specifically during the process of imports and exports when the multinational companies have to convert their money in order to pay for the transactions. Some MNCs even have their own floors in the market with designated traders who help make more profits and minimize the risk involved in the exchange rates.

Individual Investors

With the level of convenience and accessibility available to people around the world, individual traders have been flocking to the Forex market like people rushing to the electronics store on a Black Friday weekend. And you are going to be joining the platform as well. The only difference is, you will be better informed than most people.

Small Businesses

When it comes to managing cash flow on an international level, then the task becomes challenging for small businesses. What rules do they adhere to? How can they conduct a transaction while being completely aware of currency exchange rates? By using Forex, SMEs can leverage the currency information readily available on the platform and also hedge currency risk. When SMEs begin to deal with transactions on an international level, one of the biggest challenges that they face is currency risk. In order to either minimize or eliminate the currency risk, they use a process called hedging where they will lock in on an exchange rate today. When they conduct transactions in the future, they will be using the locked-in currency exchange rate and not whatever rate is present at the time of the transaction. This way, even if the value of their currency drops in the future, they are not going to risk facing the repercussions of it. They have already locked their exchange rate.

What's in It For You?

Another way to ask that question: is Forex profitable?

The short answer is that yes, it is profitable. The long answer is that there is no easy way to make profits.

Many people enter the Forex market thinking that they are not going to make the same mistakes as someone else, only to end up losing their investments and feeling like they were swindled.

But Forex is about big risks and big rewards.

In fact, one of the biggest roles that you will be adopting while working in Forex is risk management. You need to be constantly thinking about the options you will take to mitigate a specific risk and what strategies you will utilize. If you are trying to risk too much in a trade in order to make sure you can face losses in the future, then you are going to find yourself exiting Forex faster than you can say "risky business".

Here is something that most traders don't realize when they enter Forex: you have to expect losses.

You might experience losses in a single day, over multiple days, or even across weeks. Those are the situations that every trader must face because the end goal is to make profits over the long-term.

This is why you need to enter Forex with proper control over your emotions and the right frame of mind. We are going to explore this further in the coming chapters, but for now, you need to know this: you have to be prepared for the Forex market.

Remember this, at the end of the day, you are going to be making the decisions that will dictate the direction of your trades. When things do not look good, Forex traders often end up blaming the government, the trading platform, luck, God, the fate of the universe, or whatever else they can find to blame. But the end result is that they are the ones who take the final actions. Sometimes it pays off and at other times, it may not.

However, there are a few steps you can take to give you an edge in the market. One of them is choosing your broker. Whatever trading platform you choose, make sure that you have done your research about that platform. Giving you numerous features and speedy execution of trades is important, but at the same time, they need to provide you with honesty and transparency as well. You should also ideally choose a broker who can provide a demo account.

With a demo account, you can paper trade (demo trade). Take advantage of it and practice your demo trades. Make as many mistakes as you can. Learn how to work the system properly.

You need to reach a point where you should be getting consistent results over the long-term. Once you have found your strategy, you can implement it in real trades.

Are there any other tricks or information that could be useful for you?

Of course there are. We are going to look at all of them. From the basics that you need to be aware of before starting your trade to getting into the mindset of a winner, you are going to get an edge over others in the market.

Chapter 2: The Basics that Everyone Needs to Know Before They Start

Where Do You Trade Forex?

To trade in Forex, you are going to be using special platforms that are essentially labeled as "brokers". This is why there was an emphasis on choosing the right broker as this can impact how effectively you trade and how much knowledge you are privy to at any point.

Additionally, you should be picking your broker based on the strategy you are using in Forex (discussed further). For some strategies, you need to have low spreads and speedy executions while for other strategies that are focused on the long-term, you might need to focus on swapping. When you evaluate platforms, you will find out that some are better than others not because of the overall features, but mainly due to the suitability of the platform to your strategies.

When you have matched the broker to the strategy, look for some additional features that you can get from the platform as well. These don't change the way you work on the platforms but simply provide you with convenience.

Finally, do check if your broker is regulated in its home country. This allows you to check that they are following a certain set of criteria and requirements, which is important to make sure that they are not going to break rules during their operation.

What Exactly is a Currency Pair?

A currency pair, in essence, is a quote. You are being quoted one currency against the other.

In such a manner, you are comparing the value of one currency against the other. When you discover that the value of one currency appreciates, you then conduct a sale to net yourself some profits.

When you are trading with currencies, you are using "contracts". The contracts are essentially lot sizes of the units of currency that you are going to purchase. Typically, the usual contract or lot size is 100,000. This means that you are going to purchase 100,000 units of a particular currency. But many trading firms and platforms also offer what are known as mini lots (which have a size of 10,000 units) and micro lots (which have a unit size of 1,000).

Now let us see how this works and how you typically make a profit with an example.

Since we have familiarized ourselves with the EUR/USD pair, we are going to use it for our example here. Let us imagine that the exchange rate of EUR/USD is 1.13 and you have made a purchase of 10,000 units of euros. What this means is that each euro is equivalent to $1.13. You have spent $11,300 to purchase 10,000 units of euros (10,000 x 1.13).

You have all these units of euros with you and you decide to wait. After two weeks, you notice that the value of the euro has appreciated. The EUR/USD is now going for 1.2, or in other words, one euro is now equivalent to $1.2. At this point, you decide that you are going to sell the units of euros that you have with you.

What happens now?

Well, you exchange the euros and receive $12,000 in return (10,000 x 1.2).

You made a profit of $700 on your trade.

Of course, the reality is not as simple as that. If it was, then we would have a lot more people striking it rich on the platform and a lot more Ferraris rolling down our neighborhood.

However, that example gives you the gist of what you can expect from a Forex trade.

The Basic Terms of the Forex Market

Now that you are ready to become a trader, you should also learn some of the Forex lingo that you are going to come across.

In other words, time to walk the walk and talk the talk.

Long/Short

When you have a currency pair with you, then you have an important decision to make. Are you going to buy that currency pair or sell it?

If you are aiming to buy the currency pair, then you are hoping that the base currency increases in value so that you can sell it at a profit in the future.

In trading long, this action is commonly referred to as "taking the long position" or "going long". Traders usually shorten it to "long".

When you sell, then what you are doing is that you are selling the base currency in the hopes that it decreases in value at a future date. This way, you can buy it back and make a profit out of it.

Trading lingo refers to this action as "taking a short position" or "going short". In short, it is called "short" (see what we did there?).

The best way to remember the above terms is to know this:

- Buy = long

- Sell = short

Pip? Pipettes? What the Pip Are They?

It is recommended that you take your time to digest the information presented here. This is truly important if you would like to understand what the values of the currencies mean. Even a slight shift in the currencies can affect the trade.

When there is a change in the value between the currency pairs, then that change is expressed as a "pip".

For example, let us take an earlier example and say that 1 euro = 1.1388 U.S. dollars. After a couple of days, you see a change in the value; it has risen to 1.1389. That 0.0001 rise in the value of the currency is called "1 pip".

That is why the pip usually indicates the last decimal in a currency exchange value. Usually, you see currencies expressed to a maximum of four decimal places, but there are exceptions to the rule. One such exception is the Japanese yen, which is shown up to two decimal places.

So if a 1 pip increase in the value of a U.S. dollar is shown as 0.0001, then the same pip value is shown as 0.01 for the Japanese yen.

Still confused? Let's try and use an example.

Let's see what we know so far.

1 euro = 1.1388 U.S. dollars.

However, for the Japanese yen: 1 euro = 122.26 yen.

The currency itself is expressed up to two decimal places. Now if there was a rise in value by one pip, then the new exchange rate would be:

1 euro = 122.27 yen.

Which brings us to pipettes.

On some platforms and for certain brokers, currencies are not represented using the standard 4 and 2 decimal place positions. Rather, they are expressed up to 5 or 3 decimal places.

This means that the EUR/USD will be: 1 euro = 1.13886 U.S. dollars.

Similarly, EUR/JPY (where JPY is the Japanese yen) will be expressed as: 1 euro = 122.278 Japanese yen.

When you use the above format, then an increase in a single value is no longer referred to as a pip. It will become a fraction of a pip or a "pipette".

Thus, an increase in value by 1 pip will be shown as 0.0001 or 0.01, depending on the currency, while an increase in value by 1 pipette is shown as 0.00001 or 0.001, depending on the currency.

So how can you use these terms to express the currencies you are dealing with? It's simple.

Let us take this example:

1 euro = 1.13886 U.S. dollars.

With the above currency, you have (starting from the right at 6 and moving to the left):

- 6 pipettes

- 8 pips

- 80 pips

- 300 pips

- 1,000 pips

- 10,000 pips

Therefore, if the value increases from 1.13886 dollars to 1.13986, then the change in the value is 10 pips.

Now comes the rather complicated part of measuring the value of each pip. How can we do that? Well, we use the below formula:

The change in the value of the quote currency x current exchange rate = value of the pip in the base currency.

Time for another example and this time, let's see something other than EUR/USD. We will use GBP/USD (British pounds and U.S. dollars).

Let us assume that GBP/USD = 1.27299.

We are now going to calculate the value of 1 pip.

What do we know so far?

- 1 pip = 0.0001

- 1 British pound= 1.27299 U.S. dollars

We simply add the information above into the formula. We get:

0.0001 x 1/1.27299 = value of the pip in base currency.

In other words, 1 pip = 0.000127299 USD

Why is it so important to calculate the pip value? Simple, it expresses the shift in the value of your lot size.

Let us imagine that you have purchased 1,000 units of GBP/USD. Then you calculate the shift in lot value by multiplying the pip value by the number of lots you have with you. This is translated as:

1,000 x 0.000127299 = 0.127299 USD.

This means that every time the value of the currency pair changes by 1 pip, the value of your lot size changes by 0.127299 USD. Therefore, if your currency increases by 8 pips, then you have made a profit of 1.018392 USD (8 x 0.127299 USD).

This little calculation helps you keep track of your investment, find out patterns, and strategize for the future more effectively.

The Bid, The Ask, and The Spread

When you are given a quote in Forex, you are provided with two prices: the bid price and the ask price.

Basically, the bid price refers to the amount your broker is willing to pay to purchase the base currency for the quote currency.

The ask price on the other hand simply refers to the price at which your broker will sell the base currency.

Usually, the bid price is lower than the ask price, but that is not always the case.

Now let's look at it with an example.

EUR/USD:

- Selling price = 1.1257

- Buying price = 1.1240

So we know that the bid price is the buying rate of the broker. So guess which of the above two numbers is the bid price?

If you guessed that the "buying price" is the bid price, then you are wrong.

Using the numbers above, you have to understand that the "Selling price" refers to the amount at which *you* are going to sell to the broker (a.k.a. the *buying price* of the broker).

It could get confusing if you did not know about the distinction between the two prices. It is always recommended that you take some time to just look at the selling price and buying price of currencies to figure out the bid and ask price of the brokers. This helps you get comfortable with the numbers to a point where you can easily make connections on your platform and you won't forget what you are supposed to be looking at when someone says "bid price".

Finally, we come to the term "spread". When someone mentions this term, then you are looking at the difference between the bid and the ask price.

Let's take a moment to do a quick recap.

EUR/USD

1.1257/1.1240

Base currency = EUR

Quote currency = USD

Bid price = 1.1257

Ask price = 1.1240

Spread = 17 pips (1.1257 - 1.1240)

Margin

When you are trading in Forex, you are required to set a "Margin". This term refers to the minimum deposit or collateral that you are going to place for your trades.

When you set your margin, you will be able to understand what size loan you can take so that you can access a larger amount of capital.

Leverage

A trader uses the term "leverage" to define how much of the loan he or she can use in order to receive a boost in trading capital. Because you are increasing your capital, you not only increase your profits but even your losses exponentially. This is why most trading platforms will provide you with advice on your margin and leverage. If they don't, then you are on the wrong platform!

Stop-loss Order

Simply put, a stop-loss order is a limit or condition placed the trader to commit to a sell action when the order reaches a certain point or price. You typically give the stop-loss order to your broker and they do the rest. A trader usually develops a stop-loss order when he or she would like to minimize the loss that they incur on a particular trade. This is useful when traders are unable to monitor the progress of the currency for a long time or they have to step away from their platform. It allows them to avoid any unexpected surprises.

Elements That Affect the Forex Market

When you are trading in Forex, then you must be aware of certain factors that affect the market. Being aware of these factors or elements helps you stay ahead of the game and look for the right information to gain an advantage in your trade.

Interest Rates

When there is an increase in the interest rate of a country's currency, then there is an appreciation in the value of the currency. This is because it provides money lenders with higher rates to work with, which in turn attracts more foreign investment. The culmination of this process is an increase in the exchange rate of the currencies.

Inflation

In typical circumstances, when a country consistently has a low rate of inflation, then that is an indication that the country's currency value is rising. The opposite is true for those countries whose inflation rates rise at unexpected levels.

Public Debt

When nations have high debts or public deficits, then they become unattractive in the eyes of foreign investors. When a country has a large debt, then there is a potential for high inflation rates. In many cases, the government has to manage the debts and to do so, they will end up increasing the supply of money. However, this has consequences as increasing money supply results in high inflation. In other words, it shows that the country is unable to manage its deficits by relying on domestic factors. This, in turn, shows instability within the country. Additionally, when countries are in debt for a long time, then investors become apprehensive, thinking that if the country cannot make due on their obligations, then what are the chances for investors to receive their money?

Eventually, their currency value drops and you might notice it in the Forex market.

Trade Terms

Trade is an important indicator of a country's financial situation. If the rate of a country's exports increases much higher than its rate of imports, then it is an indication that there are more favorable terms of trade. Foreign nations are always looking for trade terms that are favorable to them. When this happens, the demand for the exports of the host country increases. This increases revenue, which increases the demand for the currency of that country. Eventually, this demand is reflected in the Forex market in the form of increasing values.

Economic Performance

This is probably one of the more obvious factors that affect the currency in a Forex market. When the economic performance of the country improves, then more and more investors are ready to spend their capital in the country. Other countries who provide higher risks for investors will find that their foreign investments reduce.

Chapter 3: The Foreign Exchange: What Will You Really Trade?

Money, Money, Money: A Brief History

It all started with chaos.

Currency exchange has been in place for a long time now. And by a long time, we are not talking about a couple of hundred years or even a few thousand years. We are referring to the BC period. More specifically, to around 10,000 BC. The only difference was that at that time people used the barter system to exchange goods and services. But this created feelings of dissatisfaction among the traders. How can one gauge the value of objects? Even if they were referring to a specific object, how can they say that the object from one place is better than another? For example, let us assume that you were providing two bags of rice for a fine carpet. (I"m not sure if this was the exchange rate, but let's pretend that it is. Though if you are giving two bags of rice for a carpet, then that carpet better fly!) Now, you know that in your little village or town, carpets are of the finest quality. But does that mean all the carpets around the world have the same quality? Does that mean you are getting a fair return for your two bags of rice? Now imagine this scenario playing out between the countries. How can one set accurate values for each country's "currencies"? How can exchanges take place that are fair and governed by the right rules?

This situation created a system of bias and prejudice. This started to disrupt whatever form of economy was used during those times.

Eventually, the earliest coins were made in parts of what we now refer to as Turkey. Empires and nations around the world began to manufacture their own coins using precious materials like gold and silver.

This controlled the chaos of exchanges that took place between traders because everything had a proper value. If you are going to purchase something, you knew how much you had to pay for it.

Fast forward to the 19th century. More specifically, to the year 1847. Up until now, countries were commonly utilizing gold and silver to make international payments. But that changed with the introduction of the Gold Standard Monetary System. With this system in place, the paper currencies of the countries had a value directly linked to gold. This means that a certain value of money from a country could be converted into a specific amount of gold, depending on that country's currency value.

Over time, this system was dropped in order to give each country a degree of autonomy when managing their affairs. This means that each country is responsible for creating their own currencies without leveraging it against anything. When governments began issuing their own paper currencies that were not attached to a physical commodity like gold or silver, that currency was given the term "fiat money".

Why is this significant? As we had seen, autonomy.

But once again, what does this actually mean?

With the presence of fiat money, the value of the money is dependant on the relationship between the supply and demand of the country along with the stability of the government. Rather than using gold and silver to decide the value of the money, the situation of the country would derive the value of the money.

Enter World War II.

And once again, it started with chaos.

The whole world was experiencing unprecedented levels of chaos. Governments were scrambling to find a solution to stabilize the economies of the world. They turned their eyes to the U.S. dollar.

In order to provide a solution, the Bretton Woods Agreement was established. According to this agreement, the U.S. dollar was set as the exchange rate for gold, giving nations around the world one currency to work with when managing international trades. Other currencies were eventually pegged against the U.S. dollar.

Once again, another solution to control the chaos of exchanges was formed. But did it last? Sadly, no.

History has a strange habit of repeating itself. Because even the Bretton Woods Agreement became obsolete as it became apparent that countries progressed at different speeds. In fact, it was observed that new rules introduced in countries could change trade laws and currency values.

In 1971, the Bretton Woods Agreement was dropped. The world needed a different system of currency valuation.

The U.S. was once again placed in the pilot seat and with the country's guidance, a free-floating market was introduced that would actually determine the *exchange value* of currencies based on the demand and supply in a particular country.

Of course, this innovative way of looking at currencies brought with it a whole new set of problems, the most prominent being the fact that it was not always easy to establish fair exchange rates. Additionally, gathering information about a country and its governmental policies, domestic situations, and trade policies could not be done quickly enough.

Then came the 1990s, a time we should all be thankful for. After all, it was because of the internet boom that we now have access to Facebook, online multiplayer RPGs, Netflix, and YouTube.

One of the greatest achievements of the internet was the availability of information instantly to anyone, anywhere in the world. The foundation provided by the internet allowed people to create new and innovative technologies.

These innovations led to the establishment of various trading platforms.

As we saw earlier, prior to the availability of trading platforms, the Forex market was simply something only certain entities or individuals with high net worth could access. It was never really available to everyone and the thought of joining it probably meant you had to have a million dollars, take a loan, perform an ancient ritual to the god of money, and maybe even sacrifice a few goats.

It was like a realm that everyone wanted to be in but no one had any access to.

But trading platforms changed all that. Because of these platforms, there was a paradigm shift in the way people approached the Forex market.

This brings us to the concept of institutional and retail trading.

Institutional Versus Retail Trading

In the world of trading, there are basically two forms of traders: institutional and retail. The difference between them dictates the way they approach their trades. For example, institutional traders usually make large trades as compared to retail traders. But what are they exactly?

Their names might just give you a clue as to what you can understand about them.

Retail traders refers to individual traders. These traders can be anyone in the world who has the ability to get in on a trade. On the other hand, institutional traders are those who represent large financial institutions, hedge funds, banks, or other big firms that manage money. You could say that institutional traders are "corporate" traders whereas retail traders are "home" traders.

So does the amount invested in the trade dictate the type of trader one becomes? Is that the only point of distinction?

Not quite.

Analysis

A retail trader usually prefers to use some sort of technical analysis system for their trades. They utilize price patterns and behaviors in the past or indicators in the present that dictate future price scenarios. On the other hand, institutional traders do not usually refer to only technical patterns or systems to show them opportunities in their trade.

Focus

As institutional traders have been dealing with the system for a long time, their experience has led them to hone their skills well. They make use of market sentiments and fundamentals. They make use of trading psychology (which is a firm grasp on their emotions and keeping an analytical mind despite the situation) and understanding of overall responses towards a currency. They are keeping a close eye on the news to see if there are certain trends or reactions that they can pick up on.

Retail traders are not experienced in managing risks or having a proper psychological mind for trading. However, this is a situation that happens to everyone who gets started in Forex trading. No one can be prepared for what they will experience. They have to experience it first before they can decide how to keep their minds sharp.

Leverage

Institutional traders do not usually use leverage. Their main attention is spent on risk management. Even if a situation were to occur where they had to make use of leverages, they would be careful about how much leverage they are going to use.

On the other hand, retail traders make the mistake of looking for brokers that provide them with high leverages. While that act in itself is not wrong, it does pose a problem to those retailers who choose their brokers solely on the criteria of how much leverage those brokers provide them.

Now that we have understood more about the Forex market and its players, it is time we look at the most essential component of the market, currencies. More importantly, we are going to look at some of the major players in the Forex market.

Popular Currencies

U.S. Dollar

The U.S. dollar is combined with numerous currencies to either form the base or quote currency. Some of the combinations involve:

- USD/JPY (Japanese yen)

- USD/CAD (Canadian dollar)

- USD/CHF (Swiss franc)

- EUR/USD (Euro, but you already knew that with the number of times we have used this in our examples. It wouldn't be surprising if this will be the first pair your trade in.)

- GBP/USD (British pound)

- AUD/USD (Australian dollar)

- NZD/USD (New Zealand dollar)

The U.S. dollar becomes the base currency when used in exotic pairs (and by exotic, we are referring to the fact that these combinations are not very common on the trading platform). These currencies include the below:

- SEK (Swedish krona)

- SGD (Singapore dollar)

- NOK (Norwegian krone)

- DKK (Danish krone)

- MXN (Mexican peso)

- BRL (Brazilian real)

- ZAR (South African rand)

The U.S. dollar is also considered the standard currency unit that is used in many of the commodity markets around the world (especially in the crude oil and gold markets). Currently, it also takes the important position of being the most employed reserve currency in the world. These features of the U.S. dollar allows it to have trade deficits with many countries in the world without facing the problem of depreciation.

Because the economy of the US has a strong influence on the rest of the world the volatility of the currency ranges from low to medium. Because of its market orientation, many corporations and business lead their decision-making processes using the US dollar.

Euro

The Euro becomes the base or quote currency when included in the below pairs:

- EUR/GBP

- EUR/AUD

- EUR/USD

- EUR/NZD

- EUR/CHF

- EUR/CAD

- EUR/JPY

It solely becomes the base currency when you pair it with the following currencies:

- SEK

- NOK

- CNY (Chinese yuan)

- DKK

- MXN

- BRL

- ZAR

- SGD

After the Euro was formed in the year 1999 and then officially implemented in 2002, it quickly became fairly commonly used in most of the countries of the European Union (EU).

One of the main reasons for bringing about the implementation of the euro was to make sure that there was easy free trade between the member countries of the Eurozone. It was also set up to boost public relations and political integration.

The currency pair EUR/USD is commonly referred to as "fiber". This is because the Eurozone includes the greatest fiber optic network in the world.

The Central banks of the member countries of the EU along with the European Central Bank (ECB) form policies and rules to manage the currency. The euro is managed through the European System of Central Banks (ESCB).

The power to make monetary policies concerning the euro lies with the ECB only. However, other members of the ESCB also have the ability to issue and then distribute the coins and notes of the currency. Because the euro has been adopted by numerous countries, the Eurozone has been able to become one of the largest economies in the world. For this reason, the euro is a stronger currency than the U.S. dollar.

Australian Dollar

The Australian dollar becomes the base or quote currency in the following pairs:

- AUD/CAD

- GBP/AUD

- EUR/AUD

- AUD/CHF

- AUD/JPY

- AUD/NZD

- AUD/USD

It becomes the base currency along with a few exotic currencies. However, it is not as popular with other currencies as the U.S. dollar and euro.

In the world of trading, the Australian dollar or AUD is also known as "Aussie". This nickname is also used when it is paired with the U.S. dollar in AUD/USD. In the Forex market, it is the 6th most traded currency and also amounts to nearly 5% of the foreign exchange transactions conducted around the world.

One of the reasons why the currency is so popular is the fact that the intervention from the Australian government in the Forex market is practically nonexistent. Add to that the fact there is usually stability in the politics and economics of Australia, and you have a currency with low volatility.

Canadian Dollar

The Canadian dollar becomes the base or quote currency in the following pairs:

- GBP/CAD

- EUR/CAD

- AUD/CAD

- NZD/CAD

- CAD/JPY

- USD/CAD

- CAD/CHF

The Canadian dollar, or CAD, is also commonly referred to as "loonie". The nickname is also used when it forms a pair with the U.S. dollar to create the USD/CAD. The use of the nickname is due to the fact that there is an image of a loon (which is a form of aquatic bird) on the face of the currency note.

One of the notable features of the Canadian economy is how similar it is to the United States in many ways. For example, it is mostly production - and market - oriented. It has also evolved a lot since World War II, mainly focusing on being industrial. It also pays heavy attention to its mining, manufacturing, and service sectors.

British Pound

The British pound sterling, or the GBP, forms the base or quote currency in the following pairs:

- GBP/CAD

- GBP/AUD

- GBP/NZD

- EUR/GBP

- GBP/CHF

- GBP/USD

- GBP/JPY

It also becomes the base currency with few of the other exotic currencies in the world such as the ones below:

- BRL

- DKK

- CNY

- MXN

- ZAR

- SGD

- SEK

- NOK

The GBP is one of the most widely traded currencies in the world, along with the U.S. dollar, the euro, and the Japanese yen. Of the major currencies in the world, the GBP has the highest value. When paired with the U.S. dollar to form the GBP/USD, the pair is given the nickname "cable". This is mainly due to the fact that, at one point, the rates of the currency pair were transmitted using the trans-Atlantic cable.

Japanese Yen

The Japanese yen, or the JPY, forms the base or quote currency in the following pairs:

- NZD/JPY

- AUD/JPY

- EUR/JPY

- USD/JPY

- CAD/JPY

- CHF/JPY

- GBP/JPY

The Japanese yen was originally pegged to the U.S. dollar at the end of World War II, but that was changed in the year 1971. The Japanese economy mainly revolves around the manufacturing industry. Initially, the currency of Japan had been weak because it was mainly circulated within its borders. This restriction in its currency prevented it from attaining a favorable position in foreign trade. Eventually, the rise in industrial production and the increase in foreign investments in other countries have given it an edge.

Swiss Franc

The Swiss franc, or CHF, forms the base or quote currency in the following pairs:

- NZD/CHF
- AUD/CHF
- CAD/CHF

- GBP/CHF

- EUR/CHF

- CHF/JPY

- USD/CHF

The first thing that people notice about the Swiss franc is the initials of the currency. CHF is used to denote the currency because it stands for "Confederatio Helvetica Franc". Although the currency does not have a nickname when it stands on its own, it does have a nickname when in pair with the U.S. dollar. The USD/CHF pair is commonly referred to as the "Swissie".

One of the most attractive features of the Swiss franc is that it is a rather stable currency. This is because of Switzerland's political and economic stability. Additionally, the currency is mostly used as a form of reserve currency by numerous financial institutions and individuals who are highly wealthy.

New Zealand Dollar

The New Zealand dollar, or the NZD, forms the base or quote currency in the following pairs:

- NZD/CAD

- NZD/CHF

- EUR/NZD

- GBP/NZD

- NZD/JPY

- NZD/USD

Informally, the currency is also referred to as "kiwi" by traders because of the fact that a picture of a kiwi appears on the $1 coin. Additionally, traders also use the nickname to refer to the NZD/USD pair. Typically, the New Zealand dollar's validity hovers in the low to medium levels.

New Zealand and Australia share the same change in direction for their economy. Initially, the country was dependent on its agriculture market which was limited to British concessionaires. It then shifted its focus to becoming a free and industrialized market whose presence is felt all over the globe and is even going toe-to-toe with some of the big economies. One of the things that set New Zealand apart is that despite the improvements in technology, the country still has a large percentage of agricultural exports.

With all the focus on the market, trade, and currencies, there is still another vital cog in this machine, you. That is why, in the next chapter, we are going to focus on helping you think like a winner.

Chapter 4 - The Mindset of a Winner: What They Do and How They Do It

By now, you are slowly getting a picture of the complex world of Forex trading. You have probably understood that there is more to it than just putting all your money in one place and returning to it at a later time, hoping that your money has doubled or maybe quadrupled in size.

Here is the truth: what you have read is just the tip of the iceberg. There is a lot more ground to cover.

Which is why, before going any further, it is important to cover one vital component in all of this.

You.

You Are Not Other Forex Traders

Remember how we compared institutional traders and retail traders? When you look at the traits that retail traders carry with themselves, you might realize that those are probably the ways new traders, or "newbies", would work.

You might be doing the same.

And that is completely alright. You need to get a feel for the system. You might figure out a few things on your own, while others might require some prompts and assistance from other sources. But there are certain characteristics of other traders that are best not adopted. Let us look at a few of them.

The Blame Game

One of the things that a lot of beginner traders do is blame the market for any unfortunate circumstances. It takes a lot to admit that you have made a mistake. Because you see, the market is just numbers. It was not designed to predict your mind and make sure you fail. It's not a Jedi.

Take a lesson from the workings of institutional traders. They always analyze the market. When things do not go their way, they start figuring out the solution to the problem. That should be your focus as well.

Track Record

One of the important things to note is that, as much as money is the end game, it should not always be the intent of your trading. It is equally important to maintain a good track record. You cannot hope to continue to trade when you are afraid of losing what money you have. Forex involves great risks and you need the necessary capital for it. In the case of institutional traders, they have the right financial backing, so they can shrug off a loss and move on to the next plan.

But how can you gain capital without taking a loan or leveraging your account?

Easy, you keep a healthy track record. You will soon be able to accumulate capital for bigger trades.

Risk Within Your Limits

When you are managing your risk, one of the important questions that you will be asking yourself is, just how much capital can I risk for each trade?

Ideally, you should not risk more than 1% of your capital on a single trade. This serves two purposes:

- If you encounter a loss it won't put a huge dent in your capital.

- You will be able to learn valuable lessons from the trade and have enough capital to try new strategies on different trades.

News is Facts, Not Prediction

It is tempting to feel that you can make a prediction and profit from it based on what news information you have. But the reality of the situation is different.

In the wake of economic releases, you might find that currency values can either rise or fall. At that moment, it becomes tempting to anticipate the direction the pair will move and trade accordingly. Seems like a sure way to nab an easy quarter of a million dollars.

But that is a big mistake. The news is simply providing you with the latest information. Do not anticipate what direction the news will take the market. Rather, create a strategy that you can use to trade after the news comes out.

No Plan. No Trade.

You need to make sure that you have a trading plan prepared for yourself. Essentially, this is a document that you have written or created that gives a direction for your strategy. It lets you know what, how, and when you day trade in the Forex market.

When you create this plan, make sure it includes suggestions for the type of currencies you should trade, what time you will conduct your trade, and what time of the day you have allotted for analyzing your trades or for conducting research.

Additionally, you should also cover all the rules you have for risk management. You should be able to tell how you are able to enter and exit the trades.

When You Are Starting, Forget Fundamental Analysis

Despite what many people might think, do not focus on economic or fundamental analysis. You are starting out. Your first priority is to get used to the lay of the land.

In many cases, traders get caught up in the news. This compels them to form certain biases about trades, especially when they watch or read information that claims that the economic situation of a country is good or bad.

Remember this: when you are day trading, forget the long-term repercussions and outlook. Your mission, should you choose to accept (and you probably should), is to focus on implementing your strategy effectively. This message will not self-destruct in 5 seconds (we still have a lot of topics to cover).

This does not mean that fundamental analysis is not preferable. In fact, quite the opposite: fundamental analysis plays an extremely vital role in trading. But you need to first begin by gaining a sense of mastery over one form of analysis.

In the short-run, good investments can go bad and bad investments can turn around. When you have long-term biases, you tend to move away from your trading strategy and simply shifting to a new strategy is like nosediving into loss territory without a parachute.

Emotional Wreck

If you cannot keep your emotions in check, then you are on a path to destroy everything you have built during your trades. Successful traders understand how to manage their frustrations and their temper, knowing full well that any hasty decision taken in the "heat of the moment" is only going to create further problems.

There are many ways you can keep your emotions in check. However, today we shall try and examine this from another perspective.

We are going to learn how to build your confidence and in turn, explain how you can manage your emotions.

Step 1: Be Disciplined

Remember that we just talked about all the things that other traders often do that you should probably not be doing.

One of the things that is common among traders is the lack of discipline. Most traders are not brilliant. They are not the people in the movies who can perform quick calculations in their mind as though they have a Mac operating system installed in their brain.

In real life, the most successful traders are those who have discipline. Take bank traders for example.

In banks, traders usually work under a risk manager. It is the job of the risk manager to make sure that the bank traders know the boundaries within which they should operate.

These bank traders follow one fundamental rule: they are not allowed to take on more risks than they are granted. Each trader is given a specific number or amount. All risks must be below the number specified. The risk manager is present to oversee the risks taken by the traders. If a trader exceeds the amount mentioned, then he or she is given a single warning. If the trader repeats the error again, he or she is fired.

Here is a surprising fact: even traders who bring in millions of dollars to the bank are shown the door if they mess with this rule.

We do not have risk managers in our lives (unless you can afford one). But we do have risk management capabilities.

Step 2: Change Your Beliefs

Your belief system is what establishes, to an extent, your mental fitness. These beliefs tune your attention toward a specific idea and change your attitude towards the things that surround you. They help you figure out how to deal with life's many components.

But most importantly, they help you form your emotions.

You can agree or disagree with a certain idea or point of view. You determine if something is right or wrong based on your beliefs. But here is a question that needs to be asked: how many of these beliefs are helping you see the bigger picture or, even more importantly, the right picture?

Psychology has identified a tendency in human beings called confirmation bias.

According to this bias, people generally look for ideas and facts that confirm their viewpoints and ignore everything else that opposes them. In other words, they seek out facts to confirm what they already believe, even though the same people claim to be objective. In fact, if you go ahead and check your browser history, you might find some traces of confirmation bias. In many cases, even though we look for contradictory ideas, we generally find more information that supports our theories, suppositions, and viewpoints than opposing ideas.

Having confirmation bias is harmless when it comes to supporting your favorite music genre or explaining which Teenage Mutant Ninja Turtle is the best (Donatello for the win, by the way).

But when it comes to Forex, having confirmation bias is not just folly, it's perilous.

When you have flexible beliefs, you will approach a situation with an analytical mind. You will see every mistake as a learning experience and losing trades as lessons. Instead of feeling disappointed, angry, or frustrated, you will be focused on getting better.

Step 3: Evaluate Your Mistakes

But you should not stop simply at your beliefs. Once you have entered into the right frame of mind, it is time to focus it in the right direction.

Examine the situation that led to the loss. Identify what mistake was made. Consult with your broker and other traders if you have to.

You should be able to understand what happened, what conditions led to the loss, why you did or did not take a particular action. Were you following your strategy? Did you break any of the rules you have established for your plan?

If you made a successful trade, then you should look for the steps that led to that success. When you examine both your successes and failures, you will be able to make connections that teach you how to proceed further in Forex.

Step 4: Write Down the Consequences

Your mistakes have consequences and you need to be aware of them. Make a list of the consequences, both bad and good. This helps remind you what steps you should not be taking in future trades and why.

Step 5: Create an Action Plan

At this point, you are ready to create a different approach to your trading. Remember this: every mistake is an opportunity to create a trading success. The more mistakes you make, the more clearly defined your next course of action will be until all you have is a path that helps you get to your next success.

If you realize that the mistake comes from your strategy, then redefine and refine the strategy. Work on it until you are able to employ it without committing any errors.

Step 6: Master Your Stress and Confusion

Just google stress management and you will be bombarded with a horde of self-help books, systems, stress management gurus, and indicators. Eventually, you have traders equipping themselves with multi-screen monitors, fast computers, the latest software, and abundant data. And does that help them?

Nope.

It's like someone with no knowledge of tech found the Iron Man suit of armor and is now tasked with going mano-a-mano against Thanos.

Exactly. Time to count your prayers because you are going to get snapped into oblivion.

It is not about what equipment you have. That hardly matters when you haven't even reached the root cause of what might be compelling you to make mistakes: your own stress and confusion.

In fact, have you ever gone on YouTube and seen those ads where this guy pops up claiming that he can get you earning millions in just a short time using a secret technique that has a fancy name? None of those work. Think about it, if people really knew the secret to earning millions (or if anyone did), would they actually go on sharing it to get *more* money? In fact, would they actually have a subscription model or high product prices?

This is what happens to people who are under a lot of stress or who get confused; they begin to look for alternatives and fall prey to any advertising.

What you should be doing is studying your own techniques and strategies. If you feel like things are getting overwhelming, do not go ahead and make another trade. Take a short break until you can figure out what is causing your stress and disappointment.

Was it a loss that you did not expect? Then focus on what caused that loss.

What is a sudden shift in the market? Find out how and why that shift happened. Discover methods to predict that shift in the future.

Incorrect news and information? Change the channel!

Commonly Used Platforms for Day Trading

To have the right trade, you need to have the right tools. These usually come in the form of the trading platform you utilize for your trades. We have compiled a few that are not just popular but recommended by many traders around the world.

TD Ameritrade

One of the most attractive features of this platform is the ability to stream news, giving you more power over the information you would like to receive. The platform also provides you with numerous educational materials made to help you get started on the trading platform. You can use its "Social Signals" feature, which extracts information about your trades from Twitter. These tweets could be from other experienced traders or industry experts as well.

Fidelity Investments

Fidelity is known to have one of the best trade-routing systems, which helps provide their customers with lower trade costs when compared to most platforms.

The platform has technology integrated into its operation to make sure that there is a visible improvement on orders placed by customers. This gives the customers on the platform the ability to make a "Buy" trade at a considerably lower price than shown in the market. Additionally, it also allows traders to commit to a "Sell" option at a slightly higher price.

The whole platform is easy to navigate and might we also add, rather aesthetically pleasing.

You even have educational materials and features, such as tax planning, to help you with your trades. You can examine your financial health by connecting to outside accounts on other platforms.

IG

IG has been setting up to become one of the most trusted and regulated platforms for trading around the globe. You are able to make use of their real-time exchange data to power up your research and trading. IG is also used to publicly trade in many of the countries around the world. Because of this global presence, there are proper jurisdictions and regulations that they adhere to. As their platform keeps on improving, IG manages to add in more features to ensure that traders have commission-based spreads in the Forex market.

CMC Markets

Founded in 1989, CMC Markets is a popular trading platform in the UK that is now making its presence known around the world. It is also listed in the London Stock Exchange, which means it provides you with a layer of transparency. When using the platform, you might as well be spoilt for choice as it offers you 300+ currency pairs to choose from.

You will also find out comprehensive spreads that offer you different bet sizes and trade options to work with. This allows you to fine-tune your strategy to match their offerings.

FOREX.com

This platform was founded more recently than others, in the year 2001. But it has quickly risen up the ranks to become a trusted platform among traders. It is designed to meet the requirements of both new and seasoned traders.

The pricing is transparent, allowing you to choose the option that fits your capital availability. You also get to work with different kinds of accounts and each account gives you a unique benefit. In one account, traders pay the spread for every trade that they make while in another, traders are charged a small commission, but the spreads are smaller. Each account has its own benefits and spread types. However, one of the things that you should be cautious about when using the platform is that there are high levels of risk involved. Sure, you do get bigger rewards for it, but you have to have a proper strategy in place to work on the platform.

City Index

The platform is regulated according to the rules established by the European Securities and Markets Authority (ESMA). This allows the platform to provide you with features such as leverage limit, where you cannot simply apply for any amount of leverage, and negative protection, where you do not lose more money than you place into the platform. You can also apply for stop-loss protection, but you have to shell out a premium amount for the feature. Ideal for beginners, City Index provides you an opportunity to test out your strategies.

XTB

XTB is almost like a one-stop platform to cater to a wide variety of investment needs. You can enter into markets such as shares, indices, forex, metals, and even cryptocurrencies. It also follows certain regulations as it is registered with the Financial Conduct Authority (FCA). You get to use the xStation 5, the primary interface of the XTB, which is easy to use and provides all the pertinent information through charts, watchlists, menus, and notifications. The layout is friendly for new users and provides enough information to attract seasoned traders.

With your chosen platform ready, let us get down to one of the most important steps in Forex trading: determining your position size.

Determining a Position Size and the Importance of Using a Formula

Most traders are of the opinion that you need to pay attention to your entry and exit as they are the most important factors. That is not entirely true.

Determining your position is more important.

You may have created the best strategy in the world. In fact, you might be a math genius whose mind works like Sherlock Holmes, but if you do not know your position size, then all those math tricks won't help you. That's because if you know your position size, then you will be able to gauge how much risk you are about to take.

We have already seen how you can choose between different options for your position size, which are indicated by lots. You have your standard, mini, and micro lots, each one provided you with specific units of a currency (with standard giving you 100,000 units, mini giving 10,000 units, and micro 1,000 units).

When you are looking at the risk, they are further divided into two forms: account risk and trade risk.

Let us see how all of these factors fit into the entire idea of picking the ideal position.

Step 1: Establish Your Account Risk

Before you can even determine your position size, make sure that you have a clear rule for your account risk. You need to set a percentage of your capital as the risk limit. Professional traders often stick by the 1% rule where they only risk 1% of their account for a trade.

Let us assume that you have around $5,000 in your account. If you use the 1% risk rule, then you are only going to risk about $50 per trade. If you like, you can even go lower and perhaps only choose 0.75% as a risk rule, but as long as you do not exceed 1%, you should be fine.

However, the 1% rule is not one set in stone. You can even choose to have a 3% risk rule or a 5% risk rule. One of the most important things to remember is that you do not change your rules between trades or it might become difficult to keep track of your risks.

Step 2: Find Out Your Pip Risk

Your next step is to focus on the trade itself.

You need to establish your stop-loss point and your entry location. Ideally, your stop-loss point should be close to your entry point. But make sure that you do not place it too close or else your trade might stop even when a small loss occurs. In the long run, a small degree of loss is always part of the trade. Let them happen.

To calculate the pip risk, you simply have to take the difference between the entry point and the stop-loss point.

When you have established the distance between your entry point and the stop-loss point, then you can choose the ideal position size for your trade.

Step 3: Get Ready to Determine Your Position Size

Now you can finally determine your position size. To do so, you have to utilize the below formula:

Pip Risk Value x Pip Value x Number of Lots in Trade = Amount Placed For Risk

Here is all the information that we already know:

- We know the amount placed for risk, because that depends on the risk value we have set for ourselves, whether that is 1% or 3% of the capital (refer to Step 1).

- We also know the Pip Risk Value which we calculated using Step 2.

- Finally, we know the pip value which we can find out by simply referring to the currency pair itself.

When you put in the numbers, you finally get your Lots in Trade, which is your position size.

Time for an example.

Let us take the earlier example where you have $5,000 in your account. You have decided to use a risk percentage of 1%. This means that for each trade, you are going to risk just $50. What can you do with this amount? You can get a mini lot.

Each lot has a fixed amount for pips, or the pip value. You can find this out on your trading platform itself or your broker will be able to supply you with the information.

Now, you decide that you are going to trade with EUR/USD which is selling at 1.1366 (bid price) and buying at 1.1370 (sell price). Let us assume that you have placed your stop-loss point at 1.1360, which means your pip risk is now set at 10 pips (1.1370 - 1.1360).

You now have all the information required to fill in the formula. Simply substitute the numbers and you will be able to find your position size.

Chapter 5 - How to Tackle Trading: So Many Approaches You Can Choose From!

The First Option: Technical Analysis

When you are using technical analysis, you are making use of volume and price data to make a speculation about future movements. The fundamental idea of technical analysis was established by Charles H. Dow, who based his techniques on the behavioral patterns of investors, movement or prices, and on psychology. If you choose the movement of prices as your criteria for making an analysis, then that becomes a technical analysis.

When you look at charts that do not feature anything more than the price movements of a specific currency, you will notice that the market moves during trends. Which means that all the information you require for conducting technical analysis is available within the charts of a currency.

We have already seen how we can gain whether we are in a bull market or a bear market. But in order to make the gain, you need to understand the trend lines and make informed speculations.

Technical analysis makes use of patterns and indicators. Patterns are certain forms that are repeated over time while indicators are mathematical functions that are used on the range of prices available in a chart.

One of the important components of a technical analysis is the support and resistance levels. When levels break downward, then they are referred to as support and when they break upwards, then they are referred to as resistance.

Price Action

Price action occurs because of the flow of orders, which in turn comes from the buyers and sellers in a market. Price action will reveal to you how fast operations are taking place in the market, where trades are buying and selling (and what currency they are focused on), and also any specific bias in the market (if any exist). Price action relies on finding patterns.

Patterns are recognized on charts by drawing geometric shapes around certain areas to indicate a pattern. These shapes are not drawn by the platform. Rather, you might find yourself applying a circle here, a triangle there, or a semicircle on another spot to see if there is any underlying meaning in the chart data.

Pattern recognition is not easy. You have to be used to the platform you are using until you can start recognizing patterns or trends.

Another point to remember is that technical analysis is rather subjective. John and Mary may be looking at the same chart, but that does not mean that John and Mary will come to the same conclusion. Who are John and Mary? We don't know. Just pretend they are two traders who are not as smart as you (because you have this book after all).

Advance and Retreat

When you are looking at a chart, you will notice two types of moves: impulsive and corrective.

An impulsive move happens when there is a sharp movement in the direction of a particular trend.

On the other hand, a corrective move happens when the movement occurs in the opposite direction.

When there is an impulsive move, then it usually indicates the fact that there has been an influx of large amounts of capital into the market. This causes sellers and buyers to arrive at a particular level and have a specific direction in mind. It could also be caused by a cascade in the price, occurring due to a large number of stop-losses that are still pending. Impulsive moves have the most consistency because the flow of order is tuned towards one direction (and a rather predictable one at that). If you can identify impulsive moves, then you will be able to gain some incredible trading opportunities (translation: money money!).

On the other hand, you have corrective moves. These could happen because of two situations:

- Profits have been taken after the occurrence of an impulsive move.

- A mixed number of buyers and sellers are present at a certain level and that level has the potential to become a reversal point.

When a corrective move occurs, then there are usually not many opportunities to conduct a good trade.

When you understand the duration it takes from one move to another, then you might receive an idea of just how long you might have to wait for the next continuous move.

What are the different trends that you can derive from a technical analysis? Let us focus on some.

Trend Indicators

Moving Averages

Moving Averages is a type of indicator that shows you the average value of a currency pair over a specific period of time. Moving Averages, or MA for short, are best used for identifying momentum and seeking out areas of potential resistance and support. Traders also use MA for checking the direction a particular trend is taking.

When using Moving Averages, you can make use of several variations.

Simple Moving Average (SMA): You calculate this MA by adding the closing price of a particular trade or currency across a number of time periods and then divide that by the number of time periods.

Exponential Moving Average (EMA): There is no significant difference between SMA and EMA, except that EMA gives more weight to the latest data and information.

Limited Weighted Moving Average (LWMA): The LWMA also gives priority to the latest data.

However, the way to use it is completely different than EMA. The price of a particular period of time is multiplied by the position that price takes in the series of data. All the results are added and the final number is divided by the number of time periods.

Bollinger Bands

These indicators were developed by John Bollinger and they allow traders to compare the relative price levels and the volatility over a particular time period. The name of the indicator is actually apt: it includes three bands that focus on the price trends of a given currency pair.

Bollinger bands are useful for traders in identifying periods of extremely low and high volatility. They are able to provide insights into the fact that prices can reach such extremes that they cannot be sustained, eventually allowing the trader to decide if he or she would like to cut losses or use another strategy in place.

Commodity Channel Index (CCI)

This indicator was developed by Donald Lambert and plays a particularly important role in determining whether a currency has been oversold or overbought. Traders have also used the CCI to figure out the troughs and peaks in the prices of currencies and to find out what possible changes can occur in the trend line.

The Second Option: Fundamental Analysis

Economic Release

To understand fundamental analysis, it is better to start with an economic release. Basically, this release is an official report released by the central banks to the press. Other parties involved in the creation of this report includes governments, the Federal Reserve, large financial institutions, and analytical and research departments who are responsible for working with economic data. These releases are always made available to the public. And this becomes useful for Forex traders.

When traders work their trade based on the news, they need to have reliable information to make quick judgments. These traders are very attentive to the economic release, absorbing the information like a sponge. Some of the main components of the economic release that concern the traders are gross domestic product (GDP), balance of payments, sentiment and confidence reports, prices, leading indicators, spending figures, employment, housing, and monetary policies.

Entering Fundamental Analysis

We are now ready to explore fundamental analysis more. The reason we talked about the economic release is that one of the main sources of data for fundamental analysis is the information provided by the release. But additionally, fundamental analysis also includes political data as sometimes politics can influence the economic regulations and advancements of a country. In fact, the politics of the country can indicate the confidence various factions have with the government of the country and this, in turn, can reveal the status of factors such as foreign investments.

Fundamental analysis also includes the review of macroeconomic indicators and the stock market as well.

When working with fundamental analysis, the existing inflation rate, foreign currency, and monetary mass all come into play. For this reason, governments have increased the frequency of the releases so that traders are able to compare them easily with previous reports. This makes it easier to generate forecasts about the direction the currency is taking and how it could evolve in the near future.

Traders typically start with the primary analysis of data and several factors are important for this analysis:

Economic growth: Traders usually discover this by using the quarterly published figure of the country's GDP. When traders notice that the GDP of a country is rising, then that typically signifies a shift in the capital. This shift occurs because there has been a rise in the savings and consumption in the country. Traders value the consumption increase and make their trades accordingly, having positive sentiments about the currency. However, an excess of growth is not a good indicator. This is because there are chances that the country could eventually deal with inflation tensions and force the Central Banks to change their interest rates.

Inflation: Typically, when currencies have high-interest rates they are considered favorable because of the fact that they can contain inflation rates and of course, the chance to attain high profits. Which is why, when looking at inflation, traders will also look at the Central Bank's changes.

Unemployment: The rate of unemployment is sometimes difficult to measure accurately, but it is nonetheless a very important component and indicator for traders. The main reason for this is that it determines the consumption and income levels for families. If the unemployment rates rise, then the currency of the country falls so hard that it might just punch a hole through the financial basement. When the unemployment rates drop, it helps elevate the currency's value.

Trade Balance: A currency quote can attain an equilibrium, which happens when there is stability in the balance of payments. If the country has a trade deficit, then it suffers due to a drop in the currency reserves, which eventually causes a drop in the value of the currency as well.

Stock market: Inflation, growth, and even unemployment are just some of the factors that are involved in finding out the value of the currency. Every single day, the evolution of a currency has a big impact on the assets markets, in particular, stocks. When investors have positive sentiments about a country, then they increase investments into that country, which in turn propels the stocks and assets to new heights. With the arrival of different currencies into the market, the value of the currency of the home country will become strong.

The Third Option: Market Analysis

When you are performing market analysis, you are taking into consideration a lot of factors.

Let us look at a few of them.

Gross National Product (GNP)

The GNP is an indicator of the performance of the global economy. However, when used on a macroeconomic scale, then it is the total of the investments, consumptions, the net volume of transactions, and government spending. In the U.S., the GNP refers to the total of the goods and services provided by the residents of the country, either within its borders or in international territories. When the GNP increases, it improves the situation of the currency.

Gross Domestic Product (GDP)

The total number of goods and services produced by companies in the United States, whether they are domestic companies or foreign entities is indicated by the GDP. Within the U.S., there is little difference between the GDP and the GNP. However, in countries outside the United States, GDP figures are more popular. For this reason, the U.S. release data in both GNP and GDP. When it comes to the currency, the higher the GDP, the better it is for the currency.

Consumption Spending

While the fact is that the spending habits of consumers are purely psychological, it is still a powerful indicator of the economy. Consumer spending habits indicate the confidence they have with the country. Consumer confidence is also calculated as a method to explain why they have a tendency to replace their saving habits with spending habits. When the consumer's spending index increases, the consumer's confidence increases, and that eventually leads to a rise in the value of the currency.

Investment Spending

The gross domestic spending or investment spending consists of inventories and fixed investments. When investment spending increases, it improves the economy, which eventually causes improvements in the value of the currency.

Government Spending

When the government spends, it spends! The sizeable amount of money that the government works with impacts various other factors. Let us take an example to highlight this point. Before 1990, the military expense of the United States had a significant role in the employment rate of the country. The higher the government spending, the better it is for the currency.

Net Trade

Another important factor of the GNP is the net trade volume. After the rise in globalization in the 90s, the United States received a great boost in its ability to compete abroad. However, GNP did not catch on in other countries of the world. So while it does play an important role in the economy of the United States, for all intents and purposes, the GDP is presented to the world. And an increase in the net trade figure always shows an increase in the value of the currency.

Industrial Production

When countries shift away from agriculture to industry, this factor becomes an important indicator of the economy. Industrialization also allows the country to grow, improving its technology and adding more employment opportunities. For this reason, Forex traders often use this indicator as a signal for commencing trading. The higher the industrial production, the better the economy.

Capacity Utilization

This term refers to the highest output of production that industries and factories are capable of under normal working conditions and operations. Typically, capacity utilization is not an important indicator in the Forex market. It's just that there are certain conditions where it might provide information to traders. For a stable economy, the normal capacity utilization is around 81.5%. If the number exceeds the 81% mark, then it is an indication that the industry is about to reach a boiling point and is close to hitting its maximum capacity.

When capacity is maxed out, then the traders in the markets are looking for signs of inflation. This is why, the higher the capacity utilization of a country is, the higher the value of its currency.

However, if it becomes too high, then caution is the name of the game.

Factory Orders

This indicator reveals the total number of orders made by factories for the manufacturing process. Typically, Forex traders do not use this indicator. However, when there is a sharp rise in factory orders, then it usually means that there is going to be a boost in the production of goods and services in the economy, which is typically a good sign. High factory orders are always good for the economy and therefore, improve the value of the currency.

Construction Data

When it comes to the U.S. GDP, construction data is often included and if you look at history, then you might notice that it was housing that pulled the United States out of the recession that happened after World War II.

Why is construction data important? Well, the main reason is that this data is linked to the interest-rate levels and the income level of the people. In the United States, the data is represented by the number of home units. The higher the home unit figures are (referred to people actually occupying units, else these units simply become houses), the better the indication of the economy.

Producer Price Index (PPI)

When the U.S. compiles data for the PPI, then it includes numbers from various sectors such as agriculture, mining, and manufacturing. This is why, the higher the number of the PPI, the better it is for the currency.

Consumer Price Index (CPI)

This indicator reveals the change in prices of the goods and services produced in an economy. But we are not talking about any goods and services. We are referring to those elements that are considered vital for the basic needs and requirements of the people. This includes food, internet, transportation, and others.

Fourth Option: Intermarket Analysis

In an intermarket analysis, the traders focus on more than just one single asset or market to figure out the strengths and weaknesses of the markets. What this means is that, instead of analyzing markets individually, this form of analysis looks at the correlations between four of the major markets: currencies, commodities, bonds, and stocks. So instead of looking at, say the bonds, we also take a look at the commodities market along with it to find any connecting trends that we can use for our trades. But there is no point in looking at these markets without understanding how they influence the country's market.

How Does Intermarket Analysis Work?

To perform an intermarket analysis, we are going to require a few tools of the trade, which include a convenient charting program along with detailed and widely available data.

When you start correlating, then you can give the whole results certain scores. When you discover a positive correlation, then your score can go as high as 1.0. On the other hand, a negative correlation can bring down the score to as low as -1.0. If the score hovers around zero, then it means that there aren't a lot of correlations for you to uncover.

The intermarket analysis depends on the forces of inflation and deflation. During a normal inflationary situation, bond and stocks are positively correlated. In other words, they both move in the same direction. What happens when they move in different directions? In that case, they are known to move in inverse directions, where one factor goes up while the other goes down. This is also termed as a deflationary movement. If they have a more positive direction, then you are going to give them a positive score if they have an inverse direction, they receive a negative score. The scoring process is something that is done by traders solely for the purpose of getting a better understanding of the market.

Chapter 6 - Your New Journey's First Steps - How to Start and What to Do

Fundamentals of Trading

Many brokers provide you with numerous options when it comes to trading accounts. In many of these accounts, you might find a demo account which will allow you to familiarize yourself with that broker's particular features and platform presentation. This means that you can use the demo account to get comfortable working with your broker.

The demo account not only allows you to work with your broker's platform, but also exercise your strategies within a safe environment without the worry of losing any of your funds.

When you practice using a demo account, you begin to build up confidence. More confidence means less emotions. Less emotions means you have laser-like focus.

Once you have perfected your strategy using the demo account, then you have to implement it in your actual trade. Too often, you find traders who end up using a completely different strategy once they begin trading with actual money. They end up losing big time, wondering where they went wrong and unwilling to admit that they had simply not followed the rules that they established for themselves.

This is why, when you are practicing in your demo account, you are creating a battle plan for yourself. This plan is what makes you confident about your trades. Do not change track when you get started on the actual platform unless you are absolutely confident that the new direction is where you should be heading.

Another factor to remember is that, while the Forex market is mainly unregulated, individual brokers have to follow a certain set of regulations based on the country that they are operating in. For example, if the broker is located in the United States, then they should be registered with the Commodity Futures Trading Commission (CFTC). By doing so, traders can verify the status of the broker. Some brokers who are not regulated with the aforementioned commission when located in the U.S. do not have any financial regulations. This means that they could stop operations and disappear without a trace with all your money. You, on the other hand, will be left without legal recourse.

Of course, this is not true for all brokers. There are many brokers who have a strong reputation but are not regulated by a particular commission. But ideally, knowing about these regulatory bodies will allow you to choose your broker more effectively. We have already shown you many points you should consider when selecting your broker. This additional step is to ensure that you are trading without any problems.

Before you even think of placing your order, make sure that you have a stable and fast internet connection on all your devices. Sure, your internet connection might be working perfectly on your computer. But what about your smartphone? Does your service provider provide you with stability and speed on your smartphone? If it doesn't, do you think you could choose a better data package or a better service provider?

What about multiple monitors? It definitely sounds cool when others do it.

It is not exactly mandatory, but it might help you when you are multitasking. You could use one monitor just for your trading platform. The other monitor can be used for other activities such as listening to your music, chatting with other traders, watching videos (whether they are for trading or simply catching up on the latest episode of your favorite TV show), or completing any of your daily tasks. There are many traders who work off their computers from home, whether they are freelancing or have the ability to carry out their work at home. In such cases, they make use of two monitors so that they can perform their daily tasks but also stay tuned to the price fluctuations happening in the market.

Also, make sure that you are in an environment that allows you to trade properly. It might seem convenient when you think about working from home. But if you have family obligations that could interrupt work, then you are better off working from somewhere else that could provide you with privacy. Remember what we discussed earlier: Forex is a business. It cannot be taken as a hobby.

Once you have decided where you would like to trade, then examine yourself. Make note of your habits and your life patterns. These factors help you decide what kind of trader you are. When you understand your daily habits, then you can arrange a strategy accordingly. This will not only help you trade better but will allow you to adjust to your habits. Additionally, we have just shown you a multitude of ways to perform analysis. Don't go into a trade and then figure out what kind of analysis you would like to do. Why not try each of the analysis methods and find out which one fits your trading.

Placing an Order

We are going to start placing your orders. Perhaps you should try today's best, fresh currency with a side order of pips.

Okay, maybe not that kind of order, but on the trading platform, you are going to be dealing with orders a lot, so let's first get down to the fundamentals.

Essentially, you should be aware of the fact that there are different types of orders available for you to place. When choosing your broker, make sure that they are able to provide you with the order that will want to place in the future.

Let's look at these orders and how they work.

Market Order

This is a common type of order placed by traders. In a market order, you buy or sell the currency at the best available price, but you perform the buy/sell action immediately. As in, now!

With a market order, you can either enter a position or exit from an already held position.

Let us take an example. We welcome our old friend EUR/USD and here, let us assume that the currency pair's bid price is 1.1376 and the ask price is set at 1.1377. This means that if you are going to buy the currency, it will be 1.1377.

You are going to confirm buy, upon which your platform or broker will execute the buy order.

Think of this step as heading over to an online store and confirming your purchase. You look at a product and if you are interested, you click buy.

The only difference here is that you are buying currencies instead of a blender (or whatever you use an online store for).

Limit Order

You place a limit order when you would like to enter into a new position or exit the currency position at a particular price. In most cases, you are going to buy below the market or if you are selling, you are going to sell above the market.

Let's take an example. You find out that the EUR/USD is currently trading at 1.1376. You decide that you would like to go short (or in other words, you sell) if the price reaches 1.1396.

Now there are two ways you can do this:

1. You can sit in front of your computer or your smartphone (if your trading platform provides an app) and wait for it to reach the sweet spot.

2. Or you can place a limit order where your platform will execute a sell action at 1.1396 while you go enjoy your yoga class.

There are several reasons why traders would choose to place a limit order.

- You place a limit order if you expect that the price of the currency will reverse after reaching the price that you predicted.

- Limit orders are placed when you have a clear idea of your profits. When you are creating your strategy, you will usually have an idea where you would like to collect profits when a trade is working to your benefit.

Stop Entry Order

You place this order when you would like to sell below the market and make a buy above that market.

Let us assume that the GBP/USD is currently trading at 1.2741. After conducting your research, you have the belief that the price will continue to rise up until it reaches 1.2751, which is the point at which you would like to place your stop entry order.

As with the limit order, you can choose to do one of two things

- Sit in front of your computer to execute the buy order

- Stop entry order + yoga class

Stop Loss Order

As we saw earlier, you place a stop loss order to prevent you from experiencing heavy losses on a trade if the price does not go in the direction you wanted it to.

If the position you are in is long, then you execute a sell order.

If the position is short, then the order is buy.

Let us say that you went long with the USD/CAD at 1.32185. While planning out your strategy, you decide to place a limit on the maximum loss you can bear by placing a stop-loss order at 1.32150.

This means that if the market goes against you, then your trading platform will automatically make a sell order to minimize your losses.

Trailing Stop

This is a type of stop-loss order that moves as the price fluctuates.

Let us take the above example of USD/CAD. You have decided to place a trailing stop-loss order of 20 pips. This means that at 1.32185, your stop-loss is placed at 1.32165. If the price increases to 1.32195, then the stop-loss moves up to 1.32175.

By using this method, you are ensuring that you can keep up with the rising trend but will be prepared if something out of the ordinary happens and the market decides to go against you.

Now that we have understood the various kinds of orders you can place in your trading platform, it is time to move on to the next step.

The Long and Short of It

We already know that when you go long, it means that you are going to make a buy order. When you go short, you are about to execute a sell order. But is that all there is to it?

Let us dive further so you are clear on both concepts.

When a particular currency pair is long, then you are purchasing the base currency and then selling the quote currency. If you go long on it, then you are making a speculation in which you hope that the price of the currency will rise in the future. The position of long is always indicated by the base currency.

On the other hand, when a currency is going short, then it means that the base currency is being sold and the quote currency is being bought. When you go short on a currency, then you are hoping that there is going to be a drop in the market price of that currency. The position of short is usually denoted by the base currency, but that does not have to be the case. Traders look at both base and quote currency when they are going short.

Exiting a Position

One of the things that traders focus on intently is fine-tuning their strategies and making sure that they have opened their position in the best way possible. However, they forget one vital component in all of this, how to exit. They simply destroy everything they have built with a poor exit strategy.

Here is how to look at it. Imagine that you have boarded an airplane that is going to take you to a far-off location. It is your holiday, after all, and you have decided on heading over to Thailand/Bali/India or if you are located on the eastern side, then you have chosen New York/London/Vancouver (if you are in the middle, well, pick any direction).

As you get comfortable in your seat and buckle up for the ride, the pilot suddenly pops up near your seat. He looks at you gravely and poses this rather strange question:

"Tell me Sir/Ma'am, do you think the take-off is important or the landing is important? I will adjust my flight preferences accordingly."

Flabbergasted, you take a moment to wonder if the pilot is playing a prank on you. His serious expression reveals that this is no joke. He really wants you to answer the question.

"Both," you respond, hoping that he can see the confusion on your face and the intention in your voice, "I prefer you take-off and land perfectly."

Smiling, the pilot nods and heads back to the cockpit while you sit in your seat wondering whether, if you hadn't answered the question, you would have doomed your life and those of your fellow passengers completely.

Think of trading as the airplane. You are the pilot. What do you think you should be doing when you are focused on your strategy? Do you think entering the position is more important than the exit or the other way around?

If you answered both, then you are keeping your passengers safe. By safe, we mean profitable.

And who are the metaphorical passengers in this rather colorful analogy? Why, the currencies of course!

Calculating Profit and Loss

Of course, the whole point of being on a plane is to reach your destination and enjoy the local beer!

In the case of Forex, the local beer is profits. What is a loss, you ask? We should give an analogy for loss as well. If that is the case, then think of loss as an unsavory dish that is about to go MMA on your digestive system.

When you have closed your trade, you take the price when you are selling the base currency and subtract it from the price of the base currency when you were buying it. You then multiply the result with the transaction size to finally show you whether you made a profit or a loss.

Let us look at an example.

Let assume that you have bought the Euro (part of the EUR/USD currency pair) at a price of $1.1278 and then you sold the currency at a value of $1.1288. Your transaction size is basically the lot size. For this example, you have bought the standard lot of 100,000 units.

So let us follow the steps in the formula to find out our profit or loss.

Step 1: Selling price - Buying price

$1.1288 - $1.1278 = $0.0010

Step 2: Take the result from above and multiply it by your transaction size. In this case, 100,000

$0.0010 x 10,000 = $10

Form the above example, we have noticed that you have made a profit of $10. Way to go trader!

Let's try a different approach to the above example. Let us assume that you are working with pounds (GBP/USD) and you have bought the currency at $1.7374 and sold it for $1.7379.

If you apply Step 1, then you will get a result of $0.0005. When you apply Step 2, then you will get $5 as a result.

You just made a profit of $5.

Of course, if your selling price was lower than your buying price, then you will find that your result is a negative number, indicating a loss in the transaction.

With just a simple formula, you can calculate your profit and loss. Here is a recommendation. Make sure that you are keeping a journal where you note down your strategy and the amount of profit or loss that you have made using that particular strategy.

This way, you can change your strategy and then check to see if your profits have improved or your losses have worsened. This method is effective to plan ahead and figure out the best tactics for your trade. Remember this: trading is a learning process and you will constantly be learning something. It is better to have a record of your transactions, strategies, and ideas so that you can apply what you learned.

Account Balance, Leverage, and Margin

Account Balance

We have already had a glimpse into what leverage and margin indicate. But here, we are going to take a step further and look at each of these terms in detail, while also understanding what your account balance means.

The first thing that you are going to do before you even start the trading process is open an account. You are going to go through the process of evaluating these brokers in such detail that even James Bond would be proud of you.

Once you have finalized your option, you are going to go ahead and open your account with the broker of your choice. Some brokers have an approval phase where they evaluate your profile and then decide if you can use their platform.

When your account is approved, you can begin to transfer funds to your account.

One recommendation at this point is to make sure that you are solely transferring the risk money you have calculated (which is 1% of your capital). Sure, having enough money for emergencies might sound like a sound plan, but having enough money to fuel your temptation is not a good way to start off your trading journey. Once you have mastered the platform and your strategies, feel free to transfer as much as you like.

Let's say that you deposit about $500 into your account, then that will be your account balance.

When you have entered into a new position, there will be no effect on your account balance until the position is closed.

Now, your account balance becomes important when you perform a rollover. Basically, when you are performing a rollover, then you are keeping your account open overnight. There is a difference between closing positions after a few hours and closing them by carrying your position to the next day.

Traders manually make sure that they are carrying their position overnight by closing their positions at the end of the day. At the same time, they will open another position for the next day. This new position that they open will be similar to the position that they closed. In other words, it might look like the same position is getting carried over to another day. This process of closing and opening positions can also be done automatically by giving specific instructions to your broker (also it depends on the fact that your broker has this feature available with them).

When they perform a rollover, then a certain calculation is performed, after which the traders have to pay or receive a certain fee known as a swap fee.

If traders pay a swap fee, then their account balance will reduce.

If traders receive a swap fee, then their balance will increase.

Regardless of the situation, both scenarios will affect your account balance. You won't have to worry about rollovers as they are meant for very experienced traders. However, as we were covering the subject of account balance, it was important to bring your attention to it.

Leverage

Leverage is used to give you a bit of a boost in your trading. If a trader intends to take advantage of leverage, then they have to first open a margin account on their platform. Typically, there is a certain amount of leverage provided that is fairly common among all brokers. You get leverage options of 50:1, 100:1 or 200:1. Which of the leverage options you can take advantage of depends on the broker and also the size of your investment. Some brokers do not allow you to take big leverage in order to protect you from incurring hefty losses. Other brokers are more lenient in that department.

But what do those ratios mean?

Essentially, it is the ability for you to control a large amount of money without actually using much of your own money.

Let us see this with an example.

Let's say that you have opened a position and are now in control of 100,000 units (or $100,000). You have chosen the 100:1 leverage option. Your broker will set aside $1,000 for you (this does not have to be the case as you could even choose $2,000 or $5,000, but we will stick with $1,000 for the sake of this example).

Technically, you are now managing $100,000 with a leverage of $1,000.

Let us say that your investment paid off. The value rose to $101,000. This is an increase of $1,000.

If you had invested in the $100,000 all by yourself, then return is $1,000. This is a 1:1 leverage.

But if you made use of a leverage of 100:1 and your broker set aside $1,000 the outcome is a bit different.

When the value increases to $101,000, then you do not just get the initial $1,000, but by banking on the 100:1 leverage, you get 100% of the profit as a bonus. That means you get $2,000 as your total return.

Sounds cool eh?!

But wait. You might have heard rumors of the fact that leverage can affect you both ways. It could harm you considerably. Are these rumors true?

Think of it this way, if you have made a gain, then you have earned $2,000. If you took a loss, then you would lose $2,000 as well.

The above example showed what happens if your loss was around $1,000. But what happens if you lost more, say $5,000? Then according to your leverage, you have lost a total of $10,000!

See where this situation becomes tricky? Think of it this way: whatever amount you gain, you are going to get an additional 100% of it extra. But whatever amount you lose, you still have to shell out an extra 100% of it as well.

It is no wonder that traders are extremely careful when they are working with leverages. In fact, experienced traders never take a leverage unless they have a bank account that would make Bill Gates blush.

Margins

Now we come to the point of margins.

Let us stick to the above example. Now that you are managing 100,000 units of currency, your broker has told you that in order to have a leverage of say 100:1, they would require a margin of 1%. In this example, that would come up to $1,000.

Basically, that $1,000 that you shell out to your broker is a margin. Think of it as a deposit that you place with your broker. If you are successful in your trade, then you receive the margin back along with the profit you have made with your leverage. On the other hand, well, you already know what happens in this case.

Chapter 7 - Your Plan of Action: Crafting Your Battle Plan

How to Build Your Trading Plan

What exactly constitutes a trading plan? Essentially, you are looking at a set of rules that you are going to place before you venture forth and begin trading in the market. These rules should cover every facet of your trading and you should make them as detailed as possible.

However, here is something that you should understand. Just because you build your trading plan, it does not mean that you are going to succeed. It is not your ticket to profits. Nothing can guarantee profits in the Forex market. However, what your trading will do is help you avoid too many mistakes, prevent things shifting from bad to worse, and provide you solutions for various problems you might encounter.

You can never control the market. But you can make sure that you are in control of yourself. A trading plan is essentially a level of control that you place over yourself to ensure that you make trades based on information, keep your emotions in check, and always look for the next course of action.

A trading plan also breaks down your process into simplified chunks of actions. This allows you to work with each action with care and awareness. If an unexpected situation occurs, then you will know where the problem occurred.

Battle Stations! Building the Battle Plan

Your trading plan should fit you. So you should make sure that it fits your skills, personality, and the number of resources available to you. When you are creating your plan, it is imperative that you are honest in your evaluations. If you have a small amount of capital, you should make sure you understand it as a "small capital" and not "acceptable capital". Also, make notes about your emotional responses. Are you prone to anger easily? Do you get depressed when things go wrong?

Yes, everything is important in your trading plan. No detail is insignificant.

Parts of a Trading Plan

Your trading plan should be able to answer the below queries with clarity:

Markets

What are you aiming to sell or buy?

Position sizing

In what quantities would you like to make your purchase or sale?

Risk management

If things go wrong, how much are you willing to lose without having any impact on your life?

Entries

When do you plan to purchase or sell currencies? Include factors such as your availability, the market hours, when you can sit down and read news releases, etc.

Stops

If you are in a losing position, when do you aim to exit?

Exits

If you are in a winning position, when do you aim to exit?

Strategy

How would you like to deal with currencies?

Time frames

How much do you think you can win from a particular trade? (Make sure you place a proper evaluation.)

Now that we have gone through the basics, we are going to focus our attention on the details.

Here is an example of a checklist that you can use (you can modify some of the questions to fit your requirements):

Before entering any position (whether you are going long or short)

What currency pair are you planning to deal with?

Strategy: What are the primary indicators of this currency? What factors influence it? Can you identify any secondary indicators?

Risk areas: What does your chart look like? Are you able to identify the risk areas easily?

Break-even price: At what point would you consider that your trade has made neither a gain nor a loss?

Look into the actual market position and check out the previous activity. Answer the below queries:

Are there any prices in the current trend that are close to the high or low of the previous day?

Were there any prices that indicated a support or a resistance?

What did the economic reports and news talk about when referring to the previous day's trades?

Now, look at your chart in front of you.

Look at the point of entry of your position and speculate on where the trend will be heading.

Situations

You are going long and the trend seems to be going in an upward direction. It has a downward swing that is bigger than two previous downward swings.

You are going short and the trend seems to be going in a downward direction. It has an upward swing that is bigger than two previous upward swings.

You are going long and the secondary trend seems to be going in a downward direction. It eventually swings back up and goes in the same direction as the main trend.

You are going short and the secondary trend seems to be going in an upward direction. It eventually swings back down and goes in the same direction as the main trend.

Measure your risk management

Buy Entry Price

Your broker will set up a signal bar. This is an indicator that lets you know whether the price is reaching a high or a low. You can adjust this signal bar to your preference, but it will be available once you open your position. You might notice this as a horizontal line that goes across your chart. You should ideally buy when the prices are above the high of the signal bar.

Sell Entry Price

Look at your signal bar again. You should be selling when the price reaches below the low of the signal bar.

Risk

Have you set a stop-loss? Make sure that you do.

How much risk are you willing to take at this point with the capital that you have?

Are you going for leverage (your answer should be "no" if you are starting out)?

Situation

Never let the positive trade become negative. Establish your stop-loss points so that you can get out of a loss before it gets any worse for you.

Exit Strategy

Take your profits, or if you have still ended up with a loss, go through the checklist and see if there were any errors. Make sure that you modify your strategies where you see fit.

The above example is just one way of preparing your trading plan checklist. Essentially, you are going to have to describe in detail the what, when, and how parts of your trading.

We have mentioned this before but the point becomes more relevant in this stage: make sure that you are maintaining a journal or record of your activities. No detail should be too insignificant. Entry position, stop-loss, date, time, indicators used, leverage taken, and any other factor that was part of your trade should be recorded accurately. When you have filled out the technical data, move on to yourself.

What were you going through when you took the trade? Did you enter a trade in the right frame of mind? Were your surroundings beneficial to you? As you were making your plan, were you interrupted at any point? Did you just wake up from sleep and decide to make a trade because of a sudden surge in excitement?

Each of these factors helps you discover the weakness in your process. You can find out where you went wrong and discover steps to remedy it.

There are many traders who end up giving up after their first trade, frustrated at not knowing where they went wrong. However, with your journal, you know everything there is to know about your trade. Nothing is arbitrary. It wasn't some unknown cause that led to a poor trade.

Here is another checklist that you can prepare to gauge your readiness for the trade:

- Have you tried out the demo account? What strategy have you implemented?

- How many times have you worked with this strategy? Would you like to go and practice some more or are you confident that you can begin your trade with your strategy?

- Were you able to understand the signals and the charts?

- Do you feel confident about your skills and your ability to understand numbers? Can you replicate that confidence in your trade?

- What are your goals? (Don't say "I would like to earn a million dollars" because that is not a goal, it is a target.) You have to think about what you are going to achieve through trading. Are you planning on starting your own business? Are you going to pay for a world tour? Are you buying your house? When you define your goals, you will understand the seriousness of the situation. You will be receptive to lessons and information. You will make sure that you think of Forex trading as a business venture that requires quite a bit of hard work and dedication. More importantly, you will have an idea of when you would like to stop trading.

- Set up separate sections for the money you might make through trading (this is also based on your initial performance).

- Do you think your current technical setup is satisfactory? Do you feel that your router might break down in the near future? Will you need a faster internet connection? If you cannot upgrade your internet connection, how can you make sure that internet speed is not an issue when trading?

- Are you prepared to accept losses? If you are not, then do you require time to get into the right mental frame? This is important because you should not let losses on your trade run for a long time hoping that it might turn around. Sometimes, you just have to accept your losses, get back to the drawing board and adjust your strategy.

- Have you met the conditions that dictate whether or not your entry to the trade is ready? Once you meet these conditions, do not second guess your decision. You might not get the same opportunity again. It does not matter if the trade will head in an upward direction or a downward direction. You have made your preparation. Stick to it.

Understanding Risk-reward Ratio

Your risk-reward ratio is a measure of how much you are willing to risk in order to gain a particular reward.

Here is an example: you are about to make a trade and have set your stop-loss at 10 pips. You have also established your take-profit point at 20 pips.

So your risk-reward ratio is now 10:20 or 1:2. This means that you are planning to risk 10 pips in order to get a gain of 20 pips.

The key thing to remember when you are preparing your risk-reward ratio is to identify situations where the rewards are more than the risks. The higher the rewards you can get, the more you are capable of withstanding any future failed trades. What does that mean?

Let us look at the example above. Your risk-reward ratio is 1:2. Essentially, for every $1 that you risk, you are aiming to receive a reward of $2.

Now let us say that in your first trade you made a win. You now have a reward of $2.

You have a positive balance of $2 in your account.

In the next trade, you made a loss. You have now lost $1.

Your balance at this point is $1.

Now, you can go for another failed trade, which will send your account back to zero balance. But you cannot suffer any further losses or you will enter negative balance. (The idea of a negative balance is not referring to the balance of your account. Rather it is just a way to show that you have now incurred a loss on your investment.)

So the bigger the ratio, the more losses you can withstand.

Let's try this with a table.

We have taken a risk-reward ratio of 1:2. You trade might look something like this.

Number of Trades	Loss	Gain
1	$1,000	-
2	-	$2,000
3	$1,000	-
4	-	$2,000
5	$1,000	-
6	-	$2,000

7	$1,000	-
8	-	$2,000
9	$1,000	-
10	-	$2,000
Total	$5,000	$10,000

With the above transactions, you have made a $5,000 profit. Now, if you decided that you were going to risk 6 pips to gain 14 pips, then your risk-reward ratio is going to be 6:14, to 3:7. If you were to replace all the $1,000 in the above table with $3,000 and the $2,000 with $7,000, then you are looking at a total of $15,000 and $35,000. Which means you make a profit of at least $20,000.

The greater the margin on your risk-reward ratio. The greater the profit. However, does that mean that you will always get an equal balance of profit and loss? Let us use the 3:7 ratio and examine the problem in the below table.

Number of Trades	Loss	Gain
1	$3,000	-
2	$3,000	-
3	-	$7,000
4	$3,000	-
5	-	$7,000
6	$3,000	-
7	$3,000	-
8	$3,000	-

9	-	$7,000
10	$3,000	-
Total	$21,000	$21,000

In the above example, you have neither made a loss, nor a profit. That was because your risk-reward ratio was rather high. What if that was not the case? If you were to go back to the risk-reward ratio of 1:2, then you will have to replace the $3,000 with $1,000 and the $7,000 with $2,000. In the end, you get a total loss of $7,000 and a total gain of $6,000.

Which means, you just made a loss of $1,000.

That is essentially how the risk-reward system works. However, when you are actually trading, the situation may not be as clear-cut and simple as the above examples. There are various factors that go into revealing the loss. But to get a general idea, the above examples show you just what could happen when you have a small risk-reward ratio.

Does that mean you have to only trade with a high risk-reward ratio? Not really. Think of it from this perspective. If you suffered only losses, then with the 1:2 ratio, your total loss is $10,000. With the 3:7 ratio, your total loss is $30,000!

The manner in which you choose your risk-reward ratio is based on how prepared you are with your trade, how well you have created your trading plan, and how much capital you have with you. Additionally, some traders have a higher risk than reward. This might boggle some people but it is essentially done by traders when the market is volatile. That way, they give a bigger margin of error in the hopes that the trend bounces back up after a downward direction of the currency.

Combining all of these factors together helps you determine your risk-reward ratio.

Due Diligence – Doing Your Homework

In the current digital age, we are inundated with terms such as "fake news", "scandals", and "conspiracies".

When you look for any news information online, then the most attractive headline catches your attention. Publishers make use of these catchy headlines because they want that reaction from you: to look towards their headline and forget the competition. The news platforms want to make sure you click-through to their articles.

In many cases, the article headline seems to tell a story by itself. The idea of sensationalism means that shocking language is used to blow up a story.

In those circumstances, it becomes your duty to perform thorough research to verify the authenticity of the information you are receiving. If you react to something without due-diligence, then you are going to make some huge mistakes.

For example, one article in *USA Today* mentioned how the Justice Department spent $16 on a muffin during one of their events. The article's title simply read, "How good is a $16 muffin? Find out for yourself"[3].

Your reaction would be, "Wait! They are enjoying $16 muffins when people are starving on the streets? How could they?! #JusticeFromJusticeDepartment."

However, the reality of the situation was much different. In fact, the article was not supported by the real facts. According to Hilton Worldwide, the $16 included the following items:

- Coffee/tea

- Fresh fruit

- Drinks

- Tax

Now that paints an entirely new picture about the Justice Department. Suddenly, you might find your voice changing from #JusticeFromJusticeDepartment to #JusticeFORJusticeDepartment.

That is the case with numerous news articles from around the world. You cannot simply read a small part of the news. You need to make sure that you are performing your own thorough research.

If there was a similar article such as the $16 muffin in an economic situation, then you might assume that a country is spending heavily on something. Time to make a profit! Eventually, you might realize someone had exaggerated the entire story. Now, you have already invested a large amount of capital in the trade and you cannot back down. All you can do is watch your investment disappear into the digital sinkhole of the Forex market. #JusticeForYou

But it is not just the news and economic data that you have to focus on. Make sure that you are going through tutorials and expert feedback with the same due diligence. Research more about your broker to find out any hidden charges or regulations that might come back to haunt you in the future. Make sure that you are truly prepared before you enter a trade.

Setting Entrance and Exit Rules

A lot of traders spend a considerable amount of time trying to discover the best entry strategies. They look for the perfect buying and selling indications and forget about the exit strategy. When you are going to trade, you need to have a balance between the entrance and exit rules.

Let us take a page out of the textbook of hedge fund managers, who focus on both the entrance and exit strategies. There are four main ways you can enter or exit a particular trade.

Method 1: Single Entry. Single Exit.

In this method, traders place all their bets on a single point of entry. This means they have only one entry position at one price. When they exit, they do so entirely at one price as well.

Method 2: Single Entry. Multiple Exits.

In this strategy, traders make sure that they enter completely using one position, but for their exit strategy, they leave at different points (meaning, each point will have a different price).

Method 3: Multiple Entries. Single Exit.

In this method, traders enter into positions at different prices. However, when they close their position, they do so at a single price (which is typically the total of the various prices they used for entry positions).

Method 4: Multiple Entries. Multiple Exits.

The title says it all. Traders enter into position using different prices. When they exit, they use different prices as well.

Keeping a Trading Journal

One of the things that seasoned traders will tell you is that, more often than not, trading isn't about finding the secret "recipe" to success. It is mainly about having discipline. We have already seen why discipline plays a vital role in your trades. However, one of the ways that you can maintain discipline is by keeping a record journal. Institutional traders, regardless of their rank and their degree of success are trained to keep a journal until the habit of recording their transactions and other behaviors becomes automatic. The main reason for this was to instill a sense of accountability. After all, these traders are dealing with millions of dollars. How did these traders maintain their journal?

One of the habits that they formed was that for every long and short position that they made, for every stop-loss point they set up, every risk-reward ratio that they decided upon, they had to have a solid rationale for doing so.

It was always, "I am doing this because of the following reasons that are based on large amounts of research and information."

They never decided something without a strong foundation to carry their decisions.

Which is why this level of accountability leads to the formation of some of the best traders in the world. You might think that this is an extreme practice and only pertains to traders who are dealing with large sums of money.

On the contrary, it becomes even more important to you.

Why?

Because you are not dealing with someone else's money. You are using your own money.

For banking traders, they receive a fixed paycheck regardless of how poorly they perform. Of course, repeated mistakes mean that they are asked to leave the job. But in essence, they don't have any personal loss. In your case, forget getting a paycheck. If you lose, you are slowly drying up your own reserves. Additionally, institutional traders have multiple chances to make the money back without disrupting their personal lives. If you experience a loss, then you might find your entire life upended.

Now, your journal is different from the checklist and questions that were created when you were building your trading plan.

Here are some of the things you should include in your journal.

Currency Pair Information

In this section, you are going to make notes about the currency pairs and how you have traded with them. This will work best if you have prepared a table and then taken a print out of the sheet.

Here are some of the columns that you have to use in the sheet.

Currency Pair	Current Price	Daily High	Daily Low	10-day High	10-day Low

Target Trades

In this section, you are going to list all the trades that you are going to make. Essentially, you are waiting for the current trade to generate its results so that you can proceed with your next trade.

Let's say that currently, the date is November 1.

Your entry should look something like this:

November 2

- Buy USD/CAD at 1.1712

- Stop loss placed at 1.1700

- Target 1: 1.1760

- On reaching Target 1, Target 2: 1.1790

- No Target 3. High Risk.

With just a few instructions, you have made your next task easier. You have given yourself clear instructions. The next day, let us assume that you had one of those mornings where you just can't seem to find the energy to even move your pinky.

You force yourself out of bed and realize that you need to get back to trading. However, you are in no mood to think straight. What do you do? How can you keep your trades going? Is this the end of the world?

Wait! There is no need to panic. After all, you have already set a plan into motion. Everything will be okay!

Make sure that by the end of the day, you have taken a small portion of your time to create a plan that will help you the next day.

Completed or Existing Trades

Of course, just like you have planned for future trades, you should also be recording your completed or existing trades. Spend some time looking through the trades you have already made to find out any mistakes you may have made. However, not only can you use this section to identify the losses, you might just discover a trend that you wouldn't have otherwise noticed while looking at the charts.

Think of it this way.

When you are talking with your friend, you might inject your responses and questions with a lot of "uhms" and "ahs". However, do you know how many of these blanks are inserted into one sentence? Are you aware of the frequency of these blanks? If you start recording your conversation and then play it back later, you might be surprised by the results.

Reporters and newscasters often record the way they speak and play it back to themselves so that they can improve their speech patterns.

They can identify when they are most likely to pause and where they tend to lose track of the conversation.

In a similar way, you are using your journal to track the "uhms" and "ahs" of your trading. You might not be aware that you are making minor mistakes, but when you look through your journal, you might just be surprised by the frequency at which certain actions slip by your awareness.

Why Money Management Matters the Most

You are dealing with money.

Which is why you need to know how to handle money.

One of the key traits that you need to have in order to become a successful Forex trader is the ability to manage your money effectively.

One of the most important rules that you should apply in your life when it comes to Forex trading is to never invest money that you can't afford to lose.

If you cannot afford to invest the required capital into your trading all at one point, then keep a small portion of money that you are comfortable using for Forex trading. Even if you do have the required amount of capital, make sure that you break it into smaller chunks and use one chunk at a time. When you keep small portions, you minimize the risk.

We have already seen how Forex is all about speculation. But it can turn into gambling if you decide to spend money without being cautious about it. You are making informed decisions and one of those decisions is realizing that you cannot spend all your money in one go.

Next, try and open a small account where you are dealing with micro pips. This way, you are not investing large amounts and even if you suffer losses, it might impact you, but not to an extent where you lose big.

In the world of Forex, ensuring that you are keeping a close watch on your money is what separates a successful trader and one who suffers heavy losses.

Chapter 8 - The Best Tools for the Job: What Every Winning Trader Uses

It's All in the Software

When you are working in the Forex market, the right software helps you connect to the market, gives you regular updates, and essentially completes all the transactions that you would like to make.

You could say that your software is your portal to the world of Forex trading, and that is putting it mildly.

There are many criteria you can use to select the ideal software for your Forex requirements, but here are some of the essential points.

Regulatory Compliance

Many of the software options that you come across will be regulated by the authority in their home country. This is vital when you would like to have a level of assurance when making trades. When software follows regulations, it established a sense of integrity.

Just because the software has some cool graphics and a colorful interface, it does not mean that you should definitely trust the software. Make sure that you are performing your own background checks and checking trusted reviews.

Commissions

Different software programs have different commissions. So when choosing your software, make sure that the commission structure is right. Additionally, there are many software options that give you access to additional features for a premium amount. If this is not the kind of thing that you are comfortable with, then you are better off trying some other platform.

Software Features

Look at all the features available to you and decide if what you are provided will suffice for the work that you have to do. Sometimes, you might find out that choosing another software or a different version of the same software might give you the features that you are looking for.

Customer Service

At the end of the day, nobody is going to have a perfect experience with a software. But that is something to be expected. Which is why every software provider maintains their own team of customer servicing professionals ready to bail you out of a jam or give the occasional *"did you try turning it off and turning it back on again?"* suggestion.

You might need assistance navigating through the complex mechanisms of the software and you might even need expert help in order to guide you through it. This is why you should make sure you've checked out reviews about the customer service team working for the software.

MetaTrader 4 (MT4) and the bigger, shinier, MetaTrader 5 (MT5)

Time to go Meta!

MetaTrader is essentially a trading platform that provides you with a portal to numerous global trading markets. You might find that it is popularly used for trading online in the Forex market, although it does have a reputation for trading in CFD and futures markets as well.

Presently, you can gain access to .the MetaTrader by using two of its products, the MetaTrader 4, also known as the MT4, and the MetaTrader 5, also known as the MT5. Let us look at this platform and find out the difference between the MT4 and MT5.

A Brief History

The first version of the MetaTrader came out in 2002. Suffice it to say, it was not really popular among the masses. Ever since then, the company has focused on making changes. They rolled out the MetaTrader 2 which was also not widely accepted widely. The MT3 had the same poor response that the MT2 had.

It was not until 2005 that the MetaTrader became a renowned brand name in Forex trading with the release of the MT4.

Within two years, its popularity grew to such a tremendous scale that between the years of 2007 to 2010, many brokers began to recommend MT4 as the trading platform to use instead of the platform that they were already providing.

In 2010, the brand launched the latest version of the software, the MT5.

MT4 and MT5: What's the Difference?

One of the major differences between the MT4 and MT5 is the programming language that is used by these platforms. The Mt5 makes use of MQL5. The MT4, on the other hand, uses the previous version of the language, the MQL4. What does this upgrade bring to the table? For one, it introduces a new feature called "black box" programming.

Now there is a lot of technical know-how when it comes to explaining what black box programming can do, but it boils down to one thing: the program is easy to use and provides a better foundation for developers of trading platforms and users.

Additionally, the MT5 is faster, allowing for multiple trades to be carried out easily on its platform.

TradingView - The Best Overall Forex Charts Software

We have been talking about how you should refer to charts when you are conducting your Forex transactions. But that begs the question, is there Forex software that will meet your needs and at the same time provide you with tons of features?

The satisfying answer is that there is!

That software is TradingView.

Let's start with a brief summary of what TradingView is all about.

Check out the Awesome View of TradingView!

No, the above title is not their slogan. Although, if they would like to purchase the tagline…

Ahem, we digress.

So what exactly is the TradingView?

It is convenient charting software that also provides traders with the ability to network on the platform. TradingView is ideal for all kinds of trades, whether they are beginners or veterans. It is meant to provide you with a visual representation your trading (which is what we want after all) and supplements that view with tons of information about the trade.

Here are some of the cool features of the software:

Depending on how you would like to approach your trade, you can create simple charts or complex dynamic and multi-layered charts to track a plethora of markets. Additionally, if you feel like it, you can even create your own charts on the platform.

The software comes with different kinds of alerts that you can modify on the platform. Based on what kind of information you require urgent updates about, you can adjust up to 12 different notification settings.

For those who have honed their skills in charting software, TradingView also provides the feature of "Pine Script". What this script allows you to do is create your indicators and charts.

The platform also gives you access to over 50 exchanges around the world, enough to fulfill all your trading needs.

Finally, to add the cherry on the cake, TradingView provides a lot of educational materials. They have everything from videos to podcasts to articles giving you details on how you can trade and how you can manage finances, to how you should be looking at the various charts. Simply put, you have all the information you need to get started on the platform and become acclimated to the Forex world.

You can sign up for a free account, but it is not necessary to view some of the information on the platform. If you would like to simply make a quick reference, then head over to TradingView and you will spot a ticker on the top of the website giving you updates about the popular currency pairs.

Mobile Charting Platforms

Today's world is all about going mobile. If you have a business, it has become vital to target mobile users. It is for this reason that platforms such as Facebook, Google, YouTube, and Instagram all have special marketing campaigns that target mobile users.

In the same way, there are numerous mobile versions of charting platforms that you can access from anywhere in the world, as long as you are connected to a network.

But out of all the platforms available to you, which ones are actually worth looking into? Here are the ones you should consider if you are going to work on charts.

Netdania

One of the highlights of this app is that it provides you with trading strategies and ideas. The creators of the app have marketed the platform as a "personal trading assistant" and in many ways, it does function that way. For example, the app actually gives you a notification to let you know when the right time to go long or go short is. While doing this, it accumulates real-time news and economic information from around the world. Through social networking features, it shares strategies between various traders. This means that you can use the app to copy someone else's trading techniques if they have been successful.

As the app is connected to a cloud platform, you can easily share your info and details between multiple devices. Meaning that if you lose your mobile device, you can always download the app on another phone and get your data back.

Forex Time FXTM

What does Forex Time FXTM have in its favor that most other platforms do not? It has a degree of trustworthiness. After all, it has been used in nearly 180 countries and regulated in numerous regions as well. The platform is designed to work for both beginners, as the app itself is fairly easy to use, and for professionals, as it gives access to advanced features and educational materials. It also offers speedy functionalities and is able to make trades with just a percentage of a second difference between the time you execute and the time the order has been confirmed.

Trade Interceptor

Trade Interceptor is mainly made for advanced users. Though it does have a friendly interface and numerous educational materials to use, it is targeted to those who have more experience dealing with the Forex market. Its main charm is the fact that it provides access to a myriad of indicators that you can use for your trades. The app is also powered by the cloud network, allowing you to transfer your profile to any device. You can even play around with a trading simulator, designed to try out your strategies before you get down to working on real trades.

TD *Ameritrade*

TD Ameritrade makes a comeback! Earlier, we talked about the desktop version of the app. Here, we are going to focus on the mobile version. Not only is the app one of the most established and trusted platforms in the U.S., but it is also regulated (as we have seen before). The information on the app is presented in a clear manner. TD Ameritrade also focuses on other products such as futures, stocks, and options.

Chapter 9 - Making Your First Trade: Step By Step

The Initial Analysis

We have four different analysis options for you to use. Now the question is, is there a way for you to perform an analysis of the market? Is there a secret technique passed down from one Forex sensei to another, finally available to those worthy of seeking its power? Can you do the "Kamehameha" and get your Forex to give you a lot of profits?

The answer to the last two questions is no.

The answer to the first one is, well of course!

Here is a four-step process to help you apply any of the Forex analysis methods you choose.

Step 1: Understanding What Drives the Market

Your first step should be to familiarize yourself with the reasons why many markets are related to each other and what those relationships mean. For example, how do stocks, currencies, and options contribute to the country's market? What factors do each of them share between themselves that allow them to boost or affect an economy?

When something happens to the market, it is not arbitrary. There is always a reason behind it.

For example, when you notice that the stock market is slowly recovering, don't think of it as a good sign and be done with it. Think of why there is a recovery. Is it because investors are hopeful about an upward trend in the economy? If so, what caused this positive sentiment among them?

Step 2: Keep a Record of Trends

Having historical data not only helps you in the short-term, but also in the long-run.

Let's take an example here. Did you know that in the year 2009, Gold prices had risen to a record high? They had practically shot up by 300%.

In fact, one cannot call that a rise. It's like the difference between choosing to climb the stairs to the top and choosing to take the elevator. The Gold prices took the elevator. And that elevator had rocket boosters on the bottom of it.

Now when you look at that information, your immediate thought might be, "wow! I wish I was Scrooge McDuck and I had all his gold. I would have sold them all!"

But then there are those who are skeptical about the rise. Most people consider these skeptics as party poopers, but they have a point.

Ask yourself this, why did the Gold prices rise anyway?

Here is a free life lesson for you: if something is too good to be true, then it usually is.

When The Guardian covered this story, they had a very interesting angle[4]. While there could have been many reasons for the sudden rise in Gold prices, one of the most debated ones was the fact that the U.S. dollar had lost status.

Now imagine if the situation were to happen again. What would you do? What would your reaction be?

Step 3: Look for Trends in Other Markets

If you are trading the USD/JPY, then you should not just be focused on the U.S. market. You should look at what is happening in the Japanese market. Check out factors such as their exports, whether the Bank of Japan is planning to intervene in the Forex market, if trade relations between the U.S. and Japan are steady (in fact, check if their relationship has turned sour in any area) or if there has been a new fiscal policy in Japan. Any information that you can gather is beneficial to you.

Step 4: Timing is Everything

Know that you don't have to only use analysis to look at trends or information.

You can actually find out when to trade.

If you are still skeptical about making a move, then perhaps the best way to enter into the trade is to let the analysis give you a story.

Starting the Platform

You are now ready to enter the Matrix.

Think of yourself as Neo about to kick some Forex posterior. Be confident. Be analytical. Leave your emotions at the door.

Before you boot up the platform, make sure you are following the steps mentioned in this book. Keep your journal near you. Start up any charting platform that you may need.

Once you are ready, think of the opening position. Know that from this point onwards, you are going to be making calculated decisions. So be prepared for it.

Opening the Chart

At this point, we could let you know that having two monitors might be useful for you. But it is not vital. There are many traders who only need their trusty MacBook to work with their trades.

You might have already booted up your chart. But make sure that everything is running smoothly. Keeping both the trading platform and the chart open, switch between the two and see if there is any lag in the computing speed. When you are in the moment, looking at prices and making calculations, you are going to be switching between the two software a lot. So make sure everything is running smoothly.

Adding Indicators

If you are using the MT4 or MT5, then you can download custom indicators directly from their website.

- Once you have downloaded them, head over to the install directory in your computer and open the "Data" folder.

- In the Data folder, open the folder named MT4 or MT5. Then open the Indicators file.

- Now open the files that you have downloaded from the website and copy them.

- Paste them into the Indicators file.

You are done.

How do you use these indicators?

- Boot up the MT4 or MT5.

- On the top, choose the "View" option and then head down to the "Navigator" option. Click on it. A window will pop up. Navigate to the Custom Indicators folder. You should be able to see your newly installed Indicator.

- Simply double click it to activate it.

Placing the Order

When you are ready to place orders, simply head over to the "New Order" button. You should be able to spot it in the standard toolbar that comes with the software.

- You will typically be shown a new window. In this window, you are able to select the currency pair that you would like to trade in. Go ahead and make your selection.

- You might notice an "Order Type" option in the same window. Click on it and then select the "Market Execution" option.

- Time to enter your position size. Remember your lesson on lot sizes. This is where it comes in handy. For example, you know that one standard lot is equal to 100,000 units. What should you do if would like to purchase only 2,000 units of a standard lot? You simply enter 0.02 in the volume field.

- You also get the opportunity to add any comments about your trade in the space provided. Here, you can make any important notes that you think you might need to refer to in the future.

- Finally, you have to choose whether you would like to execute a Sell order or a Buy order. Make your selection and click Accept. A new dialog box will pop-up to confirm your order.

Wait a minute! What about stop-loss and take-profit options? Hit the panic button!

Calm down Grasshopper. We got you covered.

If you would like to add a stop-loss command or a take-profit command, then you have to edit your existing trade. To do so, head over to the tab that says "Trade".

- Here, you will be able to see all your trades. Find the trade that you would like to modify.

- Right click on your trade and then select the option "Modify or Delete".

- Next, you simply have to navigate to the stop-loss or take-profit field and then enter the value you would like to establish.

- Simply click on the "Modify" button and you are done!

Order Confirmation

Now you might be thinking to yourself, "Why couldn't I just add the stop-loss and take-profit order while I was creating the order?"

The main reason is that when you create your first trade, you will notice that these options are actually disabled by the system. The reason? To make sure that you get to jump into the trade as soon as possible.

Should you like, you can always enter the stop-loss or take-profit values by enabling the options in the beginning. But it is better to get your trade going and then add the changes later.

The Waiting Period

Remember how we talked about the fact that the Forex market is a three-step market? This is why you won't have to wait for too long before your order is confirmed. Typically, it is a matter of minutes, depending on the currency that you have chosen, the values you have entered, and the other options you have enabled.

Trade Complete

Once everything checks out, you will receive a notification letting you know that the trade has been completed. From this point onwards, you are going to use all the tricks that you have learned so far to make sure that you are going to get the most out of your trade. Do not go with the expectation that you are going to get a successful trade on your first try. Have a mindset in which you are aware that your trade could go both ways.

When you have the right mindset, you won't be emotionally distraught or disappointed.

Chapter 10 - The Scalping Strategy: What Winning Traders Do to Profit Quickly

Why scalping and how does FOREX scalping work?

In the world of Forex, scalping is a method of trading where you engage in taking small amounts of profits on a regular basis. How do you accomplish this?

You go long and short several times a day, only choosing to take in small amounts of profit but aiming to rack them up so that, by the end of the day, you have a large enough total profit in your hands.

When you scalp in the Forex market, then you are using real-time analysis to work on the currencies. The reason you use this type of analysis is that you are going to hold the position for a really short time and then close it with the aim of making a quick, but small, profit.

You essentially work during those times of the day when there is a large amount of traffic and quickly buy a small number of pips.

What you should remember about this method is that you have to be in front of your computer the whole time. You are not going to be playing the long game here. You need to make sure that you are not going to get distracted while you are engaged in scalping.

Forex Scalping Strategies VS Other Trading Strategies

People who engage in scalping are specifically called scalpers while those traders who use any other form of strategy are collectively labeled "day traders". So why is there a distinction between these two forms of trading, as though scalping is a unique strategy on its own?

Let us examine this.

The best way to understand the differences is by categorizing them based on certain factors. We'll start with the time.

Timeframes Used by the Two Forms of Trading Strategies

There is a major difference in the timeframe adopted by scalping in comparison to other strategies. What exactly is the time used by the scalping and the others? Well, when a trader engages in scalping, then he or she opens a trade and closes it in a matter of minutes. Most traders aim to complete the trade within 1 or 2 minutes while some others (especially those who are getting started on the platform), take about 4 to 5 minutes to complete the trade.

Regarding The Others (we are going to use this term to describe every other strategy that is not scalping), the trade takes place over the course of 1 to 2 hours (or more).

Some traders use both strategies. They open up a trade using The Others and while that is open, they engage in some scalping. However, doing that is a big risk as it involves more capital, the capital being split into different directions, and the requirement of extra attention. In fact, if you are not used to it, you are going to be overwhelmed really quickly.

Account Sizes

Scalping involves high risk. Because you are trading within such a short timeframe, you are not giving the trade a lot of time to go in a particular direction. This is why scalpers have a large account size.

On the other hand, The Others are used by traders who have a fairly average account size. This is because traders can work with small amounts and then keep their trade active for a fair amount of time.

Difference in Experience

Scalpers are highly focused on their trade. They are well-versed in the knowledge of the market. This is because they are not waiting for a result. They have a strategy and they are in and out of the trade quickly. This is why scalping is a strategy based on skill and a fair bit of experience on the trading platform.

Quick Results

As scalping involves quick trades, it also yields quick results. It could be a profit or a loss and once the scalper recognizes the result, he or she has already moved on to the next trade.

Most scalpers keep a particular target for a day. This could be the number of trades carried out or a certain amount of profit earned (which typically falls into a particular range).

If trading in The Others is like watching Dwayne "The Rock" Johnson fight, full of big impacts and methodical movements, using scalping is like watching Bruce Lee, in and out before you know it.

What makes for a good FOREX scalping system?

In order to have a proper scalping strategy, there are a few points that you need to take into consideration. Let us look at some of these points.

Liquid Pairs

Some of the most liquid pairs are listed below:

- EUR/USD

- USD/CHF

- USD/JPY

- GBP/USD

Why is it important to focus on liquid currencies? This is because these pairs have a tight spread or in other words, they usually have high trading volumes (ideal for scalpers).

Getting Busy

You need to make sure that you are trading at the busiest times of the day or else you are not going to get a lot of action. And you need a lot of action! Here are some of the busiest times of the day:

- 2:00 am - 4:00 am EST

- 8:00 am - 12:00 pm EST

Therefore, your best bet is to make as many trades as possible during the first time frame and then wait till the second time frame to continue with your trades.

Spread

Spread will play an important role in your overall returns. This is why you will need to pay close attention to your spreads.

Test the Waters

Try working with one pair first before moving on to the others. Many traders end up trading with two or more currency pairs and the tactic backfires on them. Furthermore, if you put all your energy into one pair, then you have a better chance of getting a successful trade.

No Need for the News

Do not pay too much attention to any big news announcement. They can confuse you about your trade and you might make a move out of sheer panic. And that is not something we want. After all, we are doing everything possible to control our emotions. However, the news does play an important role in future trades (either in the next time frame or the next day).

The Simple Scalping Strategy - Scalping At Resistance and Support Levels

This is a really simple method to scalp. What you do is that you buy the lows and then fade the highs.

For this scalping strategy, you need to be aware of two very vital points:

- Trading range

- Low volatility

The trading range allows you to select where you would like to place your longs, shorts, and stops. On the other hand, the low volatility helps you avoid the risk of a market or trade going against you sharply.

This method is not only used by seasoned scalpers, but it is perfect for beginners who are getting introduced to the platform.

1-Minute Scalping Strategy

In this strategy, you make use of a special indicator that comes with the MT4 known as the predictive EMA. Typically, this indicator is already available with the system when you get the MT4. This strategy makes use of the typical MA indicator but is slightly modified so that it works on charts that are based on 1-minute durations.

The first thing you are going to do is set up the EMA. To do that, make sure that your MT4 or MT5 is open in front of you. Head over to the Insert option, then work your way over to the Indicators section. Move to the option titled Trend and click on Moving Average.

In the dialog box that pops open, you will see two options: Period and Shift.

Enter the following values:

- Period - 25

- Shift - 8

Then continue clicking OK until the EMA has been set up.

Next, you have to set up two more EMAs. Follow the same steps as above but for the second EMA, the values are:

- Period - 50

- Shift - 15

For the third EMA, the values are

- Period - 100

- Shift - 30

Once the EMA has been set-up follow the below strategies.

Long

- Go Long when the 25 EMA first crosses the 50 EMA. Eventually, both the 25 and 50 have to cross the 100 EMA.

- Buy on the "candle" indicator (this is the shape of the various bars in the indicator, they look like candles).

- Your target should be from 5 to 10 pips and you should have placed a stop-loss order of anywhere from 9 to 12 pips.

Short

- Go Short when the 25 EMA first crosses below the 50 EMA. Eventually, both the 25 and 50 have to cross below the 100 EMA.

- Sell on the "candle" indicator.

- Your target at this point should be the same as for the Long strategy, from 5 to 10 pips with anywhere from 9 to 12 pips for a stop-loss order.

Conclusion

What you have seen is just the beginning.

But the beginning is essential to lay down the foundation for future successes. Too often, traders fail in the basics and then continue to struggle when they are trading in the future.

One of the things that you should understand is that Forex is a real market. It is also one of the largest financial markets in the world. Which is why every strategy you implement matters. Every move you make could make or break the trade.

People are often looking for the "treasure chest". The once in a lifetime move that will get them millions of dollars in their bank accounts. Forex does not work that way. In fact, the "treasure chest" you are looking for - the big treasure - is right there within you. It is your brain.

Every lesson you learned here - from understanding the Forex market to getting into the mindset of a winner to knowing about different analysis methods - are there to power up your brain.

And within there lies your biggest treasure: the knowledge that you have which is the rubies, diamonds, and other precious gems of your treasure chest.

All you have to do is know how to transform those rubies and precious gems into dollars.

This book has given you all the resources you need to get you started on your Forex journey. It is your primer into the world. Your handbook to understanding the variety of information you are going to face.

At the end of the day, you are going to take that with you.

Happy trading.

The end… almost!

Reviews are not easy to come by.

As an independent author with a tiny marketing budget, I rely on readers, like you, to leave a short review on Amazon.

Even if it's just a sentence or two!

Customer Reviews

★★★★★ 2
5.0 out of 5 stars ▾

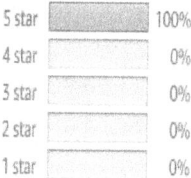

5 star		100%
4 star		0%
3 star		0%
2 star		0%
1 star		0%

Share your thoughts with other customers

Write a customer review

See all verified purchase reviews ›

So if you enjoyed the book, please...

>> Click here to leave a brief review on Amazon.

I am very appreciative for your review as it truly makes a difference.

Thank you from the bottom of my heart for purchasing this book and reading it to the end.

References

Scutt, D. (2016). Here's how much currency is traded every day. Retrieved from https://www.businessinsider.com/heres-how-much-currency-is-traded-every-day-2016-9/?IR=T

Malito, A. (2018). This guy lost $10,000 trying to time this volatile market — using his credit card. Retrieved from https://www.marketwatch.com/story/this-guy-lost-10000-trying-to-time-the-market-volatility-using-his-credit-card-2018-02-06

Douglas, M. (2001). Trading in the Zone. Penguin Group US.

Lien, K. (2008). Day Trading and Swing Trading the Currency Market: Technical and Fundamental. John Wiley & Sons.

Tharp, V. (2007). Trade your way to financial freedom. New York: McGraw-Hill.

Brown, J. (2019). MT4 high probability forex trading method. CA: San Bernardino.

Notes

[←1]

Scutt, D. (2016). Here's how much currency is traded every day. Retrieved from https://www.businessinsider.com/heres-how-much-currency-is-traded-every-day-2016-9/?IR=T

[←2]

Malito, A. (2018). This guy lost $10,000 trying to time this volatile market — using his credit card. Retrieved from https://www.marketwatch.com/story/this-guy-lost-10000-trying-to-time-the-market-volatility-using-his-credit-card-2018-02-06

[←3]

Hirsch, J. (2011). How good is a $16 muffin? Find out for yourself. Retrieved from https://usatoday30.usatoday.com/money/industries/food/story/2011-09-28/16-dollar-muffin-recipe/50590060/1

[←4]

Rogoff, K. (2010). Why has the price of gold risen 300%? | Kenneth Rogoff. Retrieved from https://www.theguardian.com/commentisfree/2010/oct/03/gold-price-rise-us-dollar-euro

www.ingramcontent.com/pod-product-compliance
Lightning Source LLC
Chambersburg PA
CBHW030449210326
41597CB00013B/590